本书由贵州开放大学（贵州职业技术学院）高层次人才科研启动经费资助。

Global Awareness and Metrolingualism in English Textbooks and Curriculum for Primary Education in China

我国小学英语教材中的全球意识教育与都市语言现象研究

孙婷婷　著

中国海洋大学出版社

· 青岛 ·

图书在版编目（CIP）数据

我国小学英语教材中的全球意识教育与都市语言现象研究：英文／孙婷婷著 . -- 青岛：中国海洋大学出版社，2024.4

ISBN 978-7-5670-3814-1

Ⅰ. ①我…　Ⅱ. ①孙…　Ⅲ. ①英语课－教材－研究－小学　Ⅳ. ①G623.312

中国国家版本馆 CIP 数据核字（2024）第 061536 号

出版发行	中国海洋大学出版社		
社　　址	青岛市香港东路 23 号	邮政编码	266071
出 版 人	刘文菁		
网　　址	http://pub.ouc.edu.cn		
订购电话	0532－82032573（传真）		
责任编辑	邵成军	电　　话	0532－85902533
印　　制	青岛国彩印刷股份有限公司		
版　　次	2024 年 4 月第 1 版		
印　　次	2024 年 4 月第 1 次印刷		
成品尺寸	170 mm ×230 mm		
印　　张	16.5		
字　　数	330 千		
印　　数	1—1 000		
定　　价	69.00 元		

总序（一）

　　中国海洋大学出版社将国内外国语言学及应用语言学博士研究生的优秀论文集中出版建立文库，对学界来说是件极好的事。目前已经出版了第一辑总计15本专著，在学界引起了很大的反响和广泛的关注。现在，第二辑论文专著正在筹划与编辑中。希望挑选出来的优秀博士学位论文能够丰富该文库的学术内容，促进该领域的学术争鸣。

　　作为一门学科，外国语言学及应用语言学涉及面极为广泛，几乎包罗万象。因此，要规划好第二辑论文主题，先要对该学科有个明确的范围界定，以期有的放矢地挑选相关的优秀论文。

　　外国语言学及应用语言学，顾名思义，是指与外国语言紧密相关的语言研究学说及用来解释语言问题的相关理论。这样界定似乎较为完整，但仔细分析发现，其中存在着概念界定模糊、内容划分不明等问题。

　　首先，学科名称"外国语言学及应用语言学"就值得商榷。外国语言学是个大概念，其他的语言学分支包含其中，如心理语言学、社会语言学、应用语言学，不应把语言学和其分支并列作为学科名称。因此，外国语言学及应用语言学似有概念混淆之嫌。其次，语言学有国内国外之分虽也说得过去，但时常造成共性语言现象研究的归类困难。而且应用语言学因涉及领域过于广泛而很难界定其确切的研究范围。当然，现在外国语言学及应用语言学作为学科名称已约定俗成，人们心目中也已经有了一个大概的范畴，但鉴于中国海洋大学出版社要出版此学科的第二辑博士学位论文专著，理应对这一学科有一个理性的解读。

　　语言学的研究（无论国内国外），大致分为理论层面的研究和应用层面的研究。理论层面的研究主要集中于对语言的描述以及人类语言的普遍规律或语言与某一领域的结合,如语音研究有音位学,词汇研究有词汇学,句子研究有句法学,还有语法学;与某一领域结合起来的研究有心理语言学、社会语言学、神经语言学、计算语言学、系统功能语言学等。应用层面的研究又可以分为宏观、中观和微观三个研究视角。宏观研究视角主要与语言政策及语言教育政策的研究有关,如语言的地位规划、语言的本体规划、语言的习得规划以及教育上使用何种语言等问题。中观研究视角大多关注语言在社会生活中的使用,如语言的翻译、语言的社会交际、语言的态度、专门领域中的语言使用以及方言、民族语言和外国语言的和谐共存与发展。而微观研究视角与外语教育教学有关,包括语言课程、教学方法、教学大纲、课堂教学、信息技术与外语教学、教育技术与外语教学等。综上所述,外国语言学及应用语言学与语言的理论研究和应用研究息息相关,并涉及上述的方方面面。

可见,学科研究范围的解读界定了博士文库所包含的内容。第一辑的15本博士论文专著主要涵盖两个方面:语言本体研究与语言教学研究,符合学科的理论研究和应用研究。即将出版的第二辑博士学位论文专著,除了涵盖第一辑的研究内容外,其研究焦点应集中在以下几个方面:语言和认知的结合、语言的普遍规律、语言的变化与发展(理论层面);语言政策与语言规划、课程开发与课堂教学、信息技术与语言教学、"互联网+"语言教学解决方案(应用层面)等。

博士文库的建立主要是为了把相关领域的最新研究成果集中展示,供人参考、研究和借鉴。因此,必须体现文库的开放性、内容的完整性、论述的创新性以及研究的科学性。这样才能充分发挥博士文库应有的学术价值!

中国海洋大学出版社以先进的编辑理念和敏锐的学术意识策划并设计了外国语言学及应用语言学博士文库,为广大的优秀博士人才提供了展示自己学术研究成果的交流平台。相信博士文库的不断丰富和完善,必将极大地促进该领域的研究和发展。

陈坚林

上海外国语大学教授、博士生导师

《外语电化教学》主编

总序（二）

　　在我国外语研究中，语言学自20世纪80年代后期开始蓬勃发展，先是作为英语语言文学、日语语言文学、俄语语言文学等二级学科的一个研究方向，之后外国语言学及应用语言学被列为外国语言文学一级学科下面的二级学科。当前，在外语语言学方面具有较强实力的院校一般拥有数个二级学科或一级学科。语言学蓬勃发展的另一个表现是研究生培养规模的扩大。90年代初，语言学硕士研究生还不多，博士研究生更是凤毛麟角。当时招博士研究生的只有北大、北外、上外、广外等院校，招生人数也是屈指可数。后来，增设外语博士点的院校数量稳步增加，现在招收外语语言学博士研究生的院校已经超过40所，每年招生人数在200人左右，学制一般为3～4年，最长不超过8年。随着高校对外语教师水平和学历要求的不断提高，广大教师考博的热情高涨，20余人竞争1个名额已属常见。报考语言学方面的博士研究生一般需要对语言学有一定的兴趣和热情，硕士研究生阶段已打下较好的基础，其后能经常研读相关学刊，最好有1篇或数篇较高质量的论文在外语类核心期刊上发表。被录取后，通常要刻苦钻研，潜心修炼，短则3～4年，长则5～8年。其博士学位论文要经过开题、预答辩、盲审、答辩等严格环节，所以往往具有较高水平，甚至能达到国内外的领先水平。对个人来说，博士学位论文也代表了学术生涯的一个高峰，其后要超越并非易事。正是因为博士学位论文的质量较高，对其加工出版能有效促进学术发展，国内外出版界也时常为之。这些以博士论文为基础的专著经常能为出版社赢得美誉。

　　在过去10多年间，国内几家出版社，如河南大学出版社、上海交通大学出版社、科学出版社、陕西师范大学出版社、中国海洋大学(简称海大)出版社出版了一系列外语方面的博士学位论文,其中有很大一部分属于语言学,产生了良好的影响。其中,海大出版社自 2008 年开始重视外语语言学研究,建立了外国语言学及应用语言学博士文库,共计 15 本,并通过多种方式进行推广,产生了良好的社会效益。

近几年来,我因工作关系与海大出版社邵成军老师交往较多。2015 年下半年,邵老师打电话与我商量,想对外语语言学博士学位论文进行新的策划,后商定为"外国语言学及应用语言学博士文库(第二辑)",以国内高质量的相关博士论文为对象,为专业性开放式学术系列,旨在为广大外语教师和研究生呈上丰盛的学术大餐。这套文库具有以下特点:① 加强策划——限定选题范围,请知名学者作序,统一开本、封面,加强后期宣传等;② 严把质量——对申请出版的博士论文呈送两位相关领域的专家进行指导,以进一步提高其学术水平;③ 精心编辑——由专业编辑对书稿进行高质量的编辑,确保其文字无差错,体例与规范等符合国家的出版要求;④ 立体推广——文库的专著出版后会通过书目推送、网络营销、会议赠送、撰写书评等多种方式向广大读者推介。

对广大外语教师和研究生来说,仔细阅读这套文库,将会在以下方面获益匪浅。

第一,能快速了解某一专题的国内外研究现状。博士学位论文要求有创新,前提是对国内外相关研究了如指掌。因此,通过答辩的博士学位论文的文献综述部分通常会对国内外相关论著进行梳理,并有的放矢地进行批判性评论。阅读这一部分可以使读者快速掌握某一专题的最新情况,为自己今后开展相关研究打下初步基础。

第二,了解所读专著的创新之处及创新思路。细读作者在对前人研究评论后所提出的研究内容、思路以及具体研究方法,可以窥见作者为什么选定某一专题的某个侧面,用什么理论框架及原因,研究方法有何创新等。了解这些内容并思考背后的原因能帮助读者提升在研究选题方面的功力,而好的选题对高质量研究而言是第一步。

第三,独立思考,发现其不足。阅读专著仅仅停留在吸收知识层面是不够的,还要对所读内容进行批判性思考。孔子也说过"学而不思则罔,思而不学则殆",强调了思考的重要性。我们阅读专著时,只怀着学习的态度是不够的,还要有质疑和批判精神。可以思考以下问题：选题是否有意义？理论框架是否能为研究内容服务？受试是否有代表性？数据收集方法是否可靠？统计分析方法是否恰当？是否对结果进行了深入讨论？能否较好地解释所得出的结论？只有通过思考，发现所读专著存在的不足，我们才能在今后研究中予以克服，加以超越，学术才能发展。就阅读方法而言，读者适当关注博士学位论文的最后一章往往有事半功倍之效，因为作者通常会在该部分指出其研究的不足，并对以后的研究进行展望。

第四，写书评与综述，并进行原创研究。读了一本专著及相关论文，有些收获，对某个专题产生了兴趣，这是非常难得的。此时宜趁热打铁，有所行动。比较容易入手的是对所读专著撰写书评，写好后既可以向期刊投稿，也可以在网络上发布。此后，应进一步阅读相关文献，特别是最新论文，针对该专题撰写综述性论文。综述性论文要写好并不容易，首先选题要有意义，其次要具备全面性、逻辑性、批判性，若能适当采用一些新方法，如元分析、CiteSpace 软件，往往显得不落俗套。前两步只是做学问的"练手"步骤，更重要的是做原创研究，这最能体现一个学者的水平和贡献。原创研究一般具备以下特点：选题新、方法新、结论新，但如何实现要靠自己的琢磨与钻研，"纸上得来终觉浅，绝知此事要躬行"。

在海大出版社推出"外国语言学及应用语言学博士文库(第二辑)"之际，我应约作序，很是惶恐，同时也为这份信任所感动，遂不揣浅陋，与大家分享一点治学的体会。

蔡金亭

上海财经大学教授、博士生导师

《第二语言学习研究》主编

· Preface ·

I have been invited by Dr. Sun Tingting to write a preface for her upcoming publication, and I am honored to accept. This is not only due to our shared research interests in sociolinguistics and language education, but also because of her unwavering commitment to the pursuit of knowledge. Pursuing a doctoral degree is a challenging endeavor that requires wholehearted dedication. Dr. Sun's decision to embark on this arduous journey while managing the demands of a professional career speaks volumes about her extraordinary passion for knowledge and dedication to academic excellence. Her forthcoming book is a testament to her rigorous and exceptional academic pursuits, work ethic, and intellectual ability. Readers of the book will gain insight into the critical intersections of global citizenship education (GCE), metrolingualism, and English language teaching (ELT) within the Chinese primary education system. Dr. Sun's research extensively examines the representation and impact of GCE and metrolingualism in English textbooks and curriculum development, illuminating their various manifestations within the educational landscape.

This book acknowledges the growing recognition of our interconnected world in the face of challenges posed by globalization. As a result, the educational system plays a pivotal role in cultivating global citizenship and equipping students with the necessary skills and knowledge to navigate the complexities of our interconnected reality. Within this framework, the concept of metrolingualism emerges as a significant facet of language understanding. The book emphasizes the diversity and fluidity of languages, not only in relation to each other but also within the local contexts where they are employed. This understanding becomes essential when discussing "globalization from below", acknowledging that global phenomena occur within specific local frameworks. Furthermore, the book underscores the significance of teachers' awareness and understanding of critical GCE and metrolingualism, emphasizing the need for a more inclusive GCE framework in ELT practices. It encourages teachers to embrace a balanced distribution of global perspectives and local realities in their pedagogical approaches.

This book, based on Dr. Sun's PhD thesis, not only contributes to the theoretical dimensions of GCE and metrolingualism, but also offers practical implications for the advancement of Chinese GCE and metrolingualism within ELT. It explores the potential for interdisciplinary implementation, particularly in the initial stages of education. Moreover, it provides a foundation for further research and understanding of how ELT can contribute to China's context-specific endeavors in GCE and metrolingualism during the process of "glocalization". This book enhances our understanding of how ELT can align with and support China's efforts to foster GCE and metrolingualism, offering valuable insights into the implementation of GCE and metrolingualism within the Chinese educational landscape. More importantly, it paves the way for future research and development in this field. Undoubtedly, this book will serve as an indispensable resource for researchers and educators for more cutting-edge academic discussions, which can potentially lead to further impacts in language education. Finally, I would like to express my sincere congratulations to Dr. Sun Tingting for her outstanding achievements and wish her continued success in her academic pursuits.

Dr. Fang Fan (方帆)
Professor, Shantou University
13/03/2024

· **Abstract** ·

Problems associated with globalization made us more aware of the interconnected nature of the world. Addressing global problems necessitates global solutions, prompting the educational system to transcend national boundaries and advocate for GCE as a means to provide such solutions. Besides, Pennycook and Otsuji (2015a) argued that metrolingualism raises questions about how we understand languages not only in relation to each other but also in relation to what is happening in a particular place, since we cannot talk about globalization without acknowledging that everything happens locally (Otsuji & Pennycook, 2013). In this regard, GCE and metrolingualism share the fundamental essence of globality coexisting and living together of the whole world. Both of them emphasize the interconnectedness of the entire world and the imperative of fostering a collective global consciousness. By acknowledging the interplay between global perspectives and local realities, these concepts could provide insights into how to navigate the complexities of the interconnected world.

However, it is still underexplored that in what ways Chinese elementary school English textbooks and curriculum reflect the notions of GCE and metrolingualism, as well as how English teachers perceive Chinese GCE and metrolingualism in primary ELT textbooks and curriculum. To address the research gap, a qualitative study was conducted to examine the global awareness from the perspectives of GCE and metrolingualism embedded in two series of textbooks published by People's Education Press (PEP) and Yilin Press, as well as the English Curriculum Standards for Compulsory Education (ECSCE), and to explore teachers' perceptions.

Qualitative content analysis, critical discourse analysis, and code preference analysis were adopted to analyze the collected data in this study.

The findings of the study indicate that the themes of GCE and metrolingualism are incorporated into ELT textbooks and curriculum to varying degrees, with a prevailing influence of soft GCE. Regarding this, it is recommended that the materials could consider the principles of critical GCE and metrolingualism to facilitate the full realization of global citizenship values. Furthermore, the content analysis reveals that there are more similarities than differences in terms of the salient GCE themes across the two textbook series and among different grade levels. The interview results align with the analysis of textbooks and curriculum, indicating a predominant emphasis on soft GCE in teaching practices. Teachers' limited awareness of critical GCE and metrolingualism may impede the full realization of inclusive GCE in ELT. Recognizing the significance of promoting critical GCE and metrolingualism among teachers can contribute to a more comprehensive and inclusive GCE framework in ELT.

To this end, this study places emphasis on the representation of GCE and metrolingualism in ELT materials. It also highlights the importance of achieving a more balanced distribution and fostering increased awareness of critical GCE and metrolingualism among teachers, thereby promoting an inclusive GCE approach in ELT. The findings of this study could provide some theoretical, pedagogical, and methodological implications for the development of Chinese GCE and metrolingualism in ELT. It contributes to expanding the relevant theories on GCE and metrolingualism within a national state, while also exploring the feasibility of interdisciplinary implementation, particularly at the initial stages of education. Besides, this study could provide grounds for further research and a growing understanding regarding how ELT contributes to China's context-specific GCE and metrolingualism endeavors during the "glocalization". By examining the interplay between global and local influences, this study enriches the understanding of how ELT can align with and support China's context in fostering GCE and metrolingualism. Additionally, it provides insights into the implementation of GCE and metrolingualism within the Chinese educational landscape, paving the way for future research in this area.

· Table of Contents ·

CHAPTER 1
INTRODUCTION

This chapter consists of ten sections which include the background of the study, the problem statement, rationales of the study, research purposes, research questions, theoretical frameworks, conceptual framework, significance, as well as definitions of some key terms. Then the summary of this chapter comes last.

1.1 Background of the study

1.1.1 Globalization

Since the late 1980s, there has been a tendency toward globalization in the world economy, and the growth of the economies of all nations has become increasingly intertwined. Under the influence of globalization, mankind has entered a period of rapid integration including economic, educational, cultural and political dimensions. People are paying closer attention to other countries as science and technology advance, as well as the flow of personnel and capital. The world is narrowing, and the globe is progressively becoming a tightly connected "global village". People ought to be more vigilant about the challenges that arise during the process of globalization, such as injustice, racial discrimination, violation of human rights, poverty, climate change, environmental pollution, while enjoying the global exchange and development. Moreover, the global challenges we have faced in recent years have highlighted the interconnectedness of the world. It is evident that collaboration and cooperation on both national and international levels are crucial in addressing these challenges (Lourenço, 2021).

Besides, the acceleration of globalization sparked great challenges of citizenship education for countries in the world, which appealed them to not only adhere to cultivate citizens' national patriotism and national identity, but also pay attention to their global views, international awareness and inclusive minds toward different cultures, etc. To meet the challenges of globalization, the United Nations Educational, Scientific, and Cultural Organization (UNESCO) promoted the respect for the world's diversity and distinctions, the abolition of racial and national discrimination, and the establishment of a diversified but equal society through GCE (UNESCO, 2014). Global challenges require global solutions, and the educational system should urge for GCE to provide such solutions by looking beyond the borders of individual countries, so that students, as the critical characters, can see the relevance of global concerns in their own lives, recognize their "glocal" obligations (Starkey, 2012), communicate with the attitude of respect across cultural distance, commit to social justice and equity, and act towards more inclusive and sustainable communities.

For another, due to the force of globalization, English rose to fill the need to strengthen the international connections, which made it as native or second or foreign language of many communities (Galloway & Rose, 2015). Moreover, with the increasing of non-native English speakers, communication in English is more happened among non-native English speakers than native speakers (ibid.). English has been becoming a global language, which results in multiculturalism in the global context. English interlocutors are mostly come from multilingual background and multicultural communities in both inter-national and intra-national communications (McKay, 2002). Thus, linguistic and cultural diversities require ELT educate students to bear inclusive and open attitudes toward differences, as well as to bring global and local forces together in a dual process for the "glocalization".

More significantly, increasing evidence showed that people use a mixture of languages in their daily lives, displaying transcultural and trans-territorial positions (Otsuji & Pennycook, 2011). Unlike the policy-driven of UNESCO's GCE which is focused on the globalization from top, those transnational and transcultural flows in urban cities are emergent languages from the contexts of interactions, addressing the globalization from below and challenging the orthodoxy of monolingualism. This kind of local language practice in the city was named as metrolingualism by Pennycook and Otsuji (2015a), which addresses the capacity of metrolingual practices to enhance social inclusion and provide possibilities for mobility in a global world (Otsuji & Pennycook, 2011). Underlining languages from people's daily life (Pennycook & Otsuji, 2015a), metrolingualism and GCE share the core essence of globality coexisting and living together of the whole world.

Against the backdrop of globalization, the Chinese educational system is undergoing a process of integration with the world. While incorporating global elements, it also strives to preserve its unique cultural characteristics. Consequently, it is important to provide a brief overview of the Chinese educational system in the following subsection, laying the necessary background knowledge for the subsequent progress of this study.

1.1.2 Chinese educational system

The Chinese educational system consists of five stages, which include preschool education, primary school education, junior high school education, senior high school education, and higher education. Among them, primary school and junior high school education are compulsory phases mandated by the state. Generally, students commence their primary education around the age of six to seven and undergo six years of primary school education. Subsequently, they progress to three years of junior high school education. Primary schools typically offer a comprehensive curriculum that covers subjects such as Chinese language, mathematics, English, science, social studies, and physical education. The primary school phase aims to provide students with a solid academic foundation and essential life skills. Upon completing primary school, students progress to the next phase of compulsory education, known as junior high school. Junior high school education lasts for three years and forms the bridge between primary and senior high school. During this phase, students continue to study a wide range of subjects, with an increased focus on preparing for the senior high school entrance examination, which plays a significant role in determining their future educational trajectory.

It's important to note that while primary and junior high school education are compulsory, senior high school education is not mandatory. However, it is highly encouraged, as it provides students with further academic and vocational pathways. Senior high school education typically lasts for three years and offers various tracks, including academic, technical, and vocational streams, catering to students' diverse interests and career aspirations. Finally, higher education in China encompasses universities, colleges, and vocational institutions. It offers undergraduate and postgraduate programs across a wide range of disciplines, providing students with opportunities for advanced learning and specialization in their chosen fields. The Chinese educational system provides a comprehensive framework that ensures students receive compulsory education during the primary and junior high school phases, setting a strong foundation for their future academic and professional endeavors.

Since the beginning of the 21st century, the Chinese government has placed significant emphasis on education, implementing a strategic policy known as "Rejuvenating the country through science and education" (科教兴国) since 1995. This policy has sparked extensive reforms within the educational system, with a strong focus on quality-oriented education and a firm commitment to achieving universal nine-year compulsory education. Additionally, the government has prioritized efforts to eradicate illiteracy among young and middle-aged individuals. At the core of Chinese education reform since the "Reform and Opening up" period is the guiding principle that "Education should be oriented towards modernization, the world, and the future" (教育要面向现代化, 面向世界, 面向未来). This principle underscores the importance of aligning education with the demands of a rapidly changing society, the globalized world, and the evolving needs of the future. Under this strategic policy, China has witnessed remarkable progress in expanding access to education and improving its quality. Efforts have been made to ensure that education is accessible to all, regardless of socioeconomic background or geographical location. The implementation of inclusive educational policies and initiatives has played a crucial role in narrowing educational disparities and promoting equal opportunities for students across the nation. Furthermore, the Chinese government has actively fostered a culture of innovation and creativity within the educational system. Emphasis has been placed on cultivating critical thinking skills, problem-solving abilities, and fostering an entrepreneurial spirit among students. This approach aims to equip learners with the necessary competencies to thrive in an increasingly dynamic and knowledge-driven society.

In June 2001, the Chinese Ministry of Education (MOE) issued the *Outline of Curriculum Reform for Basic Education (Trial)*, marking the beginning of a comprehensive curriculum reform for basic education throughout China. This reform aimed to bring about significant changes in the educational landscape, particularly in terms of curriculum content and teaching materials. As a result, there was a notable diversification of textbooks used in schools across the country. Following the curriculum reform, English courses were introduced in primary schools starting from the third grade, which typically meant students began learning English around the age of eight or nine. To align with the English curriculum standards for primary education, various publishing institutions released a wide array of English textbooks specifically designed for primary school students. These textbooks were accompanied by corresponding teaching references to support educators in delivering effective English language instruction.

Among the publishers, two prominent entities that gained significant popularity in the educational field were PEP and Yilin Press. These publishing houses have been actively involved in the research and development of textbooks for compulsory education in China. Their commitment to providing high-quality educational materials has earned them a reputation for excellence. Over the years, PEP and Yilin Press have consistently demonstrated their dedication to meeting the evolving needs of Chinese students and educators. They have contributed significantly to the advancement of educational resources in the country, ensuring that the textbooks they produce align with the curriculum standards and cater to the diverse learning styles and preferences of students. Furthermore, the textbooks published by PEP and Yilin Press have been widely adopted in primary schools across China, making them household names in the field of education. These textbooks not only provide comprehensive language learning content but also incorporate interactive activities, engaging illustrations, and culturally relevant materials to enhance students' language acquisition and overall learning experience. The commitment of PEP, Yilin Press, and other publishing institutions to the research and development of educational materials has played a vital role in supporting the implementation of the curriculum reform and the improvement of English language education in primary schools. Their contributions have helped shape the educational landscape and ensure the availability of quality resources for teachers and students throughout China.

In 2019, the Chinese government released the *Modernization of Chinese Education 2035*, a strategic blueprint that sets forth the primary goals for educational development in China over the next 15 years. This document serves as a comprehensive framework guiding educational initiatives at all levels, from early childhood education to higher education and beyond. The *Modernization of Chinese Education 2035* places a strong emphasis on the implementation of innovative, coordinated, green, open, and shared scientific development concepts. These principles highlight the importance of embracing cutting-edge technologies, fostering collaboration between different educational institutions and sectors, promoting environmental sustainability, embracing openness and inclusivity, and creating a shared learning ecosystem that benefits all members of society. Central to the vision outlined in the *Modernization of Chinese Education 2035* is the establishment of a lifelong learning system that is accessible to all individuals.

This commitment reflects the recognition that education is a lifelong journey and that continuous learning is essential for personal growth, career advancement, and societal progress. The aim is to create a learning society where people of all ages and backgrounds have equal opportunities to acquire knowledge, develop skills, and pursue their aspirations.

It is worth noting that these educational concepts in China bear certain parallels with UNESCO's GCE framework, which emphasizes the development of knowledge, skills, attitudes, and values necessary for individuals to thrive in a globalized and interconnected world. The convergence between the principles outlined in the *Modernization of Chinese Education 2035* and the ideals of GCE reflects the recognition of the importance of preparing students to be active global citizens who can contribute positively to the world. The discourse within Chinese education, influenced by both national and cosmopolitan perspectives, further underscores the interconnectedness of these concepts. The Chinese government prioritizes the development of a robust and competitive education system that aligns with national goals and values, and there is also a recognition of the need to cultivate global awareness, cross-cultural understanding, and a sense of shared humanity among Chinese students. This connection between the national and cosmopolitan perspectives within Chinese education will be explored in greater detail in Chapter 2, where this study will delve into the ways in which these perspectives intersect and shape educational practices and policies in China.

Nevertheless, it is important to acknowledge that despite the release of various policy documents aimed at educational reform, the examination system continues to hold a prominent position in the mindset of teachers, students, parents, and other stakeholders within the education system. This includes the senior high school entrance examination, college entrance examination, and post-graduate entrance examination, etc. Undoubtedly, English plays a pivotal role within these examinations, further emphasizing its significance in the education landscape. Moreover, it is worth noting that certain English proficiency tests, such as CET 4 and CET 6, which are required for college education, as well as internationally recognized tests like TOEFL, GRE, IELTS, and others, contribute to the perpetuation of an exam-oriented approach to ELT in China. While it is important to acknowledge this reality, it is crucial to approach the topic with sensitivity, recognizing the multifaceted factors that contribute to the prevalence of exam-focused education. By understanding the context in which these examinations and tests are situated, educators and policymakers can better navigate the challenges and explore opportunities to strike a balance between exam preparation and broader educational objectives. It is essential to adopt a comprehensive approach to ELT that encompasses not only exam-oriented skills but also fosters critical thinking, communicative competence, and a deep understanding of the English language and its cultural contexts. Furthermore, creating awareness among stakeholders about the limitations of an exam-oriented approach and the benefits of a well-rounded education can help shift the focus towards holistic development and lifelong learning. Encouraging the cultivation of creativity, critical thinking, and problem-solving skills alongside exam preparation can empower students to excel not only in examinations but also in their future endeavors.

1.2 Statement of the Problem

Based on the research background, this study aims to address four specific issues. Firstly, while GCE and metrolingualism have gained traction in the global context, they are still relatively new concepts in China. The extent to which these concepts have been incorporated into Chinese ELT, especially at the primary education level, remains largely unknown. This is particularly important as primary school students are highly impressionable and susceptible to conforming to some stereotypical expectations regarding ELT.

Secondly, researchers have placed considerable emphasis on uncovering hidden Western paradigms and assumptions that may contribute to Anglocentrism and Eurocentrism (Byram & Parmenter, 2015), as well as the impact of capitalist hegemony on peripheralization, which exacerbates socio-economic disparities. It is important to recognize that the global discourse on global citizenship may not always be globally representative (Akkari & Maleq, 2020). Therefore, another crucial issue related to GCE is whether the values embedded in Chinese ELT truly represent the inclusiveness of GCE.

Thirdly, while there exists a universalism of humanistic values within the concept of global citizenship, the practice of citizenship is inherently tied to national contexts. GCE requires adaptation and operationalization across various local, regional, and global dimensions of citizenship to address the challenges posed by national educational policies. This entails reflecting the complex reality rather than assuming a universally valid approach (ibid.). UNESCO (2018) also aimed to root the concept of GCE both globally and locally, acknowledging the importance of indigeneity and diversity in addressing its agendas. Therefore, it is necessary to further explore the extent to which GCE, as embedded in Chinese ELT, aligns with the local context in China.

Fourthly, metrolingualism raises questions about how we understand languages not only in relation to each other, but also in relation to what is happening in a particular place (Pennycook & Otsuji, 2015a). With a focus on local practices, metrolingualism underpins those resourceful metrolingual repertoires rather than systematic languages (Pennycook, 2012). It is crucial for educators to challenge the prevailing routines in ELT, which often prioritize linguistic skills, and instead incorporate people's metrolingual practices into classrooms, since we cannot discuss globalization without acknowledging that all interactions occur locally (Otsuji & Pennycook, 2013). Failing to address this issue may hinder the development of GCE from below and risk furthering the gap between language of school and language of life. However, an issue remains as to whether Chinese ELT challenges traditional approaches that prioritize linguistic skills education and make it relevant to students' daily lives. This is crucial for enabling students to adapt to different contexts during the process of "glocalization".

1.3   Rationales of the Study

Motivated by the aforementioned problems, this study is conducted for the following four primary reasons. Firstly, it is driven by the influence of educational policies. Secondly, it recognizes the crucial role of ELT in promoting GCE. Thirdly, ELT textbooks and curriculum really do matter for ELT to foster GCE and metrolingualism. Fourthly, the existing gap between the ELT reality and the ideals of GCE and metrolingualism necessitates pedagogical reforms. Moreover, this study aims to fill the research gap in this area of inquiry.

1.3.1   Policies driven

In 2014, UNESCO formally put forward GCE in its publication titled *Global Citizenship Education: Preparing Learners for the Challenges of the 21st Century*. UNESCO called for the importance of education in developing learners' knowledge, skills, values, and attitudes necessary to create a more just, peaceful, tolerant, inclusive, secure, and sustainable world (UNESCO, 2014). GCE plays a crucial role in equipping learners with the competencies needed to understand and navigate the dynamic and interconnected nature of the 21st century. Furthermore, the United Nations (UN) established 17 Sustainable Development Goals (SDGs) to address various social issues by 2030 (UN, 2015). These goals have been endorsed by all

UN member states, and GCE is considered a vital component, particularly for SDG 4, which focuses on quality education. Education has the power to transform the world, and GCE can be seen as an initiative and pedagogical framework that contributes to the achievement of the SDGs by 2030.

More significantly, the concept of "Community with a Shared Future for Mankind" (人类命运共同体) was put forward during the 18th CPC National Congress in 2012,which involves a cognizance of interconnectedness, mutual understanding and responsibility derived from Confucian ethics (Wang, 2023). This concept transcends national boundaries, highlights global responsibilities, and expresses the desire for peaceful development throughout the world. Therewith this concept was formalized in UN resolutions in 2017, demonstrating that it has gained significance in the system of global discourse (宋强 , 2018b). The concept of "Community with a Shared Future for Mankind" aligns closely with UNESCO's GCE, as both emphasize the coexistence and interconnectedness of the global community (Wang, 2023). The emphasis and promotion of the concept, both internationally and nationally, provide a top-down impetus for this study to delve deeper into GCE.

On the other hand, the educational philosophy of GCE is gradually being integrated into China's educational policies. Since the "Reform and Opening up" in 1978, the Chinese educational system has undergone significant changes, with a focus on education that is oriented towards modernization, the world, and the future. In 2016, the educational policy document *"Several Opinions on the Opening up of Education in the New Era"* was issued, advocating for a more open and inclusive approach to Chinese education. It emphasized the importance of both internationalization and the incorporation of global perspectives. Furthermore, the educational policy document *"Outline of the National Plan for Medium and Long-Term Education Reform and Development (2010-2020)"* highlighted the need to strengthen international understanding education, enhance students' awareness of global issues, and foster their understanding of different cultures. In 2019, the policy document *"Modernization of Chinese Education 2035"* further emphasized the importance of inclusiveness and opening up in the educational system. These policies reflect a growing recognition of the significance of global perspectives, intercultural understanding, and GCE in Chinese education. GCE statements with Chinese collective traditions embedded in Chinese educational policies aim to explore Chinese approach to solve global problems, and to cultivate a global perspective.

However, notwithstanding the incorporation of the concept of GCE within general Chinese government policies and educational policies, there is currently a lack of specific GCE policies or strategies in China, as well as a lack of curriculumization specifically focused on GCE within the Chinese context (Li, 2021). Thus, the objective of this study is to examine how GCE values are represented in Chinese ELT materials and to gain a deeper understanding of GCE in the Chinese context. By exploring these aspects, this study seeks to contribute to the GCE in China and shed light on its implementation within the field of ELT.

1.3.2 Role of ELT in GCE

The intricate relationship between "language" and "citizenship" has always been intertwined, and this connection is particularly evident in educational policies, especially those pertaining to language education (Guilherme, 2007). ELT serves both instrumental purposes, such as employment, travel, and business, as well as educational goals that encompass moral and civic dimensions (Williams, 2017). ELT educators bear the responsibility of fulfilling educational and political obligations, as they strive to bridge the gap between English classrooms and social communities by inspiring students to actively participate in civic and social initiatives at local, regional, and global levels, thus promoting intercultural citizenship (Byram et al., 2017). In this context, the inherently cross-cultural nature of ELT presents a fertile ground for fostering GCE, while simultaneously strengthening local identity and cultivating understanding, tolerance, and acceptance of diversity on local, regional, national, and international scales (Calle Díaz, 2017). Consequently, the distinctive role of ELT serves as a driving force behind this research, as it aims to investigate the integration of GCE within a specific discipline. By exploring the potential of GCE within ELT, this research seeks to uncover opportunities for meaningful engagement that transcends language acquisition and encompasses broader educational objectives. By intertwining language learning with the development of global citizenship competencies, ELT can become a powerful platform for nurturing socially responsible individuals who possess the knowledge, skills, and attitudes necessary to actively participate in an increasingly interconnected world. This study aims to shed light on the transformative potential of ELT in promoting GCE, and to contribute to the ongoing discourse surrounding the role of education in fostering global citizenship and building a more inclusive and sustainable future.

1.3.3 ELT curriculum and textbooks do matter

According to Kelly (1989), curriculum can be regarded as the overall rationale of an institutional educational program, reflecting planners' intentions, the procedures used to implement these intentions, the practical experience of students, direct attempts of teachers to achieve their or planners' intentions, and a by-product of curriculum organization, or even the "hidden learning" in schools. ELT curriculum is the product of English language education, following the language policy designed by the government that stipulates what educators should teach and what students should learn. It is the guiding document and a logical framework for ELT as well as the foundation for compilation of ELT textbooks. Besides, a national language curriculum may subconsciously influence learners across the country, as it authoritatively and compulsorily establishes standards of language use, teaching and learning methods, as well as language proficiency test criteria (Liu & Fang, 2022). Also, any divergence from such norms may be regarded as incorrect or inaccurate.

While ELT textbooks, as the silent partner of teachers', are the key starting points of teaching practice and educational transformation, following the national policy and being a mirror of national curriculum standards as well as reflecting the official knowledge of the society through purposely content selection and editing (Apple, 2014), through which the worldviews of dominant groups could be reflected (Nasser & Nasser, 2008). Moreover, ELT textbooks are often regarded as a crucial starting point for educators to promote learners' worldviews since they have a significant impact on the impression of foreign cultures by learners who are not exposed to English in their daily life in China where English is a foreign language (Rashidi & Ghaedsharafi, 2015). Besides, it is worth noting that education can sometimes limit students' competences by providing them with limited access to semiotic resources. In addition, ELT textbooks may tend to regulate students' identities rather than empowering them with language that enables them to exercise agency and exert their power (Mahboob, 2017).

The analysis of ELT curriculum and textbooks is regarded as a valuable approach to gaining insights into the construction of official knowledge about society and the world (Choi & Kim, 2018). This analytical process can provide valuable perspectives on how these materials either support or hinder the promotion of GCE and metrolingualism while maintaining a national focus. Furthermore, ELT curriculum and textbooks often communicate underlying ideologies that may not be immediately apparent to those who utilize or develop these materials. Consequently, this study seeks to examine the presence of these hidden ideologies within ELT curriculum and textbooks, aiming to raise awareness among stakeholders about their existence. By engaging in a critical examination of ELT curriculum and textbooks, this study could uncover the implicit values, perspectives, and assumptions that shape the content and pedagogical approaches. This analysis allows for an exploration of how these materials contribute to shaping learners' perceptions of culture and global issues. Moreover, it provides an opportunity for reflection on whether these materials effectively address the complexities of the interconnected world and promote inclusive and equitable perspectives. This study endeavors to draw attention to potential limitations that may be embedded within ELT curriculum and textbooks. By identifying and analyzing the hidden ideologies present in these materials, this research aims to foster a more nuanced understanding among stakeholders, including educators, curriculum developers, policymakers, and learners themselves. Raising awareness about the presence of these hidden ideologies can encourage a critical engagement with educational materials and promote a more inclusive and culturally sensitive approach to ELT.

Especially nowadays, there has been growing scrutiny towards the native speakerism approach in ELT, and there is a shift towards embracing multilingualism and multiculturalism as the norm, challenging the traditional focus on native-oriented language education (Fang et al., 2022). Acknowledging and valuing linguistic and cultural diversities in ELT, as advocated by GCE, can provide the groundwork for fostering a more just and socially inclusive society (Zhang et al., 2022). Consequently, there is a need to transition from the conventional monolithic cultural framework in ELT to cultivate an egalitarian and multicultural decolonizing pedagogy. This pedagogical approach enables learners to experience personal fulfillment, mutual understanding, and develop a sense of global citizenship. Furthermore, the advancement of GCE has prompted certain reforms in curriculum development, although the incorporation of cultural diversity associated with GCE is yet to be fully reflected in the curriculum (Fang et al., 2022). It is crucial to recognize the importance of including diverse cultural perspectives and experiences in the curriculum to foster a comprehensive understanding of global issues and to promote intercultural competence among learners. By integrating culturally diverse content and perspectives into the curriculum, ELT can provide learners with the opportunity to develop open-mindedness, empathy, and respect for different cultures, ultimately nurturing them as global citizens who can actively contribute to a harmonious and interconnected world.

1.3.4　The ELT reality & research gap in China

English has been conducted as a mandatory subject for students in China starting from the third grade, and the number of individuals learning it as a foreign language has surpassed 400 million, with this figure steadily increasing (Wang, 2015). As English continues to gain prominence as a global language, it becomes imperative to transition the paradigm of ELT from traditional Anglocentrism to one that embraces pluralism and multiculturalism (ibid.). However, the prevalent exam-oriented educational system presents obstacles to significant transformation in this regard. This situation poses challenges in nurturing students' global citizenship and fails to align with the realities of life. Given the widespread influence of English as a global language, it is crucial to move away from an Anglocentric approach in ELT and instead foster an inclusive and multicultural perspective. By recognizing and valuing diverse linguistic and cultural backgrounds, ELT can promote a more equitable and balanced understanding of the world. However, the emphasis on exams often prioritizes rote memorization and formulaic language use, which may hinder the development of critical thinking, intercultural competence, and a global perspective among students. This exam-oriented approach tends to focus on language proficiency measured through standardized tests rather than nurturing students' broader understanding of global issues, cultural diversity, and their role as global citizens. Consequently, there is a misalignment between the objectives of traditional ELT and the skills as well as knowledge necessary for students to actively engage in an interconnected world. To address this challenge, it is essential to advocate for a more comprehensive and balanced approach to ELT that goes beyond exam preparation.

Especially, the changing demand of market economy has influenced English education since the "Reform and Opening up" in 1978, which indicates that English education in China has entered the market-oriented era of simultaneous development with social economy (肖礼全, 2006). This is accompanied by the English tests fever, further reinforcing the exam-oriented approach in ELT. Meanwhile, as has been elaborated previously that the concept of GCE has been embedded in some general Chinese government policies and educational policies, English education in China should also echo those policies and be more inclusive as well as opening up to the diversity in the world. Perhaps, the exam-oriented reality of ELT suggests that bridging the gap between this reality and the inclusiveness of ELT is a long-term and challenging task for educators. More importantly, achieving GCE in ELT necessitates not only political guidance but also the cultivation of critical thinking skills, making ELT more relevant to people's daily lives and bridging the gap between globalization from the top and the below, or those marginalized voices and hidden ideologies maybe easily neglected.

Although research on GCE in the Chinese context is gradually emerging alongside the global surge in GCE studies, there is still a lack of interdisciplinary research exploring the connection between ELT and GCE in China. Additionally, little attention has been given to examining the role of English in GCE (Byram & Parmenter, 2015). Most discussions on integrating GCE into English education in China remain at the theoretical level (Baker & Fang, 2019). In particular, there is a dearth of studies that combine GCE with metrolingualism in ELT, particularly in the context of primary education. Considering that primary education is the initial stage of compulsory education in China and that primary students are highly susceptible to some stereotypical expectations, focusing on primary education is essential. Moreover, UNESCO (2015) has designated primary education as the starting point for GCE learning objectives throughout life. Therefore, this study argues that if hidden problems remain unrecognized at the initial educational level, it will become increasingly challenging to amend ingrained perceptions in subsequent educational stages.

More significantly, it is still underexplored regarding the following four specific aspects in the context of China. Firstly, it remains unclear whether Chinese primary ELT textbooks and curriculum have incorporated values related to GCE and metrolingualism, and if so, how these values are reflected. Secondly, there is a need to examine the similarities and differences in GCE and metrolingualism across different national ELT textbooks. Thirdly, it is important to investigate whether there are similarities and differences in the representation of GCE and metrolingualism in ELT textbooks used by students of different grades. Finally, as this study aims to examine the hidden ideologies concerning GCE and metrolingualism in ELT textbooks and curriculum, it is crucial to explore how teachers, who use these ELT materials, perceive the embedded ideologies. To address those research gaps, this study tried to achieve the following four research purposes.

1.4　Research Purposes

Being motivated by research problems and research gaps, this study attempted to scrutinize the issues regarding global awareness from the perspectives of GCE and metrolingualism in Chinese primary ELT textbooks and curriculum. Four research purposes are specified as follows:

(1) To explore the notions of GCE and metrolingualism embedded in ELT textbooks and curriculum for primary education in China;

(2) To compare the similarities and differences of GCE and metrolingualism represented in ELT textbooks between PEP series and Yilin series for primary education in China;

(3) To compare the similarities and differences of GCE and metrolingualism represented in ELT textbooks of different grade levels for primary education in China;

(4) To study teachers' perceptions toward GCE and metrolingualism in ELT textbooks and curriculum for primary education in China.

1.5 Research Questions

According to the research purposes, this study addresses four main research questions:

(1) In what ways do ELT textbooks and curriculum reflect the notions of GCE and metrolingualism for primary education in China?

(2) What are the similarities and differences of GCE and metrolingualism represented in ELT textbooks between PEP series and Yilin series for primary education in China?

(3) What are the similarities and differences of GCE and metrolingualism represented in ELT textbooks of different grade levels for primary education in China?

(4) What are teachers' perceptions toward GCE and metrolingualism in ELT textbooks and curriculum for primary education in China?

In order to answer the above research questions, this study employed the following theoretical frameworks to explore more about GCE and metrolingualism.

1.6 Theoretical Frameworks

Given that this study is focused on two main interdependent issues through a critical lens, namely GCE and metrolingualism, a single theoretical framework is insufficient to achieve the research purposes. Therefore, the GCE frameworks and the framework of metrolingualism will be introduced respectively, and critical discourse analysis (CDA) is regarded as another data analysis framework which will be briefly introduced in this section and further elaborated in Chapter 2.

1.6.1 Theoretical frameworks for GCE

The effective and sustainable GCE requires alignment with local traditions, culture and history, as well as the establishment of effective linkages between global, national and regional challenges. It cannot be based on a standard model or a top-down approach, but the development of local implementation plans that take into account geopolitical and local political circumstances, specific issues and requirements, and various citizenship concepts (Akkari & Maleq, 2020). To some extent, Akkari and Maleq's framework for GCE (2020) could provide the current study with reference of the tailor-made needs in China and facilitate "globalization from below" as well as translate GCE's international models into local classroom practice. This framework suggests operationalizing GCE within three domains, and each of these domains could be subdivided into a further subset of sub-domains. In this study, all the GCE themes and subthemes have been further elaborated under each GCE sub-domain, while some emerging themes that cannot fit into those domains have been categorized within the domain of emerging themes for GCE. Table 1.1 indicates the domains and sub-domains of Akkari and Maleq's framework for GCE.

Table 1.1   Domains and sub-domains of Akkari and Maleq's framework for GCE

Domain	Sub-domain
Education for sustainable development	Education for development
	Environmental education
Inter/multicultural education	Inclusive education
	Social justice and equality
	Respect for diversity
Citizenship education	Human rights education
	Education for gender equality
	Civic and moral education

Moreover, soft versus critical GCE (Andreotti, 2006) has been adopted in this study as another conceptual framework for data analysis through a soft versus critical GCE lens. The soft GCE is prone to underline the progressivism in economics and hardly sees the inequalities that arise during the globalization, while critical GCE concerns the inequalities and injustice in globalization as well as regards GCE as a way of counteracting the hegemony that is embedded in educational policies (ibid.). Thus, critical GCE can provide this study with a critical lens to examine the potential inequalities and injustice embedded in ELT and takes power, voice and difference as central notions, so as to develop learners' critical literacy to reflect on their surroundings and their own as well as others' epistemological and ontological assumptions, as well as empowering them to make better informed choices (ibid.). Critical GCE, being regarded as a critical approach to GCE in this study, will be further elaborated in Chapter 2.

1.6.2   Theoretical framework for metrolingualism

Due to GCE frameworks primarily concentrate on GCE values embedded in ELT textbooks and curriculum, they may not offer a thorough examination of metrolingualism-related issues. Consequently, this study incorporates the conceptual framework of metrolingualism proposed by Pennycook and Otsuji (2015a) to address this gap. Pennycook and Otsuji are renowned scholars in the field of metrolingualism, and their extensive body of work provides a comprehensive understanding of the subject. Therefore, their framework was adopted for this study, considering its extensive coverage and valuable insights into metrolingualism.

According to Pennycook and Otsuji (2015a), metrolingualism focuses on local language practices instead of the local implementation and appropriation of top-down language policies and it is the multilingualism and globalization from below, so it is not concerned with the extent to which local language policies and practices reflect top-down understandings of language but rather is constantly challenging those very ideas of language that are employed in language policies. It focuses not only on the linguistics of interaction but also on the city, the surrounds, the artifacts, all those other things that are equally part of the action. Thus, metrolingual pedagogy helps learners get beyond a segregational view of languages towards a more integrated one and be involved in the languages of life and the fluidity of everyday metrolingualism.

In fact, the focus of this study is not the ethnographic observation from the authentic metrolingualism, but the metrolingualism portrayed in ELT materials and its pedagogical implications which advocate incorporating "fluidity, flow and fixity of cultural movement" (Pennycook, 2007, p.157) into ELT practice as well as understanding the complexity of cultural exposure in the classroom and recognizing that cultures and identities are mixed and cosmopolitan rather than being bounded (Pennycook, 2007). Besides, everyday multilingualism is another implication to ELT brought by metrolingualism, which goes beyond the standards of native speakers and tends to linguistic realities of everyday communicative activities (Pennycook and Otsuji, 2015a). Such pedagogical implications could provide the researcher with a conceptual perspective to examine the related data in this study. Moreover, the concept of metrolingualism will be further elaborated in Chapter 2.

1.6.3 Fairclough's three-dimensional framework of CDA

This study adopted Fairclough's three-dimensional framework of CDA (1995) as another critical lens to analyze the data regarding GCE and metrolingualism, which will be briefly introduced here and further elaborated in Chapter 2. CDA can be seen as a critical approach to discourse analysis, since it tries to make evident through analysis and criticism, as well as to draw linkages between textual properties and social processes and relations (ideologies, power relations) that are generally invisible to those who generate and interpret those texts, and whose efficacy is dependent on this opacity (Fairclough, 1995). Fairclough's three-dimensional framework of CDA regards discourse as "(i) a language text, spoken or written, (ii) discourse practice (text production and text interpretation), (iii) sociocultural practice" (ibid., p.97). The discourse analysis approach contains linguistic description of the language text, interpretation of the relationship between the (productive and interpretative) discursive processes and the text, and explanation of the relationship between the discursive processes and the social processes (ibid.). Figure 1.1 is the diagrammatic representation of such an approach.

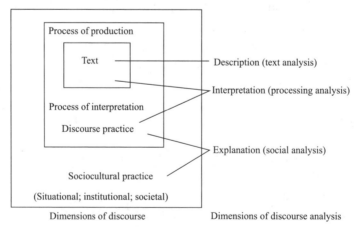

Figure 1.1   Three-dimensional framework of discourse analysis
(Fairclough, 1995, p.98)

In this study, text includes the textual and visual content in Chinese primary ELT textbooks and curriculum, and text analysis focuses on the descriptions of GCE and metrolingualism values in textbooks and curriculum. Discourse practice connects the discursive processes with the text to focus on the interpretations of GCE and metrolingualism values in textbooks and curriculum. Sociocultural practice associates the discursive processes with the social processes, that is, the results of GCE and metrolingualism in this study are explained by putting them in wider Chinese and global contexts. Figure 1.2 shows the three-dimensional framework of discourse analysis in this study, which has been adapted from Fairclough's three-dimensional framework of discourse analysis (1995, p.98).

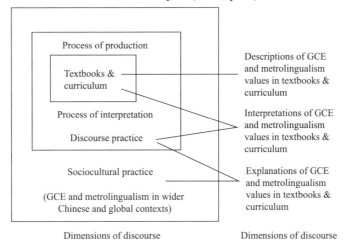

Figure 1.2   Three-dimensional framework of discourse analysis in this study
(Adapted from Fairclough, 1995, p.98)

1.7 Conceptual Framework

Building upon the aforementioned theoretical frameworks, this study endeavors to integrate the concepts of GCE and metrolingualism into a unified conceptual framework. GCE serves as the overarching concept, while metrolingualism acts as a complementary component based on the theory of globalization from below. These two concepts can mutually reinforce each other, with the ultimate goal of fostering global coexistence and harmony. Within this study, ELT textbooks and curriculum are regarded as the carriers that link these two concepts together. Consequently, the objective of this research is twofold: to explore how GCE and metrolingualism are portrayed in ELT materials and to investigate the role of metrolingualism, as embedded in textbooks and curriculum, in either facilitating or impeding GCE. The conceptual framework of this study, along with the interrelationship among the key concepts, will be further elucidated in subsection 2.4.2 of Chapter 2.

1.8   Significance of the Study

With its dual attributes of instrumental and educational goals for moral and civic dimensions (Williams, 2017), ELT holds great potential for fostering GCE, particularly within the context of globalization. However, there is still a need to examine how the theories of GCE can be effectively integrated into the Chinese educational context and implemented within ELT. Additionally, the impact of metrolingualism, as embedded in ELT textbooks and curriculum, on facilitating or hindering GCE remains largely unexplored. Therefore, this study aims to make contributions in the following three aspects regarding theoretical, pedagogical and methodological.

Theoretically, this study contributes to the development of relevant GCE theories within a nation-state and explores the feasibility of transdisciplinary implementation. While some related ideas of GCE have existed in China for a considerable time, the term itself is relatively new in the Chinese academic field and has had limited involvement within Chinese ELT. Therefore, this study aims to fill the knowledge gap regarding GCE in the Chinese context and promote the theoretical integration of GCE and ELT. Additionally, as metrolingualism is rooted in the theories of "globalization from below", this study has the potential to extend the theories of metrolingualism and further develop the concepts of "globalization from below". Moreover, this study represents an attempt to analyze and connect GCE and metrolingualism, thereby establishing a theoretical foundation for the future integration of these concepts within ELT. Furthermore, given its focus on primary school ELT textbooks and curriculum, this study may offer theoretical implications for the compilation of Chinese primary school ELT materials in relation to GCE and metrolingualism in the future.

Pedagogically, this study aims to deconstruct the notions of GCE and metrolingualism embedded in Chinese ELT textbooks and curriculum. Additionally, it seeks to explore teachers' perceptions of GCE and metrolingualism. The findings could provide a basis for future studies, contributing to a deeper understanding of how ELT contributes to China's context-specific initiatives in GCE and metrolingualism endeavors during the process of "glocalization".

For ELT teachers and students, this study aims to enhance their awareness, enabling them to transition from being passive followers to becoming critical consumers and creators of ELT materials. By exploring the GCE and metrolingualism values embedded in ELT textbooks and curriculum, this study can raise teachers' and students' critical awareness regarding these concepts. Consequently, teachers and students can become more conscious of the hidden ideologies in textbooks and curriculum, and make necessary adjustments during the implementation of ELT. They can also integrate their own language ideologies, cultural identities, and local language practices, allowing them to decode and encode additional local and global ELT content. Ultimately, this study has the potential to facilitate GCE and metrolingualism-oriented pedagogy within the Chinese ELT context, empowering teachers and students to actively engage with and contribute to these educational initiatives.

For textbook publishers and curriculum designers, this study can provide insights into incorporating the implications of GCE and metrolingualism into the revision of ELT materials. It highlights the importance of reforming ELT materials within the context of "glocalization" to make them more culturally and Englishes diversified. As ELT materials serve as teaching resources, instructors, trainers, and authorities, they play a crucial role in any ELT program (Cortazzi & Jin, 1999). Therefore, the relevant content in these materials is essential for promoting the effective implementation of GCE and metrolingualism-oriented pedagogy. This study can raise awareness among textbook publishers and curriculum designers regarding the hidden ideologies embedded within textbooks and curriculum. It encourages them to strive for a balanced and inclusive development of Chinese GCE by considering the perspectives of various stakeholders. By taking into account the implications of GCE and metrolingualism, textbook publishers and curriculum designers can contribute to the creation of materials that align with the goals of GCE and promote a more inclusive and diverse educational experience for students.

Besides, this study can provide policymakers with insights to revisit language policies by aligning them with the realities of language use, rather than adhering to a fixed vision of languages as static objects of modernity (Pennycook & Otsuji, 2015a). It aligns with Canagarajah's (2013) argument that pedagogy needs to be redesigned to accommodate the performance and cooperative personality outside classrooms and teachers should not target monolingualism, but prepare students for repertoires needed to learn cross-border contact areas. Furthermore, as teacher training is predominantly provided by government-funded institutions (Lee & Leung, 2006), this study has implications for the focus of such training programs. By incorporating the insights gained from this study, training programs can be designed to equip teachers with the necessary knowledge and skills to effectively implement

GCE and metrolingualism-oriented pedagogy. This will enable teachers to navigate the complexities of language education in a globalized context and foster students' language development and intercultural competencies.

Methodologically, this study endeavors to integrate GCE and metrolingualism through document analysis. This approach holds methodological significance as it offers insights into the potential application of metrolingualism in future GCE research. Additionally, it provides methodological implications for metrolingualism research, particularly by employing textual analysis instead of relying solely on ethnographic methodologies. This extension of methodological approaches contributes to the broader understanding and exploration of metrolingualism. Furthermore, this study can serve as a methodological reference for future ELT research that explores the connection of GCE and metrolingualism. Researchers can draw upon the methodologies employed in this study to investigate GCE and metrolingualism within the context of ELT. By adopting similar methodological approaches, researchers can gain insights into the ways in which GCE and metrolingualism are manifested in ELT materials, classroom practices, and language learning experiences.

To this end, this study is to a great extent different from previous studies regard to its new contributions in three aspects. Firstly, it combines the concepts of GCE and metrolingualism in the analysis of ELT textbooks and curriculum. By examining the presence and influence of GCE and metrolingualism values in these materials, this study offers a unique perspective that bridges the gap between GCE and ELT. Secondly, this study adopts a critical lens by exploring the dichotomy between soft and critical GCE. This critical approach enables a more comprehensive and nuanced examination of the underlying GCE values embedded in ELT textbooks and curriculum. It allows for a deeper understanding of the dynamics and ideologies within these educational resources. Thirdly, this study tries to translate the universal GCE model and metrolingualism in a new context of China from the very beginning educational level. The general goal is to highlight GCE and metrolingualism oriented pedagogies from below, and arouse stakeholders' critical awareness toward GCE while remaining a China focus, and empower students to better understand their "glocal" responsibilities, as well as bridge the gap between educational policy and daily life language practice, etc.

1.9 Definitions of Key Terms

Global citizenship supports a global view that links the local to the global, the national to the international, fostering a sense of belonging to a broader community and recognizing a shared humanity (UNESCO, 2014). In this study, this concept has been examined through a critical lens regarding the representation of this global view, particularly the promotion of diversity and plurality, within Chinese ELT textbooks and curriculum. Furthermore, it investigates how these representations intersect with sociopolitical and ideological issues specific to the context of China.

Global citizenship education is a conceptual framework that encompasses the role of education in equipping students with the knowledge, skills, values, and attitudes necessary for creating a more just, peaceful, tolerant, inclusive, secure, and sustainable world. It recognizes the importance of education in fostering students' understanding of civil, social, and political issues and preparing them to confront the challenges of an increasingly interconnected and interdependent world (UNESCO, 2014). GCE encompasses various aspects within the school community, including civil rights, diverse cultures, peace, justice, sustainable development, and environmental protection, etc. (ibid.). In this study, the representation of GCE values in Chinese primary ELT textbooks and curriculum is analyzed through the lens of soft versus critical GCE (Andreotti, 2006) and CDA (Fairclough, 1995). The study categorizes the embedded GCE values within different GCE domains, as defined by Akkari and Maleq's framework for GCE (2020). Additionally, it examines how teachers perceive these embedded GCE values in the textbooks and curriculum.

Metrolingualism in this study is primarily examined in terms of its pedagogical implications for ELT. It offers an alternative perspective for understanding language, considering the linguistic realities that emerge in everyday communicative activities (Pennycook & Otsuji, 2015a). The study adopts this pedagogical perspective of metrolingualism and analyzes how metrolingualism issues are represented in Chinese primary ELT textbooks and curriculum. Additionally, it investigates the ideologies that may be hidden within these materials. Furthermore, the study explores how teachers perceive the metrolingualism values embedded in the textbooks and curriculum through a metrolingualism lens.

ELT textbooks in this study specifically refer to the English textbooks used in Chinese primary schools by both teachers and students. There is a wide range of ELT textbook series available for primary education in China, with dozens of options on the market. Among these, the primary school ELT textbooks published by PEP and Yilin Press are very popular and widely adopted throughout the country. For the purpose of this study, the ELT textbooks examined include two series: the PEP textbooks and the Yilin textbooks used for primary English education in China.

ELT curriculum (Or ECSCE in this study) serves as an official guiding document that shapes the development of ELT textbooks and guides the implementation of ELT in classrooms. It outlines the objectives of ELT, sets standards for various language skills at each grade level, and provides implementation suggestions, among other components. In this study, ELT curriculum specifically refers to the national ECSCE (2011 Edition) in China, which is the guiding document for the compilation of PEP textbooks and Yilin textbooks that are examined in this study.

Primary education serves as the foundational stage of compulsory education. In China, primary education marks the initial phase of the nine-year compulsory education system, which is a mandated education that all school-age children and adolescents are required to receive. Typically, primary education spans six years, while junior secondary education spans three years, resulting in a total of nine years of compulsory education. In this study, primary education primarily refers to English education in grades three to six. This focus is based on the national ELT curriculum, which stipulates that English education generally commences from the third grade in primary education.

1.10   Summary of the Chapter

This chapter firstly introduced a research background for the study, including globalization and Chinese educational system. Then the researcher stated the research problem and the rationales of this study. Next, the researcher set forth the research purposes and the corresponding research questions. Theoretical frameworks of this study have been elaborated from three subsections, containing theoretical frameworks for GCE, theoretical framework for metrolingualism, and Fairclough's three-dimensional framework of CDA. The conceptual framework of this study comes next. Theoretical and pedagogical as well as methodological significance of this study have been elaborated after that. Definitions of some key terms were detailed at the end of this chapter. The next chapter will introduce some relevant literature as well as further elaborate the theoretical frameworks of this study.

CHAPTER 2
LITERATURE REVIEW

There are seven sections in this chapter. The first section is about global citizenship, containing the background of global citizenship, the concept and beliefs. The second section is about GCE, which consists of the beliefs and critiques, critical approaches to GCE, cultural awareness and intercultural awareness, global (intercultural) competence, GCE in China and national identity, GCE and English teaching & learning, GCE and textbook analysis, previous codings in textbooks regarding GCE, as well as focusing on the Chinese context. The issues concerned with metrolingualism are introduced in the third section including the concept, beliefs and pedagogical implications, previous studies regarding metrolingualism, metrolingual landscape, metrolingual citizenship and minority languages, critical multicultural education, as well as intercultural (global) sensitivity. The fourth section is focused on the theoretical conceptual relationships among some key terms in this study, containing two subsections of glocalization and ELT, GCE and metrolingualism vs. ELT textbooks and curriculum. The fifth section introduces Fairclough's three-dimensional framework of CDA and the application of this model in ELT textbooks analysis of previous studies. The sixth section focuses on the grand narratives in the discursive field of China. The summary of the whole chapter comes last.

2.1　Global Citizenship

2.1.1　Background of global citizenship

The concept of global citizenship has its roots in ancient times (宋强 , 2018a). However, it was during the emergence of capitalism in the 16th century that global citizenship took on a distinct capitalist influence, as capitalism became the dominant political and economic system in European and American countries. During this period, the notion of global citizenship became imbued with capitalist ideologies. It was not until the 19th century that Karl Marx's development of socialism from utopia to science, along with the establishment of the Soviet Union as the first socialist country and the rise of the international Communist movement in the early 20th century, posed a challenge to the capitalist global civic ideology and political system. Additionally, advancements in productivity facilitated the rise of global communication, transforming narrow national and local histories into a broader world history. Early conceptions of global citizenship expressed a yearning for the unity of human society. However, these ideas were often fragmented and lacked a systematic approach, making them difficult to implement in practice, let alone to carry out systematic education for global citizenship. Nonetheless, these early thoughts laid the groundwork for the emergence and development of GCE by providing fertile soil for its growth.

In 1945, the United Nations was established with the aim of promoting international collaboration in various areas, including international law and security, social progress, economic development, human rights, and world peace. UNESCO, as one of its specialized agencies, played a crucial role in the early development of GCE. From the 1950s to the 21st century, UNESCO released a series of documents advocating for the importance of raising awareness and enhancing the skills of citizens to address global issues arising from globalization. These issues include terrorism, ethnic conflicts, racism, prejudice, social inequality, poverty, pollution, and more. Subsequently, governments and education stakeholders in different countries began adjusting their policies and regulations on citizenship education, recognizing the significance of GCE (杨雪 , 2017). As globalization has accelerated, the concept of citizenship and its understanding have undergone changes. The distinctions between nationalities have gradually eroded (Law, 2006). The interconnectedness brought about by globalization has contributed to a shift in the perception and identity associated with citizenship.

Against this backdrop, the term "global citizenship" has garnered increasing attention from researchers. However, there is still a lack of consensus on the definition of related concepts within this field. Different scholars and experts may offer varying interpretations and understandings of global citizenship. The multifaceted nature of the concept and its broad implications contribute to the ongoing debate and lack of a universally accepted definition. Thus, further research and discourse are necessary to establish a common understanding and framework for global citizenship.

2.1.2   Concept and beliefs

There is a lack of consensus on the precise definition of global citizenship, leading to a controversial nature of the concept with multiple interpretations. Scholars have proposed various perspectives, resulting in different terms used to describe similar phenomena. For instance, "citizenship beyond borders" (Weale, 1991), "citizenship beyond the nation state" (Bellamy, 2000), "cosmopolitan citizenship" (Osler & Starkey, 2018), and "planetary citizenship" (Henderson & Ikeda, 2004) are among the diverse interpretations. As a consequence, different fields have developed their own viewpoints on global citizenship, leading to the adoption of various terms to describe similar phenomena. These terms include universal citizenship (Cavanagh, 2020), world citizenship (姜元涛 , 2015; 宋强 , 2018a), cosmopolitan citizenship (Osler & Starkey, 2018), transnational citizenship (Cavanagh, 2020), and intercultural citizenship (Byram, 2008), etc. Researchers and international organizations have provided their own definitions of global citizenship based on their respective understandings and perspectives. The lack of a universally agreed-upon definition reflects the complexity and evolving nature of the concept of global citizenship, necessitating ongoing discussions and further research in order to develop a comprehensive understanding of the term.

According to Burrow (2004), global citizenship involves recognizing the powers at play in the world and understanding their impact on human life. It also entails having an appreciation for diverse cultures, critically analyzing global issues, and generating new ideas for the betterment of the entire world. Brownlie (2001) argues that global citizens should not only be knowledgeable about global challenges but also be aware of and engaged in local issues that affect their lives and communities. Wang and Hoffman (2016) define global citizenship as individuals who act as agents of change, working towards the common good and upholding universal principles and norms. UNESCO (2014) describes global citizenship as a sense of belonging to a larger community and a shared humanity. It emphasizes the importance of adopting a global perspective that connects local and global issues, as well as national and international levels. Oxfam (2015) defines a global citizen as someone who is aware of the wider world and their role as a global citizen. They demonstrate respect for and value diversity, possess an understanding of how the world functions, are committed to social and economic justice, actively engage in both local and global communities, collaborate with others to create a fairer and more sustainable world, and take responsibility for their own actions. These different definitions highlight various aspects of global citizenship, including awareness of global issues, cultural understanding, commitment to the common good, and active participation in local and global communities. They provide diverse perspectives on what it means to be a global citizen.

Despite the multitude of definitions and perspectives, the fundamental essence of global citizenship lies in its inclusive nature towards the world. At its core, global citizenship is grounded in universal values that encompass understanding, action, and the way individuals relate to others and the environment. These values include respect for diversity, pluralism, and the recognition of the interconnectedness of the world. In the context of this study, the concept of global citizenship primarily centers around the global perspectives portrayed in Chinese ELT textbooks and curriculum, with a particular emphasis on the appreciation and respect for diversity and plurality. The analysis focuses on how these aspects of global citizenship are presented and promoted within the Chinese ELT educational context.

Subsequently, global citizenship has been increasingly incorporated into the educational system, garnering attention from educational scholars. The following section will delve into the various issues related to GCE and provide further elaboration on the subject.

2.2 Global Citizenship Education

2.2.1 Beliefs and critiques

GCE was initially proposed by Ban Ki-Moon, the former UN Secretary-General, who recognized the transformative potential of education in cultivating a deep awareness of the interconnectedness of global citizens and the interrelated nature of global problems (UNESCO, 2015). GCE provides a conceptual perspective and framework that emphasizes the essential role of education in shaping civic formation within the context of globalization. It encompasses the advancement of knowledge, skills, and values to support socio-emotional, behavioral, and cognitive aspects of learning (UNESCO, 2014). GCE is not limited to a specific stage of education but extends from primary to secondary education and into lifelong learning. It is deeply rooted in the teaching, learning, and caring aspects of schools, forming a holistic and interdisciplinary discipline that transcends narrow subject boundaries. It could promote equity, diversity, and social justice in educational settings in an increasingly interconnected world.

GCE encompasses all areas of school life, academics, and curricula (APCEIU, 2019). It connects various aspects within the school community, such as civil rights, diverse cultures, peace, justice, long-term development, and environmental protection. The ultimate aim of GCE is to empower learners to actively participate and make positive contributions at both local and global levels. It equips them with the necessary skills to confront and address global challenges, fostering their role as active agents in creating a more just, peaceful, tolerant, inclusive, safe, and sustainable world (UNESCO, 2014). In essence, GCE plays a powerful role in supporting gender equality, eliminating poverty, maintaining global equity and justice, and environmental conservation. By nurturing the growth of knowledge, skills, beliefs, and attitudes, GCE contributes to these important causes and endeavors.

However, those assumptions surrounding GCE are not without their challenges. One of the concerns is that GCE may primarily benefit elite groups, exacerbating social inequalities and widening gaps between different social groups. It is argued that GCE initiatives may inadvertently weaken national identity and further deepen social divisions (Goren & Yemini, 2017a). In recent years, higher education institutions have made significant efforts to enhance their internationalization efforts. This has involved expanding the recruitment of international students and scholars, increasing opportunities for overseas learning experiences, and implementing GCE programs such as studying abroad, international internships, and hosting visiting scholars from abroad. Nevertheless, there is a risk that some educational institutions approach GCE as a checklist of prerequisites to be fulfilled, rather than fostering a critically reflective mindset and skillset (Aktas et al., 2016). This approach may perpetuate power imbalances in the international community and reinforce elite cosmopolitanism (Caruana, 2014).

Additionally, Parmenter (2011) found that the discourse on GCE is dominated by Western English-speaking countries, which further highlights the limited representation of diverse perspectives. Critics argue that GCE, despite its positive and inclusive rhetoric, can be a concept that remains exclusive and reinforces social privilege. It is seen as a concept that separates those in positions of privilege from those in need (Jefferess, 2008). Thus, while GCE may appear to be a universal and inclusive concept on the surface, in reality, it can be highly localized and restrictive (Pais & Costa, 2017). The hidden agenda and ideological underpinnings of GCE may dilute its potential to address inherent contradictions and systemic issues. These criticisms shed light on the complex and nuanced nature of GCE, highlighting the need for a critical examination of its implementation and an inclusive approach that addresses power imbalances and ensures equitable access to it.

In response to these critical assumptions, some researchers have adopted a critical approach to GCE, aiming to uncover the hidden agenda that may be embedded within it. The subsequent subsection will introduce various critical approaches to GCE, with a focus on the soft versus critical GCE framework, which has been adopted as the theoretical framework for this study.

2.2.2 Critical approaches to GCE

GCE has long been a subject of debate and controversy, emerging as a response to the political and social realities of globalization (Choi & Kim, 2018). In recent years, researchers have argued for a more critical and theoretical approach to examine the underlying assumptions of GCE (Akkari & Maleq, 2020; Andreotti & Souza, 2012; Choi & Kim, 2018). These critical approaches to GCE can generally be categorized into three domains: neoliberal, radical/conflict, and critical/transformationalist (Shultz, 2007). Each of these approaches offers a distinct perspective on the role and objectives of GCE, while also intersecting with one another.

The neoliberal agenda has led some researchers to view GCE as an extension of national citizenship, emphasizing the cultivation of knowledge and skills necessary for global markets and connecting global citizenship to economic engagement (Choi & Kim, 2018). However, this neoliberal approach to GCE can have negative consequences. As global economic competition intensifies, neoliberal GCE runs the risk of deepening social stratification and exacerbating unequal power relations within the international community (Rizvi, 2007). Without critical awareness, neoliberal GCE may perpetuate existing inequalities while encouraging learners to view their privileged status as natural and indicative of personal success (ibid.). Further, under the influence of neoliberalism, cultural stereotypes can be reinforced in social studies, which may result in a simplistic and misguided understanding of the world, lacking critical perspectives and discussions regarding GCE (Reidel & Beck, 2016).

A radical/conflict perspective of GCE, which acknowledges the global systems that perpetuate inequality and deepen the north-south divide, seeks to challenge the hegemonic structures brought about by economic globalization and foster solidarity among marginalized populations (Aktas et al., 2016). However, critics argue that this perspective often rigidly dichotomizes global connections as global/ rich/democratic (oppressor) and local/poor/undemocratic (oppressed), with the global being associated with wealth and democracy, and the local with poverty and lack of democracy. This oversimplification fails to account for the complexities of oppression and power dynamics (ibid.). Another critique of neoliberalism comes from a postcolonial perspective, which serves as a complementary and more conciliatory approach to radicalism. The postcolonial perspective seeks to interrogate global ethnocentric hegemonies, deconstruct power relations, and challenge knowledge constructions in the field of GCE (Parmenter, 2011; Andreotti & Souza, 2012). Rizvi (2009) argues that the concept of developing global citizenship is rooted in the global inequalities perpetuated by colonial conquest. Postcolonialism examines the economic and cultural foundations of disparities in power, wealth, and labor within a complex and uncertain global system (Andreotti, 2006). This perspective offers insights and inspiration for addressing the prevailing neoliberal and imperialist frameworks within GCE (Andreotti & Souza, 2012).

In contrast to perceiving globalization solely as a path towards a globalized market, critical GCE, rooted in the postcolonial viewpoint, focuses on addressing issues of inequality and injustice while embracing diversity (Andreotti, 2006). It emphasizes the importance of critical literacy, where educators and students learn not only about different cultural backgrounds but also how power relations shape development and voices within various contexts. This approach aims to foster mutual recognition and understanding between the global North and South (Aktas et al., 2016). Critical GCE also highlights the need to reform not only institutions and systems but also personal and cultural mindsets and skill sets. Both educators and learners are encouraged to challenge and question global power structures, promoting a transformative and empowering educational experience (Andreotti, 2006).

Moreover, critical GCE calls for adapting to local, regional and global dimensions of citizenship, which makes it feasible in national educational policies challenging (Akkari and Maleq, 2020). Ho (2018) has made the case that the GCE framework differs greatly depending on the national context since it is directly tied to how states experience and react to forces of globalization, as well as realize the links between national civic and global communities, which results in the coexistence of a broad range of conceptualizations and targets for GCE (Gaudelli, 2016), and prompts people to explore alternative appropriate models of GCE around the world. Therefore, it is crucial for GCE frameworks to move beyond simplistic ideas like "bring the world into the classroom" or "send students into the world", which perpetuate to reinforce the division between "us and them" and "here and there" (Andreotti, 2006). To achieve all of this, it is necessary to prioritize critical GCE for the analysis of power relations and to address the difficulties of investigating citizenship from the viewpoint of individuals who are marginalized (Davies et al., 2018), in order to accommodate regional circumstances and needs.

More significantly, the need for more critical GCE techniques is growing (Goren & Yemini, 2017a; Reynolds et al., 2019), and more studies need to be done to bridge the gap between GCE's worldwide models and classroom practices in localities. To do this, it is possible to embed GCE in national historical legacies and citizenship development in order to provide instructional implications as tailor made models (Damiani, 2018) and to examine how instructors perceive and understand global citizenship. Furthermore, critical GCE approach has been rarely involved in ELT textbooks and curriculum analysis particularly in the Chinese context. Those issues were further addressed by employing GCE frameworks in this study. Besides, critical GCE calls for learners to have cultural awareness and intercultural awareness as well as regard communication as a cultural process, which will be underlined in the next subsection.

2.2.3　Cultural awareness and intercultural awareness

The integration of cultural dimensions into language teaching has given rise to the recognition of cultural awareness as a pivotal element. This perspective underscores the understanding that communication is inherently influenced by culture, thereby emphasizing the significance of learners comprehending their own cultural backgrounds and demonstrating sensitivity towards the cultural practices of others in the context of language use (Baker, 2012). While the incorporation of cultural awareness has been a consistent feature in language teaching, one of the most renowned frameworks is the concept of "critical cultural awareness" introduced by Byram in 1997 (ibid.). This framework serves as a fundamental principle within intercultural communicative competence, placing emphasis on the ability to critically evaluate cultural norms, standards, perspectives, actions, and outcomes within one's own culture as well as across different cultures and nations (Byram, 1997).

By emphasizing the importance of cultural awareness, language teaching endeavors to encourage learners to go beyond surface-level understanding and embrace a deeper appreciation for the intricate relationship between language and culture. It prompts learners to reflect on their own cultural backgrounds, beliefs, and values, while also fostering an open-minded attitude towards other cultures. Through the lens of critical cultural awareness, learners are encouraged to question and critically evaluate cultural assumptions and practices, recognizing that these elements are not fixed or universally applicable. The incorporation of critical cultural awareness within language teaching provides learners with the tools to navigate intercultural interactions with sensitivity, respect, and adaptability. It equips them with the ability to recognize and challenge stereotypes, biases, and ethnocentric viewpoints, thereby promoting a more inclusive and tolerant perspective. By engaging in critical reflection and analysis, learners develop a broader understanding of the cultural complexities that shape communication, enabling them to navigate cultural differences and communicate effectively in diverse settings.

In exploring the philosophical underpinnings of critical cultural awareness, Guilherme (2002) put forth critical theory and postmodernism as the foundational frameworks. Within these frameworks, cultural knowledge is perceived as a socially and interactively constructed phenomenon. Moreover, critical reflection is regarded as a vital tool for unraveling superficial cultural and social expressions and representations, while also enriching our understanding of the complex process of identity formation in multicultural global societies (Guilherme, 2002). While cultural awareness and critical cultural awareness both hold significance in language use and teaching, it is worth acknowledging that they have traditionally been rooted in the notion of a national culture and language. However, given the evolving nature of English as a lingua franca (ELF) and the emergence of more fluid and flexible communicative practices, it becomes necessary to reevaluate these concepts. In response to this dynamic context of English usage, intercultural awareness has been introduced as a more suitable concept (Baker, 2012). Intercultural awareness can be seen as an extension of cultural awareness, recognizing the need to navigate diverse cultural interactions and practices within the dynamic realm of ELF.

In the realm of language teaching, intercultural awareness takes precedence over cultural awareness as it emphasizes intercultural communication rather than focusing solely on a specific culture. To provide a comprehensive understanding of both concepts, Baker (2012) introduced twelve components of intercultural awareness, which extend cultural awareness to encompass the fluidity of intercultural interactions (refer to Table 2.1). These components encompass the knowledge, skills, and attitudes necessary for successful communication in complex intercultural contexts. The model presents a progression from a fundamental understanding of language and culture to a more intricate level, culminating in a fluid, hybrid, and emergent state that transcends critical cultural awareness. This framework recognizes the dynamic nature of intercultural communication and underscores the importance of developing the flexibility and adaptability needed to navigate ever-evolving intercultural circumstances. By embracing this expanded perspective, language learners can effectively engage with diverse cultures and foster meaningful intercultural connections.

Table 2.1   Twelve components of intercultural awareness (Baker, 2012, p.66)

Level 1: basic cultural awareness	• Culture as a set of shared behaviours, beliefs, and values • The role culture and context play in any interpretation of meaning • Our own culturally induced behaviour, values, and beliefs and the ability to articulate this • Others' culturally induced behaviour, values, and beliefs and the ability to compare this with our own culturally induced behaviour, values, and beliefs
Level 2: advanced cultural awareness	• The relative nature of cultural norms • Cultural understanding as provisional and open to revision • Multiple voices or perspectives within any cultural grouping • Individuals as members of many social groupings including cultural ones • Common ground between specific cultures as well as an awareness of possibilities for mismatch and miscommunication between specific cultures
Level 3: intercultural awareness	• Culturally based frames of reference, forms and communicative practices as being related both to specific cultures and also as emergent and hybrid in intercultural communication • Initial interaction in intercultural communication as possibly based on cultural stereotypes or generalizations but an ability to move beyond these through • A capacity to negotiate and mediate between different emergent socioculturally grounded communication modes and frames of reference based on the above understanding of culture in intercultural communication

Moreover, Pennycook (2007) described that global flows of linguistic and cultural practices, and intercultural awareness can help us approach culture as an urgent, negotiated resource in communication that flows between and across local, national and global contexts to deal with such global flows (Baker, 2009). Intercultural awareness, therefore, rejects native speakers' monolingualism as the ideal paradigm and suggests the intercultural citizen as an alternative, which regards intercultural communication as fluid, fragmented, mixed and emergent within different culture groups (Baker, 2012). Thus, intercultural awareness could also serve as the core of metrolingualism to promote intercultural communications from below as well as urge students to go beyond national-cultural affiliations and limits in order to achieve a transnational, intercultural or global citizenship (Byram, 2008). Since intercultural awareness is a prerequisite for building global competence which is the practice target for GCE, the next subsection will explore more about global (intercultural) competence.

2.2.4   Global (Intercultural) competence

All existing cultures are the results of intercultural communication, which is especially true in the era of globalization when the cultural landscape is rapidly evolving and individuals are increasingly closely connected resulting in much more diversity (UNESCO, 2013). Thus, besides intercultural awareness, the fluid, dynamic and transformative intercultural communications also require specific competences and capacities for individuals and societies to learn in order to achieve individual fulfillment and social harmony. This kind of competence, identified as intercultural competence, has been connected with various terms, such as global competence, intercultural sensitivity, multicultural competence, cross-cultural effectiveness, cultural proficiency, cross-cultural adaptation, intercultural skills, cross-cultural relations, intercultural agility (Hammer, 2015).

Fantini and Tirmizi (2006) used to define intercultural competence as the capacity to interact effectively and appropriately with individuals from various linguistic and cultural backgrounds, with the goal of releasing people from their own cultural traditions and logical constraints to interact with others and hear their thoughts. Similarly, UNESCO (2013) proposed that intercultural competence refers to having sufficient relevant knowledge about specific cultures, general knowledge about the varieties of issues that arise when interacting with different cultural members, bearing inclusive attitudes that motivate creating and keeping in touch with diversities, as well as being able to use both knowledge and attitudes when communicating with other people from various cultures. Deardorff (2006) conceptualized intercultural competence as a process that begins with an open attitude, respect and curiosity. Besides, Byram (1997, 2008) divided intercultural competence into separate skills, such as "savoirs (knowledge of the culture), savoir comprendre (skills of interpreting/relating), savoir apprendre (skills of discovery/interaction), savoir etre (attitudes of curiosity/openness), and savoir s'engager (critical cultural awareness)", which are also the core elements for his famous assumption for intercultural communicative competence.

Despite some conceptual disagreements, there is a consensus that intercultural sensitivity is a crucial capacity for effectively working and living with people from diverse cultures. It entails reducing biases, fostering inclusivity, and achieving common goals. Intercultural competence empowers individuals to engage in communication with cultural "others" by seeking to bridge differences, eliminate conflicts, and establish a foundation for peaceful coexistence (UNESCO, 2013). Therefore, intercultural competence is a key step towards promoting intercultural/global citizenship (Bodis, 2020). It plays a critical role in developing students' awareness of the interconnectedness of global issues, understanding the dynamics of multicultural settings, and enhancing their ability to work and communicate effectively in an increasingly globalized world.

Beyond intercultural competence, global competence addresses not only developing the ability to understand and deal with global and intercultural concerns, but also the cultivation of social-emotional intelligence, as well as virtues of respect, self-assurance and a feeling of togetherness, aiming to develop chances for everyone and promote a shared human dignity (OECD, 2018). OECD (2018) defined it as a multifaceted ability to investigate local, global, and multicultural concerns, understand and appreciate diverse viewpoints and world views, connect effectively and respectfully with others, and act responsibly for sustainability and everyone's well-being. The four dimensions of global competence, such as understanding and appreciating the perspectives and world views of others, engaging in open, appropriate and effective interactions across cultures, taking action for collective well-being and sustainable development as well as examining local, global and intercultural issues, are combined together and built on specific knowledge, values, attitudes and skills.

The nature of global competence defined by Reimers (2009) is to acquire the knowledge and skills that help people better understand the world they live in, as well as positively engage in global affairs and events. In the similar vein, global competency, according to the Longview Foundation (2008), is an accumulation of knowledge about regions of the world, cultures, and global concerns, as well as the skills and dispositions necessary to participate responsibly and successfully in the global environment. Thus, global citizenship needs global competence, and vice versa, students require global citizenship tendencies and diverse literacies to engage in a global world in order to be globally competent (Kerkhoff, 2017).

Besides, the OECD (2018) outlined a global competence assessment framework in PISA to encourage evidence-based decisions on improving teaching, curriculum, evaluations and schools' reactions to multiculturalism in order to prepare the youth to become global citizens. Deardorff (2013) proposed seven central themes across different cultures regarding global competence, such as listening, respect, relationship-building, self-awareness, adaptation, seeing from multiple perspectives, and cultural humility. Mansilla and Wilson (2020) created a research-informed and culturally sensitive paradigm for global competence education in China based on a culturally grounded and globally informed concept of global competence.

Moreover, since this study aimed at primary school ELT, it is necessary to briefly introduce the GCE learning objectives in *Global Citizenship Education: Topics and Learning Objectives* (UNESCO, 2015), which is the first pedagogical guidance from UNESCO on GCE. It introduces GCE-related ideas from the pre-primary or lower primary level and progresses through all stages of education via the use of a "spiral curriculum", which delivers the learning objectives according to the degree of complexity (UNESCO, 2015). The overall structure of GCE guidance has been listed in the Appendix A, which offers general information regarding the domains of learning, key learning outcomes, key learning attributes, topics, and learning objectives by age/level of education. The learning objectives have been divided into four levels according to different age groups, which are pre-primary/ lower primary (5-9 years), upper primary (9-12 years), lower secondary (12-15 years), upper secondary (15-18+ years) (refer to Appendix B for further details). Since primary school students in China are usually between 6 and 12 years old, the first two levels are the focus of this study.

All those frameworks and viewpoints provide reference for jointly promoting GCE to prepare the youth to see things from a different perspective, communicate across differences, and work cooperatively and creatively to address social, political, economic, and environmental problems (Mansilla & Wilson, 2020). While GCE has gained popularity worldwide, there is still a need for deeper exploration into its development within China and its impact on the national identity of the Chinese people. These crucial matters will be thoroughly examined in the subsequent subsection, providing a comprehensive understanding of the subject matter.

2.2.5 GCE in China and national identity

In ancient China, the concept of cosmopolitanism found its expression in various forms. One prominent manifestation was the notion of "the world under heaven" (天下), which represented the political ideal of achieving "great harmony in the world" (大同世界). Additionally, the teachings of "benevolence" (仁) and the cultivation of a virtuous character in the context of "the unity of nature and man" (天人合一) were integral to the cosmopolitan ideals of ancient Chinese society (宋强 , 2018a). Diverse schools of thought in ancient China also contributed to the discourse on cosmopolitanism. For instance, the Confucian worldview advocated for the concept of "the world is a family" (以天下为一家), while the Taoist worldview emphasized the idea of "governing the world by doing nothing" (以无事取天下), etc. Although these early notions of cosmopolitanism during the pre-Qin period were limited in scope, they served as a source of inspiration for the contemporary GCE movement in China, albeit constituting only a small fraction of its wider framework (ibid.).

Since the initiation of the "Reform and Opening up" policy in 1978, China has embarked on a path of increased engagement with the global community. It has actively expanded its presence in international economic, political, and educational spheres, while pursuing progressive international policies like the Belt and Road initiative to foster global trade and investment. In light of China's growing role on the global stage, there has been a concerted effort to prepare the younger generation for an interconnected world. Education has responded by embracing the motto "Education should be oriented towards modernization, the world, and the future" (教育要面向现代化 , 面向世界 , 面向未来). This shift in educational focus has been driven by the recognition that economic modernization, environmental challenges, rapid urbanization, and migration flows call for the development of global competence among the youth. Equipping them with the skills and knowledge to contribute to more harmonious and sustainable societies has become a pressing imperative (Mansilla & Wilson, 2020).

More significantly, the concept of "Community with a Shared Future for Mankind" was introduced during the 18th CPC National Congress in 2012. This concept transcends the boundaries of nation-states and ideologies, highlighting global responsibilities and advocating for peaceful development worldwide. Furthermore, the recognition of this concept is evident in its subsequent inclusion in UN resolutions pertaining to human rights and security. These resolutions signify the growing importance of this concept within the global discourse framework (宋强 ,

2018a). The recurring emphasis and promotion of the idea of a "Community with a Shared Future for Mankind" closely aligns with the goals of the GCE advocated by UNESCO. Both concepts underscore the coexistence and interconnectedness of the global community (宋强 , 2018b; Wang, 2023).

The word "citizen" first appeared in the People's Republic of China Constitution of 1954, which established the relationship between citizens and the government, society, and economy, as well as their responsibilities and rights within the communist system. The socialist citizenship paradigm in China has moved from exclusive to inclusive since it began to open up to the rest of the world in the late 1970s in order to address unique issues at various phases of development (Law, 2006). The term "citizenship education" has acquired popularity in the Chinese educational system and given it distinctive Chinese characteristics by elevating key communist ideas to normative status (ibid.). Global knowledge, varied cultures, and the peaceful coexistence of different races are just a few examples of how global themes have steadily been incorporated into curricular requirements and textbooks. On the other hand, China is a multiethnic country, of which the Han nationality accounts for more than 90 percent and the rest are minority ethnic groups. Therefore, GCE in China is multileveled or multidimensional (Law, 2006), embracing both global perspectives and socialist civic identities, and reflecting the regional traits of Chinese multiethnic nationalities.

Those policies and programs view GCE as a recognition of the need for global knowledge and skills to thrive in the global era, aiming to cultivate qualified citizens with global awareness and competence as defined within the Chinese discourse (Wang, 2023). However, despite the fact that the idea of global citizenship has been incorporated into the government policies, GCE is still not specifically defined in the pertinent policy on the national curriculum (Li, 2021), nor is there any explanation of what GCE should entail or how it should be implemented in China. Additionally, how China's GCE should react to the phenomenon of "glocalization" and its impact on both local and global populations is a crucial question. To this end, this study, thus, aims to address those issues by analyzing the representation of GCE embedded in Chinese ELT textbooks and curriculum.

Moreover, preparing the youth for the future world does not mean adding more continents or rivers to the already overflowing curriculum. Rather, it requires fostering a kind of learning in, about, and for the world that is deep, relevant and sustained (ibid.). GCE should be implicit in every part of the curriculum instead of an add-on. Due to both instrumental and educational roles of ELT, it plays an irreplaceable part to foster GCE (Jakubiak, 2020). The previous studies regarding

GCE and English teaching & learning have laid a disciplinary foundation for this study, which will be elaborated in the following subsection.

2.2.6 GCE and English teaching & learning

The integration of GCE across various subject areas is crucial, as each subject plays a significant role in nurturing the essential elements of active and responsible global citizenship (Oxfam, 2015). Among these subjects, ELT has emerged as an ideal domain for fostering GCE due to its instrumental and educational functions. Researchers have begun to explore the vital role of ELT in facilitating GCE (e.g., Gürsoy & Sali, 2014; Sali & Gürsoy, 2014; Omidvar & Sukumar, 2013; Erfani, 2012). Some researchers have focused on examining perceptions of GCE (e.g., Basarir, 2017; Roux, 2019), while others have emphasized pedagogical practices for GCE in ELT (e.g., Serrano, 2008; Porto, 2018) and teacher education (e.g., Ekanayake et al., 2020). Furthermore, certain researchers have explored GCE from the perspective of ELF (e.g., Cavanagh, 2020; Fang & Baker, 2017; De Costa, 2016).

In a study conducted by Basarir (2017), the attitudes of ELT instructors at a Turkish higher education institution towards incorporating GCE into ELT courses were explored using content analysis. The findings revealed that these instructors lacked the necessary knowledge, expertise, attitudes, and behaviors related to GCE. Building upon this, Roux (2019) argued that ELT instructors should move beyond a purely technical approach focused on teaching grammar, phonetics, and vocabulary. Instead, they should incorporate GCE into ELT in order to nurture students' critical thinking skills and foster their understanding of cultural diversity, thereby promoting mutual understanding among all individuals. Similarly, Pramata and Yuliati (2016) suggested that ELT instructors have a responsibility to enhance students' knowledge and understanding of global challenges while preparing them to actively participate in finding solutions. They proposed designing teaching plans that integrate GCE into classroom practices.

Recent research has highlighted the importance of intercultural knowledge, communication skills, and an inclusive attitude in promoting GCE (Pais & Costa, 2017). As a result, schools have begun to address GCE within ELT classrooms. One effective strategy for implementing GCE in ELT is to incorporate content- or theme-based instruction that addresses global challenges (Hosack, 2011; Serrano, 2008). For example, Almazova et al. (2016) analyzed the impact of globalization on foreign language teaching goals and proposed an interdisciplinary and integrative approach to enhance students' multicultural competence. This approach provides them with the necessary knowledge and skills for GCE, enabling them to become global citizens. Another case study conducted by Porto (2018) explored the connection between intercultural citizenship and language learning through the Cooperative Content and Language Integrated Learning program in Argentina and the United Kingdom. The findings, derived from content analysis, indicated that students' language and communication abilities improved as a result of embracing "cosmopolitan values" such as consensus, support, and solidarity. Furthermore, Ekanayake et al. (2020) conducted a descriptive study to examine the impact of teacher education and English language education on facilitating GCE. They emphasized the importance of establishing a strong foundation for teachers' professional skills and providing ongoing effective professional development for in-service teachers. Simultaneously, they highlighted the need to improve the professional standards of teachers.

In the context of globalization, promoting "native" English as the ideal language remains a barrier to internationalization and GCE, as highlighted by scholars investigating GCE from an ELF perspective (Saarinen & Nikula, 2013; Cavanagh, 2017). Insisting on this assumption hinders the recognition and acceptance of diverse English varieties and limits the inclusive nature of GCE. Additionally, the ideology of internationalization being equated with "Englishization" has become prevalent due to English language regulations such as English as a Medium of Instruction (EMI) policies (Botha, 2013; Piller & Cho, 2013; Botha, 2014). Consequently, the linguistic capital attributed to English in the domestic employment landscape (Park, 2016) and its associated social and economic prestige (Hu & McKay, 2012) can contribute to educational and social inequality, which in turn may have a negative impact on students' ability to fully engage in GCE. Regarding this, the importance of incorporating global Englishes in curriculum development that referenced proposal of promoting exposure to multilingualism/multiculturalism and fostering respect for diverse cultures and identities in ELT was advocated (Fang et al., 2022).

Cavanagh (2020) conducted a study using thematic analysis and discourse analysis to explore the perceptions of twenty students from two South Korean universities regarding global citizenship and how they perceive the relationship between global and Korean identities. The findings indicate that global citizenship is commonly understood in terms of English proficiency, with a strong emphasis on fluency standards that sometimes contradicts the students' Korean identity. Similarly, De Costa (2016) conducted an ethnographic study to examine identity construction in an English-medium school, analyzing how global citizenship was realized and discussing the use of ELF pedagogy to promote GCE. Furthermore, the concept of intercultural citizenship as a goal and subject in language education has been discussed (Fang & Baker, 2017) by combining intercultural and critical foreign language teaching approaches with intercultural communicative competence (Byram et al., 2017). In this context, ELF provides a solution to the conflict between native-speakerism and GCE equality (Wu, 2019). It enables students to think critically about their position in the world and how to develop compassionate and considerate relationships with others.

English teachers play a crucial role in promoting GCE and peace, as English language learning has been recognized as a vehicle for fostering global citizenship (Osler & Starkey, 2005). However, despite the aforementioned studies that have explored GCE from various perspectives within English teaching and learning, there is a lack of research on document analysis in ELT specifically related to GCE. These previous studies have yet to extensively address the gap between policies and practices, globalization from the top and the below, and the distinction between the language of school and the language of life. To some extent, this study aims to shed light on these issues. Additionally, English textbooks are a vital component of ELT materials, serving multiple purposes in the classroom, such as being a teaching resource, instructor, trainer, and a medium for conveying ideology and authority. They can be considered the heart of any ELT program (Cortazzi & Jin, 1999). Given the textbooks' significance, some researchers have turned to textbook analysis as a means to explore GCE.

2.2.7 GCE and textbook analysis

Language textbooks and other teaching materials are important curricular texts that reflect various social practices (Puspitasari et al., 2021). However, they may sometimes present distorted views of cultural and racial differences (Gay, 2015). This may explain why many teachers tend to focus only on safe themes related to cultural diversity, such as shared aspects between cultures, ethnic customs, cuisine, clothing, and holidays, while avoiding more challenging issues like inequality, injustice, and oppression (ibid.). A concerning issue is that teachers may not have a comprehensive understanding of the curriculum, which serves as a guiding document for textbooks and teaching practices. A qualitative study utilizing coding analysis was conducted to explore English teachers' understanding of the Basic Education Core Curriculum in Thailand and investigate the factors contributing to their understanding. The findings revealed that most teachers had an "impeding understanding" of the curriculum (Vibulphol et al., 2021). Therefore, the researchers called for teachers and students to critically analyze their textbooks and teaching resources and address any shortcomings when necessary (ibid.).

Ait-Bouzid (2020) conducted a content analysis of three Moroccan ELT textbooks to examine the inclusion of activities that foster students' sense of belonging to local and global communities, as well as develop skills, knowledge, and behaviors related to global citizenship. In the Iranian context, a study by Basarir (2017) revealed that ELT textbooks lacked sufficient information on global issues, hindering the development of learners' global awareness. Content analysis was also employed in this previous study. Although human rights, conflict resolution, democracy, responsibility, and diversity have been recognized as common global themes in Spanish primary school textbooks (De La Caba & Atxurra, 2006), there still exists bias in terms of the quantity and variety of contexts and perspectives they present (Ait-Bouzid, 2020).

For another, there are persistent research and practice gaps in language education policies globally, and the influence of neoliberal institutional expectations and structures often disconnect scholars from real-world issues. Therefore, critical research and reflection are necessary both within and outside the framework of neoliberal institutions to embrace more socially engaged and dynamic perspectives (Kubota, 2018). In this regard, some researchers have turned to textbook analysis to examine the influence of neoliberalism. Choi and Kim (2018) conducted a deconstruction of neoliberalism in global citizenship discourses found in South Korean social studies textbooks. They employed the concepts of soft versus critical GCE as well as CDA to analyze the textbooks, the findings of which revealed the prevalence of a neoliberal agenda and nationalist rhetoric. Similarly, Savski (2022) used CDA to explore the conceptual connections between neoliberalism and other ideologies in a Thai ELT textbook series. The findings highlighted the presence of certain elements of neoliberalism, particularly those related to consumer culture, within the textbooks. Daghigh et al. (2022) conducted a thorough qualitative analysis of content to investigate the presence of consumerism in Malaysian secondary school ELT textbooks. The results of their study provide a basis for critiquing the available ELT textbooks in Malaysia, a global South country influenced by neoliberalism.

Moreover, textbooks are widely considered as artifacts of cultural representation, making cultural representation a prominent research topic. Song (2013) conducted a content analysis of Korean ELT textbooks to examine cultural representations. The findings revealed the reproduction of social inequalities related to race, nationality, and gender, with a strong emphasis on mainstream white American male portrayals. Therefore, a critical approach is necessary to foster more inclusive and critical worldviews among students (Song, 2013). Davidson and Liu (2018) analyzed Japanese textbooks and highlighted that the cultural representation was oversimplified, failing to develop students' capacity for GCE in terms of open-mindedness, cultural awareness, and social responsibility. English textbooks used in Germany were found to depict culture and English language usage as stable and static, disregarding the dynamic nature of language change over time and across distances. This approach does not align with the fluid, diverse, and flexible cultures in lingua franca contexts, nor does it meet the needs of students in a diverse reality (Syrbe & Rose, 2016). Additionally, teachers may be unaware of the ideological messages embedded in textbooks that promote binary opposition between Japanese and foreign cultures. This lack of awareness can hinder their ability to balance these messages with more diverse perspectives, thus preparing students for a globalized society (Glasgow & Paller, 2016).

Textbooks contain both textual and visual content, and it is important to recognize that illustrations in textbooks may not be value-free. Brown and Habegger-Conti (2017) conducted a study on the depiction of indigenous cultures in visual content within ELT textbooks for Norwegian lower secondary schools. They employed visual content analysis and semiotic image analysis to examine how images of indigenous people contribute to or contradict the cultural goals outlined in the English language learning curriculum in Norway. The findings indicated a strong tendency to focus on the traditional elements of indigenous people, portray them in a lower power position compared to the viewer, and create a sense of alienation. In contrast, images of white people were more likely to invite interaction and empathy from the viewer (Brown & Habegger-Conti, 2017). Yumarnamto et al. (2020) explored the sociocultural and political dimensions of illustrations in Indonesian ELT textbooks. They employed CDA to study the imagined communities, diversity, and identities reflected by the illustrations in textbooks. The findings revealed a tendency towards a more monolithic view of Indonesian identity and imagined community. The researchers suggested that this uniformity of identity in the images served the objective of integrating character education to strengthen nationalism, which indicates the presence of a political dimension as a hidden curriculum in textbook illustrations (Yumarnamto et al., 2020).

To this end, previous studies have revealed a limited number of investigations into the analysis of textbooks concerning GCE. Most of these studies focused on college-level social science textbooks, while the analysis of primary ELT textbooks was uncommon. Furthermore, only a few studies have analyzed ELT textbooks in conjunction with the national curriculum. Content analysis and CDA have emerged as common methods employed in previous studies for textbook analysis. It is worth noting that intercultural/global citizenship education is a relatively new paradigm, particularly in the formulation of English language policies and curricula. The current ELT education should be enriched by incorporating intercultural/global citizenship education (Boonsuk & Fang, 2021). Therefore, this study aims to explore the representation of GCE in primary English education by analyzing ELT textbooks and the curriculum. By doing so, this study fills the gap in previous research and contributes to the understanding of GCE in primary-level ELT education.

Further, since this study also utilized content analysis to examine GCE in textbooks and the curriculum, it is crucial to review the codings and themes employed in previous studies on textbook analysis. This will provide valuable references for generating themes and facilitating discussions in the following subsection.

2.2.8 Previous codings in textbooks regarding GCE

Regarding the previous codings and themes in textbooks, "human rights", "conflict resolution", "responsibility", "democracy", and "diversity" were identified as popular themes in Spanish primary school textbooks regarding citizenship education (De La Caba & Atxurra, 2006). In this previous study, the researchers provide a qualitative description of the content of each theme and a quantitative assessment of their frequency of occurrence (ibid.). Choi and Kim (2018) employed soft vs. critical GCE and CDA to discuss that the GCE themes embedded in Korean public school social studies textbooks, such as "cultural diversity", "globalization", "sustainability", "peace" and "associated skills" as well as "dispositions", were marginalizing social justice and multiculturalism while continuing neoliberal economic values and nationalism. Moreover, Davidson and Liu (2018) explored teachers' and students' perceptions of global citizenship in Japanese English textbooks for primary education through content analysis and thematic analysis, and they abstracted the themes such as nascent global citizenship sentiments, (inter) cultural awareness, social responsibility, and open-mindedness.

Besides, Ait-Bouzid (2020) abstracted the GCE themes representing the learning domains in three Moroccan ELT textbooks by using UNESCO's global citizenship learning domains of cognitive, socio-emotional and behavioral, such as themes of "Moroccan Parliament structure", "culture shock", "brain drain", "environment", "unemployment", "stereotypes", "Non-Governmental Organizations", "racism", "cooperatives", "international organizations", "governmental institutions", "associations" in the cognitive domain; themes of "racial identities", "national", "gender", "immigration", "ethnic", "brain drain", "promote equality despite difference", "compare different cultures", "tourism" in the socio-emotional domain;

themes of "Non-Governmental Organizations", "community service", "youth engagement", "fight discrimination", "associations", "brain drain", "promote social justice", "voluntary work", "tolerance", "political activism", "environment" in the behavioral domain. In this previous study, the researcher adopted content analysis as the data analysis method to combine both qualitative and quantitative techniques (Ait-Bouzid, 2020). Moreover, Puspitasari et al. (2021) conducted a CDA to analyze textual and visual contents in three primary ELT textbooks in Indonesia, and they found the moral values in textbooks such as "being friendly", "helping others", "being caring", "tolerance", "politeness", "healthy lifestyle", "negotiation", "curiosity", "leisure", "cleanliness", "creativity", "curiosity", "democracy", "self-discipline", "gender equality", "honesty", "independence", "nationalism", "responsibility", and "togetherness", among which "tolerance", "helping others", as well as "being friendly and polite" are the most dominant moral values discursively depicted in textbooks which could facilitate GCE development.

The codings and themes identified in previous studies indicate that textbooks often prioritize specific issues related to GCE, such as cultural diversity, conflict resolution, gender issues, and the environment. Content analysis and CDA have been widely used as methods to code and analyze these themes in previous studies. The insights gained from these previous codings and themes can offer valuable theoretical and methodological guidance to the present study. However, the distribution and representation of these GCE-related issues in Chinese primary ELT textbooks have yet to be explored. This study aims to fill this gap by investigating how these GCE-related issues are distributed and represented in Chinese primary ELT textbooks. This research will contribute to a better understanding of GCE in the context of Chinese primary ELT education.

Despite the increasing number of studies on GCE worldwide, it remains a relatively new concept in China, and research on GCE started relatively late in China (姜元涛, 2015). While the number of relevant studies on GCE in the Chinese context may be limited, they still provide some groundwork for the implementation of this study. Therefore, it is important to focus on GCE studies conducted specifically in the Chinese context in the following subsection.

2.2.9 Focusing on the Chinese context

Relevant studies on GCE in the Chinese context can be categorized into three main aspects. Firstly, some researchers have focused on the historical development, connotations, characteristics, challenges, and opportunities faced by educators in implementing GCE in China (e.g., Qi & Shen, 2015; 姜元涛, 2015; 宋强, 2018a).

These studies provide insights into the theoretical foundations and practical considerations related to GCE in the Chinese context. Secondly, some researchers have examined the GCE experiences of countries beyond China, seeking to draw inspiration from their practices (e.g., Lu, 2010; 张超, 2020). These studies contribute to a broader understanding of GCE by exploring international perspectives and comparative analysis. Lastly, there are studies that focus on case studies of GCE or conduct comparative research in different areas within China (e.g., Lee & Leung, 2006; Liu & Wang, 2014; 杨雪, 2017; Zhu, 2013; Chen, 2020; Li, 2021). These studies provide valuable empirical evidence and insights into the implementation of GCE in specific contexts, shedding light on effective strategies and challenges.

Qi and Shen (2015) conducted a study on Chinese traditional world citizenship thoughts, such as "great harmony in the world", "the unity of nature and man", "humanitarianism" (人道主义), and "pacifism" (和平主义). They concluded that the civic consciousness of traditional Chinese society is relatively weak. Jiang (2015) explored the connotation and characteristics of GCE and analyzed its ideological tensions. The future development of GCE in the Chinese context was also discussed in this study. Song (2018a) advocated for educators to not only focus on cultivating patriotism and national identity but also emphasize the development of global perspectives, international awareness, and tolerance for different cultures. Feng (2014) proposed the construction of a multi-leveled citizenship system in line with China's social development in the era of globalization. This system includes education for individual citizenship, national citizenship, social citizenship, and global citizenship. Additionally, Song (2018b) argued that GCE is closely linked to the concept of "Community with a Shared Future for Mankind", and they share common ground in terms of their connotations.

Several researchers have drawn upon the experiences of countries outside of China in their studies. Lu (2010) examined the American GCE model, which involves a stratified and three-dimensional network of education encompassing "school-family-society". The Massachusetts Institute of Technology (MIT) was analyzed for its efforts and reforms towards GCE, providing valuable experience and reference for the international construction ideas and practices of Chinese high-level research universities (崔军 & 汪霞 , 2010). Fu (2011) explored the historical development of American civic education goals from the colonization period to the globalization period. Zhang (2020) examined the GCE curriculum in Canadian primary and secondary schools to provide inspiration and insights for China's own context. Yang (2016) argued that there is currently no curriculum in China's compulsory education that adequately addresses the goals of citizenship education.

Therefore, realizing the curriculumization of citizenship education and constructing a comprehensive curriculum system for citizenship education in compulsory education remain important tasks.

Moreover, Lee and Leung (2006) conducted a study in secondary schools in Hong Kong and Shanghai to investigate teachers' knowledge, skills, and values regarding GCE, as well as their implementation of GCE. The findings indicated that while teachers generally supported GCE, they also encountered difficulties and challenges in its implementation. Liu and Wang (2014) explored the theory and practice of GCE in a Korean international school in Beijing. They identified three dimensions of GCE implemented in the school: Beijing citizenship, Korean citizenship, and global citizenship. Yang (2017) advocated for a shift in the concept of foreign language education, moving away from viewing it solely as a tool. Instead, she emphasized the importance of establishing a global perspective to facilitate educational transformation and the pursuit of a world driven by "local positioning" and "global orientation".

Besides, Zhu (2013) conducted a comparative study between China and America using CDA, the findings of which revealed a tendency in textbooks to promote civic values primarily at the national level, rather than emphasizing the local or global perspectives. To further explore avenues for advancing the GCE agenda within the prevailing national civic education system, Chen (2020) conducted a comparative analysis of the national curricula of China and Japan. Given China's state-led citizenship education, there has been a longstanding prioritization of Chinese culture, which is a crucial element of Chinese identity (Law, 2013). In another study, Li (2021) employed a qualitative data analysis framework to conduct a case study on GCE implementation in schools of China, focusing on the perspectives of teachers. The results revealed that instructors demonstrated a comprehensive understanding of GCE, and the author argued for the promotion of critical practice within the local context (Li, 2021). Adopting a qualitative approach, Woods and Kong (2020) investigated GCE in Chinese international schools, highlighting that it often appeared as an idealized version of reality rather than a practical template for fostering new forms of citizenship and belonging. Furthermore, Baker and Fang (2019) undertook a mixed-methods study to examine how Chinese student sojourners developed their sense of intercultural or global citizenship. Their findings suggested that GCE had been a missed opportunity in the field of ELT and scholarship.

Indeed, the analysis of Chinese textbooks in relation to GCE has received limited attention. However, a few relevant studies on textbook analysis can be briefly mentioned. Tse (2011) conducted a thematic analysis comparing two series of

Chinese textbooks published in 1997 and 2005. The findings revealed that the more recent textbooks adopted a more inclusive approach towards human rights and global citizenship. They emphasized the expectation for young citizens to contribute to the mission of national revitalization and socialist modernization, reflecting the influence of official policies while also granting individuals more autonomy and rights (Tse, 2011). Chu (2018) employed content analysis and CDA to examine the construction of the Chinese concepts of minzu (ethnicity) and Zhonghua Minzu (Chinese Nation) in elementary language and social studies textbooks. The findings shed light on the multifaceted meanings of minzu within the textbooks and the discursive construction of the Zhonghua Minzu ideology, both of which play a crucial role in positioning China as a unified and multiethnic society.

Furthermore, Feng (2019) utilized a social semiotic approach to investigate the portrayal and evolution of social values in ELT textbooks in Hong Kong, the findings of which showed that social values shifted from the personal (such as maintaining good hygiene and a healthy lifestyle) to the interpersonal (such as respect and politeness) to the altruistic concern for all of humanity. However, the study also indicated a relative lack of emphasis on developing critical thinking skills in the textbooks (Feng, 2019). Therefore, it is important for teachers and students to adopt a critical stance to cultivate and exercise students' critical thinking skills (Fang & Elyas, 2021). With neoliberalism exerting significant political, economic, and ideological influence across various aspects of globalized institutions and societies, including ELT, Xiong and Yuan (2018) conducted a study on the neoliberal discourse present in Chinese ELT textbooks using CDA. The research examined how English proficiency is commodified as an ideal linguistic cultural capital, English learning is portrayed as an individualized and detached endeavor, and a vision of a monolingual and monocultural community is constructed to assimilate learners into an imagined homogeneous discourse community. Similarly, He and Buripakdi (2022) conducted a CDA-based investigation into neoliberal values embedded in a Chinese college English textbook. The study identified several values, including entrepreneurship, individualism, consumerism, and commodification, which were attributed to economic, social, and political factors in China.

To this end, previous studies conducted in the Chinese context indicate that GCE is still a relatively new research field in China. Despite the crucial role of ELT textbooks and curriculum in fostering GCE, they have received limited attention, and even fewer studies have examined GCE at the elementary school level. Existing studies in the Chinese context have primarily focused on general issues related to GCE, often neglecting its interdisciplinary nature and failing to contextualize it within specific disciplines. Consequently, there is a need for further research in China that explores the interest and relevance of intercultural citizenship education (Han et al., 2017). More significantly, the ways in which Chinese ELT textbooks and curriculum reflect the concept of GCE, as well as teachers' perceptions of GCE values, remain largely unknown. These gaps in knowledge serve as the motivation for the current study, which aims to delve deeper into these issues.

Additionally, this research also explores the concept of metrolingualism. It examines how Chinese elementary ELT textbooks and curriculum incorporate the notion of metrolingualism and how teachers implement it in classrooms. This investigation aims to shed light on how the language used in schools reflects the linguistic realities of people's daily lives. Ignoring the issue of metrolingualism may pose a stumbling block for globalization and GCE from below and impede the full realization of GCE. Subsequently, the following section will provide a comprehensive exposition of metrolingualism.

2.3 Metrolingualism

2.3.1 Concept, beliefs and pedagogical implications

The term of metrolingualism, developed by Otsuji and Pennycook (2010), was originally extended from the notion of metroethnicity (Maher, 2005), and referred to "creative linguistic conditions across space and borders of culture, history and politics, as a way to move beyond current terms such as multilingualism and multiculturalism" (Otsuji & Pennycook, 2010, p.244). Its focus is to understand about city-related language resources and to demonstrate how everyday multilingualism is practiced in streets, markets, shops, cafes and other social urban spaces (Pennycook & Otsuji, 2015a), so it is about everyday language use and local language practices in urban spaces. Metrolingualism concerns with understanding the practice of urban language, which is a part of everyday life, not through a predefined version of language in terms of equitable language policies, but through local language ideologies (ibid.). Albeit it shares some similarities with translanguaging, metrolingualism concentrates on the relation between language practices and urban space (metro) instead of centering on linguistic movement for analysis (ibid.), and it is also different from multilingualism for that it is the dynamic emergence of language and identity rather than a convergent diversity.

For another, metrolingualism links with the idea of globalization from below (Mathews & Vega, 2012) or grassroots globalization (Appadurai, 2001), which means that "globalization as experienced by most of the world's people" (Mathews & Vega, 2012, p.1) and people live in a world of movement. It is structured by movement of people, goods, information and capital between various production centers and markets that are nodes of a non-hegemonic world system, which may be associated with "the developing world", but it is actually across the whole world (ibid.). Even though globalization form below may be considered as "the transnational flow of people and goods involving relatively small amounts of capital and informal, often semi-legal or illegal transactions" (ibid., p.1), it is still beneficial since it "provides the poor of the world a taste of the goods of the rich, and enables hundreds of millions across the globe to make a living" (ibid., p.10). Ribeiro (2012) argued that below and above are metaphors of unequal relationships in the interrelationships of conflict, collaboration and contradiction. Thus, both the globalization from above and the globalization from below should be taken seriously if we hope to study the current global system (Mathews & Vega, 2012). Similar idea comes to "English from above" vs. "English from below", and the former means that the hegemonic culture promotes English to achieve the purpose of international communication, while the latter is a kind of informative active or passive manifestation of subcultural identity and style in English (Preisler, 1999).

Metrolingualism, serving as a manifestation of multilingualism from below, revolves around individuals' unique perspectives on language practices. Consequently, it remains unconcerned with the extent to which top-down interpretations of language or the alignment of language realities with linguistic ideals are mirrored in local language practices. Instead, metrolingualism serves as an ongoing challenge to the language ideals employed in language policies (Pennycook, 2013). In contrast to both monolingualism and multilingualism, metrolingualism represents a dynamic mutual relationship between language practices and the urban space (Pennycook & Otsuji, 2015a). However, it is essential to note that metrolingualism extends beyond the boundaries of cities, offering an alternative lens through which language, as well as linguistic and non-linguistic resources, can be comprehended. Consequently, metrolingual practices possess the capacity to subvert established linguistic orthodoxies and challenge assumptions concerning language, identity, and belonging (ibid.).

Besides, another significant dimension of metrolingualism is spatial repertoire, including activities, objects, place and semiotic resources, which refers to the "throwtogetherness" (Massey, 2005, p.140) of linguistic and other semiotic resources in a particular place, since metro interaction is actually the spatial organization of semiotic resources and the semiotic organization of space (Pennycook & Otsuji,

2015a). Moreover, one approach to better understanding such metro linguistic practice is to study its metrolingual franca as well, which is linked with the term of niche lingual francas referring to second languages that are not the dominant language but are used for local interactions in particular areas (Block, 2007). Metrolingual franca is not to select a language from a range of linguistic options, but specific language practices that draw on the accessible spatial repertoires at any moment, thus it contains all linguistic and non-linguistic resources that can be used at different moments rather than fixed or stable or shared (Pennycook & Otsuji, 2015a).

Furthermore, metrolingualism bears implications for ELT pedagogies. Pennycook (2007) proposed the concept of "teaching with flow" (p.155) and endeavored to incorporate the "fluidity, flow, and fixity of cultural movement" (p.157) into ELT practices. This approach acknowledges the complexity of cultural exposure in the classroom, recognizing that cultures and identities are interconnected and cosmopolitan rather than fixed within boundaries. Similarly, Canagarajah (2013) argued that educators should prepare students for the diverse repertoires required in cross-border contact zones, moving beyond a narrow focus on a single language or dialect. This enables learners to adapt to the performative competence and cooperative disposition observed outside the classroom. Consequently, the challenge for educators lies in transcending the compartmentalized view of language and adopting a more comprehensive linguistic perspective. They need to assist learners in integrating their own semiotic activities with those of their interlocutors (Pennycook & Otsuji, 2015a). In this context, an emerging target for language education may involve embracing the local practices of metrolingual speakers rather than adhering to an idealized notion of native speakers (ibid.).

This pedagogical implication emphasizes the need for language policy makers to move away from approaches that devalue certain languages in favor of recognizing and valuing diverse linguistic practices. It calls for a shift in focus towards language practices and acknowledges the linguistic realities of the contemporary world. Rather than viewing language as a fixed object of modernity, both language policy and education should engage with the dynamic nature of language repertoires, resources, practices, and mobilities (ibid.). Nevertheless, if educators disregard this world of language repertoires, resources, practices, and mobilities, it will deepen the gap between the language of schools and the language of everyday life. It will also reinforce the fixed codes of schooled multilingualism while neglecting the fluidity of everyday metrolingualism (ibid.). Metrolingualism is an emerging research field, and scholars such as Pennycook and Otsuji have made significant contributions to this area. Their studies have laid a solid theoretical foundation for research in metrolingualism. Thus, the following section of this study primarily reviews their works, along with the contributions of other researchers who have explored this field.

2.3.2 Previous studies regarding metrolingualism

As previously mentioned, the concept of metrolingualism was originally proposed by Pennycook and Otsuji and developed from the notion of metroethnicity. The book *Metrolingualism: Language in the City* (Pennycook & Otsuji, 2015a) serves as a significant milestone in the field of metrolinguistics, providing a comprehensive overview of metrolingualism. Prior to that, Pennycook and Otsuji had published a series of articles exploring this concept (e.g., Otsuji & Pennycook, 2011; Pennycook & Otsuji, 2014a; 2014b), which laid the groundwork for further research on metrolingualism. Subsequently, the study of metrolingualism has been continuously researched and expanded (e.g. Pennycook & Otsuji, 2016; 2017). As a result, the field of metrolingualism has seen further growth and exploration by scholars (e.g. Yao, 2021).

Otsuji and Pennycook (2011) collected data from "Japanese" and "Australian" interaction practices at a workplace in Sydney to explore the impact of metrolingual practices on the understanding of social inclusion, and findings showed that social inclusion has become the new multiculturalism which could provide a new way to understand language and social disadvantage if it is broadly conceived and combined with metrolingualism. Moreover, metrolingual francas were explored by collecting data from records of two urban markets to study how they were emerged from spatial repertoires through analyzing languages used by workers and customers in their daily business and paying particular attention to the ways in which linguistic resources, daily tasks, and social spaces are interwoven (Pennycook & Otsuji, 2014a). Besides, the relationship between metrolingual multitasking and spatial repertoires was also investigated through studying the intertwining of linguistic resources, daily tasks and social space in two particularly restaurants in Tokyo and Sydney, which showed that the focus on repertoires, resources, place, space and activity could facilitate the understanding of multilingualism from below (Pennycook & Otsuji, 2014b).

The publication of *Metrolingualism: Language in the City* provides a comprehensive picture of metrolingualism by exploring language within a number of contemporary urban situations in Sydney and Tokyo (Pennycook & Otsuji, 2015a). Then this concept has been further expanded in subsequent studies. The sensory landscape in urban markets has been researched to link between linguascapes and smellscapes (Pennycook & Otsuji, 2015b). Besides the fluid and fixed language use and description, Pennycook and Otsuji (2016) also focused on the negotiations around the labels used by participants themselves, and they argued that the crux of the problem lied not in the polarization between fluid language use and fixed linguistic attribution, but in the constant reconfiguration of meaning.

On the other hand, by focusing on assembling artifacts in two Bangladeshi-run stores in Tokyo and Sydney, Pennycook and Otsuji (2017) argued that those objects must be considered seriously as components of action and semiotic assemblages of material and semiotic resources, which could provide implications for social semiotics as part of a vital sociolinguistics of diversity. Similarly, Pennycook (2017) suggested including a broad range of semiotic possibilities in any analysis, as well as seeking out a way of grasping the relationships between various types of semiosis. Echoing the concept of metrolingualism on the one hand, Pennycook and Otsuji (2019) extended it to a new term for mundane metrolingualism with diverse ordinariness focus on the other hand. Combining everydayness and worldliness together, this concept is about the ordinary, the material and the tangible as well as anti-hegemony, struggle for recognition, resistance and against the dominant or normative linguistic indications (ibid.).

Besides Pennycook and Otsuji, some other researchers have also studied metrolingualism from different angles. Jaworski (2014) extended the scope of metrolingualism beyond multilingualism by including multimodal dimensions, mixture of genres, styles, accents, materiality of texts, as well as their position and pragmatic relevance, and suggested that metrolingualism be reconstructed as a manifestation of heteroglossia. For another, due to the field of linguistic landscape (LL) is rarely associated with the online digital space brought about by the growing number of metrolingualism, Yao (2021) examined the online LL of WeChat Moment posts to present a spatial repertoire consisting of innovative semiotic affordance, and findings showed that metrolingual activities have contributed to content self-policing, accessibility manipulation, and literacy compensation in the online LL, which provides a new relationship between language and space. Similar to spatial repertoires and metrolingual multitasking, Zhu, Li and Lyons (2017) investigated how spatial arrangement, merchandise display, gaze work and body movement with linguistic coding in a family retail shop in East London, and created a concept of Translanguaging Space which involves the orchestration and deployment of a variety of non-linguistic sense-making repertoires.

For another, everyday multilingualism depends on our understanding of multilingual use, which is the dynamic use of complex structures to achieve communicative goals (Matras, 2008). Thus, the dynamic everyday multilingual reality of linguistic repertoires as adjustable and adaptable instruments of communication should be advocated regarding metrolingualism, and the ownership of language forms as well as practices is best returned to language users, who should be given the skills and opportunities to manage their own multilingual repertoires (ibid.). Nonetheless, the conceptualizations of these language discourses may still indicate that the usage of English was deeply entrenched in a colonial structure of Anglophone powers' political and economic hegemony (Buripakdi, 2014). In this light, Fang and Jiang (2019), from an ELF viewpoint, argued for the necessity of overcoming the fixed relationship of language and culture, so intercultural literacy and critical language awareness should be fostered in both teachers and students by speculating and questioning during the intercultural communication process.

To sum up, while researchers have approached metrolingualism from various perspectives, the core concepts consistently revolve around key terms such as language and space, metrolingual practice, spatial repertoires, everydayness, from below, fluidity, diversity. Ethnographic approaches have been commonly used as the research method for studying metrolingualism. The importance of teaching local metrolingual practices and connecting English classrooms with the language of everyday life is emphasized in the field of metrolingualism (Pennycook & Otsuji, 2015a). However, there have been limited studies that investigate metrolingualism issues through document analysis, and the gap between the language of school and the language of everyday life has rarely been examined through the analysis of ELT textbooks and curriculum. Therefore, the current study aims to address this gap and contribute to the real inclusiveness of GCE from both the above and the below perspectives.

Moreover, as the relationship between language and space is a central aspect of metrolingualism (Pennycook & Otsuji, 2014b), this study introduces the concept of metrolingual landscape (ML) as a general term to represent the spatial repertoires found in metro places. The term "metrolingual landscape" will be further defined and elaborated upon in the subsequent subsection.

2.3.3 Metrolingual landscape

As mentioned earlier, the relationship between language and space is crucial in understanding metrolingualism. From a LL perspective, spaces are viewed as agents that carry social meaning (Yao, 2021), which can be seen as one of the spatial repertoires for metrolingualism. Spatial repertoire is a comprehensive notion that encompasses various activities, linguistic resources, and language practices in particular places. In the context of this study, people's daily interactions in cities, referred to as metrolingual interactions (MIs), are considered significant metrolingual practices. These practices involve the spatial repertoires that include the semiotic assemblages in that particular context.

Based on those assumptions, this study adopts a term of ML regarding the relationship between language and space as well as combining LL and metrolingual interaction (MI) together, since all of which represent semiotic assemblages of metrolingualism that concerned with language ideologies, resources and repertoires. Moreover, this study assumes ML as an abstract and general concept that concerns the relationship between language and space, while LL and MI being regarded as the specific metrolingual practices that can be observed from people's daily life. Figure 2.1 shows the diagram of relationship among ML, LL, and MI. The dotted circles of LL and MI in Figure 2.1 represent the uncertainty of space occupied, since the outer circle represents an abstract concept of language and space relation in which the whole spatial repertoire is the concern. Besides, the spatial repertoire of LL and MI may overlap in a particular context, since emerging assemblages may occur as spatial repertoires due to various metrolingual practices in different local contexts. Moreover, assemblages describe the new ways in which things come and function together, so focusing on semiotic assemblages is being regarded as a subset of a more comprehensive critical sociolinguistics of diversity as well (Arnaut, 2016).

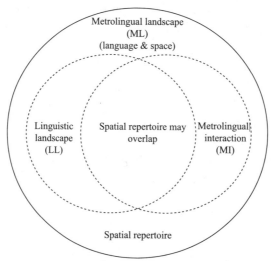

Figure 2.1   Diagram of relationship among ML, LL, MI

In order to better understand metrolingualism as an expanded version of language, LL should be moved from the traditional concept proposed by Landry and Bourhis (1997) that "the language of public road signs, advertising billboards, street names, place names, commercial shop signs, and public signs on government buildings combines to form the LL of a given territory, region, or urban agglomeration" (p.25) to a much broader one that includes "images, photos, sounds, movements, music, smells, graffiti, clothes, food, buildings, history, as well as people who are immersed and absorbed in spaces by interacting with LL in different ways" (Shohamy, 2015, pp.153-154). As a result, LL research has shifted its focus on understanding of language from countable linguistic symbols in the public domain to a larger contextual and historical level of text understanding (Pennycook, 2017), innovative and interdisciplinary studies regarding various kinds of "scapes" being appeared such as graffitiscapes (Pennycook, 2009, 2010), internetscapes (Troyer, 2012), schoolscapes (Gorter & Cenoz, 2015), the temporary landscapes of demonstrations and art installations (Blackwood et al., 2016), smellscapes (Pennycook & Otsuji, 2015b), skinscapes (Peck & Stroud, 2015), etc.

In this regard, this study attempts to adopt a term of "textbookscapes" to refer to the MLs that combine LLs and MIs in textbooks, being regarded as a new kind of semiotic assemblage to better understand diverse semiotic resources in textbooks from a metrolingualism perspective. Moreover, in order to examine the extent to which textbookscapes reflect the notion of metrolingualism, the researcher studied the textbookscapes from two aspects which are LLs and MIs in textbooks. The relationship among those concepts can be shown in Figure 2.2. In this figure, metrolingualism occupies the outermost circle and represents people's metrolingual practice in their daily life, in which the relationship between language and space is the core and is represented as MLs in this study. In order to make it more specific and feasible in the context of this study, LLs and MIs are taken as a subset of MLs, and each inner solid circle is a subset of the outer solid circle. The goal of this study is to explore the extent to which the most central dotted circle can reflect its outer circles, and the dotted line of "textbookscapes" means that such extent can be flexible and uncertain. The data collection for textbookscapes will be elaborated in Chapter 3.

Moreover, bringing metrolingualism perspectives into LL research facilitates better understanding of diverse semiotic resources so as to represent semiotic assemblages in the city. For example, the study of sensory landscape, as an integral part of linguascapes, opened up a different terrain of semiosis (Pennycook & Otsuji, 2015b), as well as the study of the relationship between language and online space through LL in WeChat Moment posts (Yao, 2021). Troyer (2012) expanded LL to

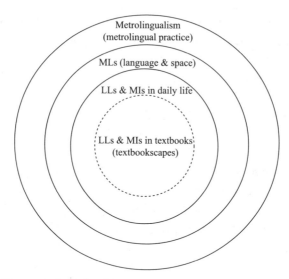

Figure 2.2   Diagram of relationship among metrolingualism, MLs, textbookscapes

encompass online newspaper in Thailand to reveal the multilingualism in online environment, and findings showed that English is more popular than any other language used in ads on Thai websites.

On the other hand, LL can be regarded as a reflection of the role that language plays in society, directly or indirectly or warped, as seen through "a carnival mirror" (Gorter, 2012, p.11), which could help us better understand the linguistic diversity in modern societies, as well as reflects the complex interaction among various factors such as ethnicity, politics, ideology, commerce or economy in a particular social context (Mensel et al., 2017). Inter alia, LL appeared to be a promising field to study issues related to globalization and multilingualism, not least because it effectively shows tensions that take place between different levels of local and global linguistic flows, the hybrids that arise from these tensions, and various policing activities that revolve around them (ibid.).

Nevertheless, the "symbolic construction" of the public space, which is referred to as LL, may not always mirror the actual use of language by the local people (Ben-Rafael et al., 2006), which may indicate the gap between the top-down ideological and political concerns and the bottom-up local practice, so some minority languages may present in or absent from the LL. The absence or presence of certain codes conveys direct or indirect information about the centrality vs. the marginality of certain languages in societies (Shohamy, 2006). Thus, the language used in LL reflects concerns about cultural globalization, identity, the increasing of English and other foreign languages, and informs us about the rise of immigrant populations or the minority languages revival (Cenoz & Gorter, 2008). LL, therefore, is an important field to study language and space for metrolingualism, which has been researched from different angles and continuously expanded its connotations from previous studies. It is commonly grounded in ethnographic method to represent policies, ideologies, and practices of languages both globally and locally.

However, there has been limited examination of the gap between top-down ideological and political concerns and bottom-up local practices within the LL framework, particularly through the analysis of textbooks where hidden ideologies can be found. This research addresses this gap by analyzing the textbookscapes to scrutinize hidden ideologies and the extent to which they reflect bottom-up local practices. Furthermore, China is a multiethnic and multilingual society, which means that metrolingual landscapes may manifest differently in Chinese local contexts. In order to make metrolingualism an adaptation to the Chinese local context and provide a background for metrolingual practice in Chinese local context, it is necessary to introduce the concept of metrolingual citizenship and consider the Chinese ethnic minority languages, as well as relevant policies concerning minority languages, in the subsequent subsection.

2.3.4 Metrolingual citizenship and minority languages

Metrolingual citizenship, which combines the concepts of metrolingualism and citizenship, expands upon the notion of "linguistic citizenship" (Stroud & Heugh, 2004) to encompass a broader discourse. It represents the identities of metrolingual speakers and carries implications for minority language revitalization, while also promoting tolerance and inclusiveness towards diversity. Metrolingualism can have complex and diverse effects on minority languages, driven by market forces, which may be beneficial or detrimental to minority language groups. Drawing on the idea of "acts of citizenship" (Jaffe, 2012), metrolingual citizenship can be understood as a stance that an individual could take through language choices and practices, such as speaking a particular language or speaking a language in a particular way, participating in a particular interaction and the sociocultural implications of relationships and belonging that come with it (Jaffe, 2009). All of these aspects aim to contribute to the process of meaning-making at that particular moment.

In this regard, it is important to acknowledge language rights, which are recognized as cultural rights, particularly for minority groups, and play a role in facilitating intercultural encounters (Beacco & Byram, 2007). Language policies have also played a significant role in supporting the preservation and implementation of minority languages by providing legitimate rights to these languages. Additionally, UNESCO, through international consensus, has released various policy documents such as the "Universal Declaration of Linguistic Rights", "Universal Declaration on Cultural Diversity", "Convention for the Protection of Intangible Cultural Heritage", and "The Declaration of Yuelu". These documents emphasize the importance of language diversity and advocate for the preservation of linguistic diversity worldwide. Turning to the Chinese context, minority languages have also been granted legitimate rights, recognizing their significance and value.

As previously mentioned, China is a culturally diverse nation consisting of 56 ethnic groups, including the Han majority and 55 ethnic minorities. Within this rich tapestry of diversity, approximately 130 languages are spoken by these ethnic minorities, belonging to more than ten distinct language families. The five major language groups in China are Chinese-Tibetan, Altai, South Asian, Austronesian, and Indo-European. These languages exhibit a wide range of linguistic structures, including isolated languages, agglutinative languages, inflectional languages, and various mixed language types. Due to their linguistic diversity and unique structural characteristics, these languages serve as invaluable linguistic resources and hold significant value for multidisciplinary research (丁石庆 , 2020).

These minority languages exhibit significant variation, with some being used by a large number of people, such as Zhuang and Uygur, with their areas of use gradually expanding. However, there are also endangered or even extinct minority languages due to their small speaker populations, such as Oroqen and Manchu (白新杰 , 2020). Many of these endangered minority languages lack a written form and rely primarily on oral transmission. Consequently, the inheritance process leads to a loss of vocabulary and a narrowing of domains due to the absence of written records. Some minority languages are confined to specific communities and families, spoken by only a small number of individuals, for instance, Hezhe, Oroqen, Manchu, Tatar. Critically endangered minority languages have lost their functions in everyday communication and are now limited to use in funerals and other rituals (ibid.). Currently, over twenty ethnic minority languages have fewer than 1,000 speakers and face the threat of extinction, with nearly half of the languages experiencing a survival crisis (ibid.).

Against this backdrop, the Chinese MOE and the State Language Commission in China initiated the "Construction of Audio Database of Chinese Language Resources" project in 2008. This project conducted extensive investigations and audio recordings of Chinese dialects, as well as the construction of audio databases in regions such as Jiangsu, Shanghai, Beijing, Guangxi, Fujian, and Shandong (Cao,

2019). The main objective of this project is to scientifically and effectively collect and preserve contemporary Chinese dialects, minority languages, and local Mandarin through actual recordings and audio corpora. In 2015, recognizing the need for comprehensive and timely preservation of language resources, the Chinese MOE and the State Language Commission launched another project named the "Chinese Language Resources Protection Project". This project focuses on nationwide investigations, displays, preservation, development, and utilization of language resources. Its aim is to "scientifically protect the spoken and written languages of all ethnic groups" while strengthening national awareness of language resource preservation (ibid.).

Furthermore, it is mandated by law that every ethnic group has the right and freedom to use and develop their own languages. This includes the use of minority languages in daily life, production, communication, and social interactions. The law also ensures that organs of ethnic autonomy can utilize minority languages in the performance of their duties. Additionally, schools and educational institutions where the majority of students belong to ethnic minorities are encouraged to use the local common ethnic language for teaching and learning purposes. Moreover, there is encouragement for ethnic groups to learn and exchange knowledge of minority languages among themselves.

In sum, current language policies in China emphasize the harmonious coexistence of unity and diversity, while adhering to two basic principles of "language equality and national equality" as well as "social unity and linguistic unity", and all ethnic languages develop together and promote mutually. The government has increasingly strengthened the protection of minority languages, and these language policies are expected to impact metrolingual practices within the Chinese local context. Further research is needed to address these issues.

Additionally, since metrolingualism advocates the complexity of cultural exposure in English classroom, it is important to briefly introduce the concept of critical multicultural education in the following subsection. Critical multicultural education can be seen as an implication of cultural education stemming from metrolingualism in ELT.

2.3.5 Critical multicultural education

Before starting introducing critical multicultural education, it is necessary to mention about the traditional multicultural perspective so as to better understand critical multicultural education. The traditional perspective is often seen as orthodox multiculturalism in education, which relates to an adversarial strain between the need to define a common community with the reaffirming of a national identity and the recognition of diversity that risks fragmentation (Gillispie, 2011). The tenets of traditional multicultural education have a propensity to view culture as immutable, essentialist, and deterministic (Taguieff, 1997, as cited in Gillispie, 2011), and are particularly focusing on the dissemination of the dominant society's cultural heritage through a definite body of information and the maintenance of the current social structure (Banks & Banks, 2016). In this light, neither racism's mechanics nor prejudices based on ethnicity that favor Westernness or Eurocentrism are called into question from a traditional viewpoint (Gillispie, 2011).

By contrast, the core of critical multiculturalism is to point out and actively challenge racism and other forms of injustice, rather than simply recognizes and celebrates differences and reduces prejudice, so the critical multiculturalism oriented English education should also be inclusive and accommodate experiences from historically marginalized communities (Sleeter, 2004). The main goal of critical multicultural education is to develop students' critical thinking and social change, improve their decision-making abilities as well as make decisions on important social issues, and support students' initiative in social change and democratic values (Banks, 2004). In this regard, critical multiculturalism could provide a transformative cultural education framework for metrolingualism oriented pedagogy by bringing diverse experience and voices to the center of students discourse and empowering students to critique and challenge the social norms that continue to favor some groups at the detriment of others (May & Sleeter, 2010; Acar-Ciftci, 2016).

For another, civism is not and never has been neutral as it is formed within the so-called "pluralistic dilemma" (May, 1999, p.30, as cited in Ferrari, 2010), which may need teachers to help students to recognize many of students' beliefs and biases from a sociohistorical perspective in critical multicultural education (Ferrari, 2010). Self-reflection and dialogue around educational concepts can be regarded as a tool of acculturation in critical multicultural education courses, which could provide students with opportunities to challenge the textbooks they have read and the context in which history has been reported and to be more inclusive to people from different cultures (ibid.). In this light, teachers may need to develop the ability of students to understand and value those points of view that are different from their own, and to see any diversity as a resource and asset, rather than a problem (Taylor & Sobel, 2001).

Moreover, it is easily to overlook such a problem that there may be big cultural differences among racially or ethnically similar groups (diversity within diversity), and such disparities within a cultural group are frequently as big as or greater than those between groups (LeRoux, 2002). At this point, another implication brought by critical multicultural education to metrolingualism oriented pedagogy is to advocate the heterogeneity both within and outside the homogeneity, so that students could gain the knowledge, skills and attitudes needed to function in an ethnically diverse country and world (Gillispie, 2011). Thus, an inclusive ELT curriculum should welcome the integration of the cultures and histories from non-Western and various minorities, and encourage students to look at problems in different ways to understand the intricate network of intercultural and intersectional relationships under the "glocalization" (ibid.).

Besides, cultivating students' intercultural sensitivity is a crucial aspect in promoting the effective implementation of critical multicultural education. Intercultural sensitivity serves as a key predictor for individuals to become successful global citizens (Wattanavorakijkul, 2020). The subsequent subsection will provide a brief overview of this concept.

2.3.6 Intercultural (global) sensitivity

According to Chen and Starosta (1997), intercultural sensitivity can be defined as "an individual's ability to develop emotion towards understanding and appreciating cultural differences that promotes appropriate and effective behavior in intercultural communication", which can be regarded as one of the dimensions of intercultural communication competence (Chen, 2010). Moreover, due to the fact that globalization has brought people from different cultures, ethnicities, regions, and religions together, understanding cultural diversity is now essential to reducing parochialism and demonstrating intercultural competency (ibid.). To put it another way, developing intercultural sensitivity means avoiding parochialism, which is essential for promoting effective global citizenship at the individual and organizational levels (Adler, 2008). In this light, people who have intercultural sensitivity are willing to integrate and accept other worldviews, as well as respect and deal with cultural differences, which are becoming increasingly important qualities for global citizens (Wattanavorakijkul, 2020).

In order to improve students' intercultural sensitivity at different stages, Bennett (1986) proposed the "Developmental Model of Intercultural Sensitivity" (DMIS) to explain people's reactions toward cultural differences. This model focuses on how individuals interpret differences on their own, and those perspectives have been arranged in a developmental chain of six stages. The first three stages of "denial", "defense", and "minimization" in DMIS are concerned with "ethnocentric", which indicates that experiencing one's own culture is considered as central; the second three stages of "acceptance", "adaptation", and "integration" are related to "ethnorelative", which means issues associated with experiencing all cultures as alternative ways of structuring reality (Bennett, 2017). Figure 2.3 shows the schematic diagram of DMIS stages.

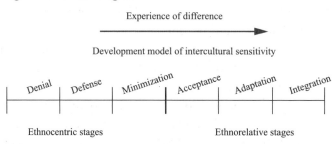

Figure 2.3   Schematic diagram of DMIS (Bennett, 1986, p.182)

DMIS regards intercultural sensitivity as a developmental process, in which people can go from being ethnocentric to being ethnorelative (Bennett, 1986). According to Bennett (1986), first, individuals in the denial stage deny the existence of cultural differences; second, they engage the perceived threat in an effort to defend their own worldviews in the defense stage; third, people disguise differences behind cultural commonalities in order to maintain their core values; fourth, they start to identify and accept cultural differences on both a cognitive and behavioral level in the stage of acceptance; fifth, people gain receptive and empathic abilities to cope with cultural differences and progress into the bicultural or multicultural phase in the adaptation stage; and ultimately, people can form an ethnorelative identity and enjoy the cultural diversity in the integration stage.

Therefore, people who could discover and identify these six stages of cultural sensitivity will be able to treat themselves with a greater awareness of and openness to the perspective of others in a variety of cultural situations, since interculturally sensitive people have the competence to project and receive favorable emotional responses before, during, and after contacts, which leads to higher levels of satisfaction and aids in the development of adequate social orientation as well as allows them to understand their own feelings and behaviors as well as those of others (Gudykunst & Kim, 2002). At the same time, the six stages of cultural sensitivity, as well as adopting a realistic perspective, can help individuals enhance their interactions with others. Moreover, having the ability to see the worldviews of other people can improve partnership and experiences with others. As a result, absorbing and being sensitive to other people's perspectives, one's own viewpoint can be developed and expanded as well (Bennett, 2017).

Nonetheless, GCE is a holistic and interdisciplinary discipline as well as connects everything within the school community related to civil rights, diverse cultures, peace, justice, long-term development and environmental protection (UNESCO, 2014), so the sensitivity in GCE should go far beyond diverse cultures or cultural differences. In this light, this study attempts to extend the intercultural sensitivity into global sensitivity to advocate individuals not only being interculturally sensitive but also being sensitive to global issues, such as global problems of poverty, racial discrimination, inequality, human rights violation, environmental pollution, climate change, and to commit towards a more inclusive and sustainable community. Thus, a successful global citizen may need both intercultural sensitivity and global sensitivity to form an ethnorelative identity as well as enjoy the cultural diversity in the integration stage, and to have the empathy for those unequal global issues as well as be willing to become active contributors to a world that is more peaceful, just, safe, tolerant, inclusive and sustainable.

Moreover, this study argues that GCE and metrolingualism are mutually reinforcing and interdependent, since we cannot talk about globalization without acknowledging that everything happens locally. Conversely, neglecting metrolingual practices in the local context may hinder educators from fully facilitating GCE. In the forthcoming section, the key terms of this study, namely GCE and metrolingualism in relation to ELT textbooks and curriculum, will be summarized to emphasize their intrinsic connections and the existing research gap in this field. The subsequent section will consist of two subsections: a concise introduction to the theory of glocalization and an exploration of the demonstrative relationship between GCE, metrolingualism, and ELT textbooks and curriculum.

2.4 Theoretical Conceptual Relationships Among Key Terms

2.4.1 Glocalization & ELT

Globalization is one of the great social influences that affect and transform every aspect of people's lives and experiences. Many major areas of human life, including education, are changing as a result of technological advancements and the impact of new media, which are perhaps the most important drivers of globalization. Globalization, though considered a buzzword, is also a controversial one. Scholars see it as an irresistible entity from the West that advocates for strict uniformity and consistency (Gray, 1998) or the proxy for "glocalization" (Robertson, 1995) as a way to connect the global and local productivity and creativity. Although historical globalization has led to the spread of cultural uniformity in the formal characteristics of nation-states on a global scale, "glocalization" is building cultural heterogeneity and national particularity.

The concept of glocalization was first emerged to describe the adaptation of goods or services of multinational companies to specific local cultural contexts in order to expand their global reach as part of the global expansion policies of these companies (Robertson, 1995). Glocalization can be seen as a template imposed by top-down template enforced with local concerns, often referred to as "MacDonaldization" (Ritzer, 2000) and "Disneyization" (Bryman, 2004), or it can build platforms for participation in culture, entertainment, and digital games (Jenkins, 2006). Ritzer (2000, p.7) defined "MacDonaldization" as "the process by which the principles of the fast-food restaurant are coming to dominate more and more sectors of American society as well as of the rest of the world". Especially, the English language culture that concerned with "MacDonaldization" becomes one thing that most inhabitants of the world have in common (Block, 2008).

Moreover, glocalization has been taken as the fragmentation of the globe while keeping its original associations as a way to experience parts of the globe either through a local lens (Roudometof, 2016), or as a form of top-down corporate control that accommodates to local circumstances (Ritzer, 2000). Alexander (2003) gave a simpler definition of "glocalization", that is, to maintain globalization by integrating local elements. Thus, glocalization is a necessary counterpart to the process of cultural homogenization, and is also the key to understanding the global expression of national and local forms (Roudometof, 2014). Besides, Delokarov (2002) believed that "glocalization" consists of two elements which are globalization and localization, the key concept that is embedded in which is the "glocality" that necessitates the presence of two streams, both global and local (Roudometof, 2016). The majority of scholars who use this word regard globalization and localization as related social transformation processes that develop together through a dynamic interactive relationship, in which each process is conceived of as influencing and changing the other, and the correlation and coevolution of the interaction between globalization and localization has resulted in the glocalization (Shi, 2013). Thus, glocalization can be taken as a way of bridging the forces for the global and the local together in a dynamic and changing way (Mehta, 2018).

Under this background, globalized phenomena are altered by different local environments they come into contact with, and those factors become the ecological environment in which new variants of those phenomena arise and evolve (Shi, 2013). English, as a social phenomenon that originated in some parts of the world became globalized via expansion to more places all over the world, where they might root themselves and become localized via imposition and/or adoption (ibid.). From this point, the globalization of social phenomena like English has always been achieved through glocalization, which entails the interplay of growing global phenomena with a variety of local situations that they confront (ibid.). Regarding the glocalization of ELT around the world, it should be realized that the purpose of glocalization is not only for international communications, but also for international interactions (Salimi & Safarzadeh, 2019).

Moreover, glocalization, as a social process, has implications for ELT. What East (2008) argued for when discussing the impact of glocalization on language education is the reciprocity between us and others advocated by the Intercultural Communication Competence approach (Rahim & Manan, 2013). The effective way of language education may be achieved through acquiring key competence to build more successful interpersonal relationships and understanding the social factors at work (East, 2008). East (2008) also emphasized that the glocalization impact is the reality that ELT should be centered on among the three major social influences of globalization, localization and glocalization. Thus, glocalization frequently causes a paradigm change in ELT from transmissive to transformative (Novak, 2005, as cited in Rahim & Manan, 2013).

In addition, recent years saw a large and growing literature being evolved on the spread of English globally, English as a lingua franca, World Englishes, English as an international language, Asian Englishes, and a variety of other topics and issues. In the ELF paradigm, the localization of English has posed a threat to English ownership, and the cultural identity of English has become more flexible and dynamic (Fang, 2018). The glocalization of ELT underlines the promotion of educational programs that take into account both worldview and neighborhood viewpoints (Sultan & Hameed, 2020). ELT should be increasingly contextualized, since people should not only approach ELT from a global viewpoint, but also integrate localized forms of English into language classrooms to encourage students to think about linguistic landscapes (LLs) in the world today (Fang, 2018). The glocalization content in ELT textbooks is a potential tool for changing English education in both native-speaking and non-native-speaking contexts (Rahim & Manan, 2013).

To this end, the backdrop of glocalization of ELT may also bring some implications to the theoretical frameworks in this study, since Akkari and Maleq's framework for GCE (2020) being adopted in this study could meet the requirements of glocalization by taking the Chinese local traditions, culture and history into consideration to translate GCE's international models into local classroom practice. Moreover, critical GCE (Andreotti, 2006), as another theoretical framework for GCE, could provide this study with a critical lens to examine how GCE findings in this study reflecting the local, regional and global dimensions of Chinese citizenship against the backdrop of glocalization, as well as to challenge the global power structures. On the other hand, Pennycook and Otsuji's conceptual framework for metrolingualism (2015a), being grounded in the theory of "globalization from below", could also enrich the glocalization of Chinese ELT by examining the linguistic and cultural exposures in Chinese ELT textbooks and curriculum through the lens of metrolingualism.

Building upon the theories of globalization and glocalization, the subsequent subsection will illustrate the relationship between GCE, metrolingualism, and ELT textbooks and curriculum. Moreover, it will revisit the research gap in this field, highlighting the need for further investigation and exploration.

2.4.2 GCE and metrolingualism vs. ELT textbooks and curriculum

In general, both GCE and metrolingualism are outcomes of globalization, aiming to foster coexistence and global interconnectedness. This study proposes two perspectives on GCE: global GCE and glocal GCE. Global GCE primarily stems from top-down policies and represents a universal model of GCE, often associated with globalization from a centralized perspective. However, the real inclusiveness in GCE cannot solely rely on top-down policies, as this approach may perpetuate unequal ideologies and reproduce asymmetrical power relations within the global community, ultimately leading to an elite cosmopolitanism devoid of critical examination. Therefore, glocal GCE emerges as an alternative that recognizes cultural diversity and national particularities, adapting GCE to different local contexts. Glocal GCE involves the simultaneous presence of both universalizing and particularizing tendencies within the GCE paradigm. It acknowledges the importance of considering local cultural heterogeneity and tailoring GCE approaches accordingly.

However, it is important to note that glocalization alone does not guarantee a conflict-free world. Nevertheless, it offers a more historically grounded and pragmatic perspective (Khondker, 2005). Additionally, glocalization falls short in challenging capitalism and comprehensively capturing the intricacies of social relationships (Roudometof, 2016). On the other hand, globalization from below can facilitate the redistribution of global wealth among marginalized segments of society. It can open avenues for career advancement and provide a means of survival in both national and global economies that are unable to provide full employment for all citizens (Ribeiro, 2012). Globalization from below is driven by the movements of people, information, goods, and capital between various production hubs and markets, which serve as the nodes within the non-hegemonic world-system (Ribeiro, 2012). This non-hegemonic world-system is composed of different components and networks solidified in a pyramid-like structure, with economic globalization from below primarily occurring at the bottom of this pyramid.

Furthermore, metrolingualism, rooted in the theory of globalization from below, primarily emerges through spontaneous and fluid multilingual practices among individuals. Metrolingualism has the potential to contribute to the revitalization of minority languages, giving voice to marginalized groups. Additionally, metrolingual pedagogies advocate for a more comprehensive linguistic perspective, embracing local metrolingual practices rather than focusing solely on mythical native speakers. These pedagogies aim to shift from traditional language-centric approaches to recognizing and valuing multiple languages, fostering true inclusiveness within society. Therefore, the complete realization of GCE requires not only critical literacy to listen to marginalized or excluded voices but also an acknowledgment of metrolingual practices. Both glocalization and globalization from below strive to achieve a state of "glocality", where individuals experience the world through local lenses. This includes considering local power relations, challenging hegemony, understanding geopolitical and geographical factors, and recognizing cultural distinctiveness, etc.

The ELT curriculum is a product of orthodox education and aligns with language policies. It serves as a guiding document and logical framework for English language instruction, forming the basis for the development of ELT textbooks. A curriculum infused with GCE values should encompass topics such as conflicts, human rights, culture, multicultural relations, socioeconomic development, interdependence, environmental sustainability, and global institutions (OECD, 2018). This approach encourages the integration of information about diverse cultures, locations, and perspectives into educational practices throughout the year, rather than adopting a superficial tourist strategy that only provides occasional glimpses into life in different countries (UNESCO, 2014). Besides, preparing youth for the future world does not mean burdening the curriculum with additional continents or rivers. Instead, it requires fostering deep, relevant, and sustained learning in, about, and for the world (Mansilla & Wilson, 2020).

ELT textbooks serve as essential resources for teachers, playing a pivotal role in educational practices and transformation. They are developed in accordance with national policies and reflect the curriculum standards and official knowledge of society (Apple, 2014). The process of selecting and editing materials for ELT textbooks is purposeful, often reflecting the worldviews of dominant groups. Moreover, ELT textbooks are considered a crucial starting point for educators in shaping students' worldviews, particularly for those who have limited exposure to English in their daily lives. These textbooks significantly influence how students perceive other cultures (Rashidi & Ghaedsharafi, 2015), which is particularly relevant in countries like China, where English is taught as a foreign language. Therefore, analyzing ELT textbooks and curriculum is a valuable practice that sheds light on how official knowledge about society and the world is constructed (Choi & Kim, 2018), as well as how they impact GCE and metrolingualism while maintaining a national perspective.

In light of the above, it is important to outline the conceptual framework that underpins the study's investigation of GCE, metrolingualism, and their relationship with ELT textbooks and curriculum. GCE serves as the overarching concept, encompassing global GCE, glocal GCE, and metrolingualism, which are rooted in theories of globalization, glocalization, and globalization from below, respectively. From a top-down perspective, globality represents the ultimate goal of the globalization process for a specific item, while glocality embodies the ideal condition of glocalization and globalization from below. Therefore, the study leans towards the broader concept of "hybrid" over "glocal", as hybrid encompasses a wider range of possibilities than glocalization alone (Roudometof, 2016). Hybrid is one of the potential outcomes of intercultural/transcultural flows, with glocality being a part of this hybrid by integrating both top-down and bottom-up approaches to globalization. Drawing from this conceptual framework, the findings of this study aim to examine how the values embedded in ELT curriculum and textbooks align with the concepts of global GCE, glocal GCE, and metrolingualism. Furthermore, the study investigates whether these notions are represented equally, unequally, or with biases.

However, notwithstanding the crucial role of ELT textbooks and curriculum in fostering GCE and promoting metrolingualism-oriented pedagogy, there has been limited research and attention given to the analysis of ELT textbooks and curriculum. Moreover, very few studies have explored these issues at the primary educational level. Currently, little is known about in what ways Chinese primary

ELT textbooks and curriculum reflect the notions of GCE and metrolingualism, as well as how teachers perceive the values embedded within these materials. To address this research gap, this study considers ELT curriculum and textbooks as the carrier for GCE and metrolingualism values. It aims to investigate how these notions are represented in ELT materials by utilizing Akkari and Maleq's framework for GCE (2020) and Pennycook and Otsuji's (2015a) conceptual framework for metrolingualism. The study employs a critical GCE perspective (Andreotti, 2006) and CDA (Fairclough, 1995) to bridge the gap between global GCE and glocal GCE, as well as metrolingualism. It also explores the connections between globalization from the top and the below, the language of school and the language of life, and the fixed codes of multilingualism and the fluidity of everyday language practices.

Moreover, this study adopted a critical perspective to expose implicit ideologies regarding GCE and metrolingualism values within ELT textbooks and curriculum. CDA approach was employed to reveal the power relations embedded in these materials. In the following section, Fairclough's three-dimensional framework for CDA will be briefly introduced as a means to examine power relations within texts.

2.5 Three-dimensional Framework of CDA & Textbooks Analysis

2.5.1 Fairclough's three-dimensional framework

Fairclough (1989) held that the relationship between language and society is not external but internal dialectic. Language is a part of society, and linguistic phenomena are special social phenomena, and social phenomenon is also a part of linguistic phenomenon, so the ways that people speak, listen, write, or read are socially determined and have social effects, as well as that language activities carried out in societies are not only the reflection or manifestation of social dynamics and behaviors, but also a component of them, while text is an aspect of the social interaction process (ibid.). From discourse analysis perspective, the form of text can be either the trace of the production process or the clue of the explanation process (ibid.). However, the meaning of the text is incomplete if one neglects how it is prevented by society in the process of text production and interpretation, so language is conditioned by other things and non-verbal social parts of social practice. Treating language as discourse and practice requires analyzing not only the process of text production and interpretation, but also the relationship between text, process and social conditions (ibid.).

Conforming to these three dimensions of discourse, Fairclough (1989) further distinguished three dimensions/stages of CDA. In the first dimension of description is to focus on the attributes of the text form. Interpretation is the second dimension which focuses on the relationship between text and interaction and views text as both a product of a production and a tool for interpretation. The third dimension is interpretation that has to do with the relationship between interaction and social context, as well as concerns the social decisions of production and interpretation processes and their social implications. Albeit the three-dimensional model shows that interaction is the link that connects social practices of discourse and text; yet, the ideas of interaction and context do not adequately capture the deep significance of social practice discourse (Fairclough, 1992). Therefore, Fairclough further developed those terms, using "social practice" instead of "context", replacing "interaction" with "discursive practice", and employing three processes of "production", "distribution", and "consumption" rather than two processes of "production" and "interpretation". Fairclough (2003) regarded discourse as a kind of social practice and a way of behavior which exists in social and historical situations and has a dialectical relationship with other elements of society, while social life is an interwoven network of various social practices. The discourse here not only refers to the social practice in an abstract sense, but also refers to the use of discourse in a specific field, such as political discourse and commercial discourse, etc.

Based on the theoretical positions above (Fairclough, 1989; Fairclough, 1992), Fairclough further developed the three-dimensional method of discourse analysis, which particularly highlights the connection between social practice and language, as well as the systematic investigation of the connection between the nature of social processes and the textual attributes of language (Fairclough, 1995). Additionally, it promotes the fusion of "macro" and "micro" analysis (ibid.). Moreover, it is a "critical" approach to discourse analysis in the sense that it seeks to expose connections between textual attributes and social processes and relations through analysis and criticism that are typically hidden from those who create and interpret those texts and whose effectiveness depends on this opacity (ibid.). In this framework, discourse has been regarded as "(i) a language text, spoken or written, (ii) discourse practice (text production and text interpretation), (iii) sociocultural practice" (Fairclough, 1995, p.97). Additionally, a discourse can be embedded within sociocultural practice on a variety of levels, including the current circumstance, the larger institution or organization, and the level of society. This approach to discourse analysis contains linguistic descriptions of the text, interpretation of the connections between the text and discursive processes, and an explanation of how the discursive processes and the social processes interact (ibid.).

A specific feature of this approach is that discourse practice mediates the relationship between sociocultural practice and text; the nature of sociocultural practice that the discourse is a part of determines how a text is produced or interpreted in terms of what discursive practices and norms are drawn from what order(s) of discourse and how they are articulated together; the nature of the discourse practice used to produce the text also shapes it and leaves "traces" in surface features of the text; and how the surface features of the text will be interpreted depends on the nature of discourse practice of text interpretation (ibid.) (refer to Figure 1.1).

In this study, text includes the textual and visual contents in Chinese primary ELT textbooks and curriculum, and text analysis focuses on the descriptions of GCE and metrolingualism values present in textbooks and curriculum. Discourse practice connects the discursive processes with the text itself, emphasizing the interpretations and meanings attributed to GCE and metrolingualism values within the textbooks and curriculum. Sociocultural practice associates the discursive processes with the social processes, that is, the results of GCE and metrolingualism in this study are explained by situating them within wider Chinese and global contexts. To visualize the three-dimensional framework of discourse analysis employed in this study, Figure 1.2 in Chapter 1 illustrates its components.

Moreover, participants in mass media discourse, such as television, newspapers, magazines, are often separated by time and place. The nature of power relations embodied in these discourses is not always clear and may even be hidden. Additionally, language is not a transparent medium for expressing ideology and power. The relationship between language, power, and ideology is often implicit. Therefore, the primary objective of CDA is to make these relationships explicit and uncover the underlying determinants of the social relationship system (Fairclough, 2001). CDA serves as an application within the field of language study, employing a specific approach to social research. It aims to provide language criticism resources for individuals engaged in social struggles. Language becomes a significant aspect of these struggles, and through CDA, the hidden power dynamics within language can be exposed (ibid.). The following subsection will introduce how previous studies have utilized this framework to reveal power relations within textbooks.

2.5.2 Fairclough's CDA in ELT textbooks analysis

Researchers and scholars often turn to CDA as a valuable tool for examining textbooks due to its ability to unveil both hidden and visible sociopolitical values and norms. CDA allows for the exposure of ideologies, social power, hegemony, and dominance within the analyzed materials (Fairclough, 2001). Within the realm of ELT textbook analysis, CDA has garnered significant interest from scholars and researchers, who have utilized it to explore various dimensions, including gender representation, cultural representation, and ethnicity (Amerian & Esmaili, 2015). This demonstrates the effectiveness and versatility of CDA as an approach for analyzing ELT textbooks.

Samadikhah and Shahrokhi (2015) conducted an analysis that compared the gender representation in two series of ELT textbooks, employing Fairclough's CDA model. The study's findings revealed that one series of textbooks achieved a more balanced gender representation compared to the other. Similarly, Gebregeorgis (2016) utilized Fairclough's three-dimensional framework of CDA to examine how gender was constructed in an ELT textbook in Ethiopia. The findings indicated that the content of the textbook reflected a struggle of discourse, attempting to uphold the existing social order in terms of gender construction while also seeking to challenge the status quo. In another study by Ahmad and Shah (2019), gender representation in an ELT textbook for grade five in Pakistan was investigated using Fairclough's CDA framework. The researchers discovered that the textbook is characterized by the dominant representation of males.

Besides, Chalak and Ghasemi (2017) utilized Fairclough's CDA to investigate and analyze the content, social relations, and subject positions within conversations found in four advanced ELT textbooks in Iran. The findings revealed that the language employed in these textbooks lacked freedom of expression and was heavily influenced by Western ideology. The discourse, tone, and intonation were all based on Western norms. Fairclough's CDA model was also applied to examine the presence of neoliberal mentality in ELT materials in Iran. The findings of this study conducted by Babaii and Sheikhi (2017) demonstrated that the ELT textbooks popularized specific neoliberal principles, such as markets, consumerism, and a superficial and non-critical form of multiculturalism. These elements were presented in a manner that aimed to portray a utopian image of the West (ibid.). In another study, Fairclough's CDA framework was employed to scrutinize the socio-economic representations within ELT textbooks used in Indonesia. The findings, conducted by Subroto et al. (2019), indicated that a significant portion of the texts still contained inaccurate and inappropriate socio-economic representations of students across various aspects.

Thus, Fairclough's CDA model offers valuable guidelines for conducting research in various fields, particularly in the analysis of textbooks. CDA effectively examines issues of injustice, inequality, racism, danger, suffering, and prejudice within specific domains. Its primary aim is to provide a comprehensive explanation, justification, and critique of the textual techniques employed by authors to normalize certain discourses (Chalak & Ghasemi, 2017). Furthermore, CDA allows for the integration of macro social structures and micro social actions by combining social and linguistic analyses of discourse. In this way, Fairclough's three-dimensional framework becomes a useful tool for researchers to uncover hidden power relations within ELT textbooks and curriculum.

Besides, to enhance the understanding of findings in this study, it is important to examine them in relation to the social discourse within the Chinese context. This involves exploring the specific grand narratives that exist in the discursive field of China and considering how the findings align with or reflect the mainstream or status quo in the country (Jensen, 2008). In the following section, grand narratives in the discursive field of China will be elaborated in the following section.

2.6 Grand Narratives in the Discursive Field of China

As mentioned earlier, the concept of GCE can be traced back to ancient China. Chinese cultural values and norms, including national identity, beliefs, and behaviors, have been significantly influenced and shaped by Confucianism, Buddhism, and Daoism (钱穆 , 2004; 梁漱溟 , 2006). Confucian education, in particular, has been dominant in China for thousands of years. Its core ideology revolves around virtues such as benevolence (仁), righteousness (义), propriety (礼), wisdom (智), and fidelity (信). Despite the changes in dynasties, the emphasis on moral cultivation and the pursuit of social harmony through the observance of etiquette and self-control in thoughts, speech, and behavior has remained relatively consistent within Confucian education (Law, 2011).

Traditional Chinese cosmopolitan thoughts, such as the concepts of "great harmony in the world", "the unity of nature and man", "humanitarianism", and "pacifism", have positively influenced Chinese GCE consciousness. Despite the passage of time, the long-lasting traditional Chinese cosmopolitan thoughts in China have had a profound influence on the mindset of the Chinese people and instilled in them a strong sense of nationhood. Since 1978, the implementation of the "Reform and Opening up" policy has spurred the development of the Chinese market economy. This policy has brought about various changes, including the reform of the ownership system, the vibrant growth of the private sector, and the emergence of an urban middle class. These changes have also given rise to new social relations and provided space for the development of individual autonomy and personality (Tse, 2011). Furthermore, China's international exchanges have become more frequent, and the interdependence between countries has deepened. Subsequent international events such as China's accession to the WTO in 2001, the Beijing 2008 Olympic Games, the Shanghai 2010 World Expo, and Beijing 2022 Winter Olympic Games have significantly broadened the horizons of Chinese citizens. Consequently, the idea of being global citizens has gained greater recognition among the Chinese population.

Especially, English education in China has undergone significant changes and regulation due to the influence of the market economy and China's booming economic growth (肖礼全, 2006). The increasing demand for English-speaking professionals in the job market has led to a surge in the popularity of English language learning. As a result, ELT training institutions have flourished, and the English book market has become enriched and diversified. These developments indicate that English education in China has entered a market-oriented era, developing in tandem with the social economy (ibid.). However, it is important to acknowledge the reality of the English testing frenzy in China. Examinations such as the college entrance examination, CET 4 and CET 6, as well as international English tests like TOEFL, GRE, and IELTS, driven by the desire to study abroad, have become an unavoidable aspect of ELT in China. Consequently, the exam-oriented nature of ELT has become a prominent reality. This has highlighted the instrumental aspect of English education, where the focus is primarily on achieving linguistic proficiency. Nevertheless, there is a growing recognition of the humanistic nature of English education, which necessitates that ELT not only focuses on language skills but also fulfills its educational function. This shift calls for a balance between the instrumental and educational aspects of English language teaching.

Moreover, it is crucial to recognize that citizenship education is dynamic rather than static, and this holds true for China's citizenship education as well, which adopts a framework of multileveled or multidimensional citizenship (Law, 2006). In

2012, during the 18th CPC National Congress, significant emphasis was placed on actively cultivating and practicing core socialist values. These values can be further classified into the value goals of the state, the value orientations of society, and the values of individuals. Simultaneously, the concept of "Community with a Shared Future for Mankind" has been repeatedly highlighted. This concept aims to establish an open and inclusive world characterized by enduring peace, universal security, and shared prosperity. In particular, the concept of "Belt and Road Initiative" (一带一 路) was introduced as a cooperative development framework to promote peaceful development and actively foster partnerships. In line with this initiative, the Chinese government issued the "Several Opinions on the Opening up of Education in the New Era" in 2016. This document emphasizes the need for China's education system in the new era to adopt a global perspective and embrace openness and inclusivity. Within the framework of the "Belt and Road Initiative", Chinese education is expected to actively participate in educational cooperation and communication, enhance educational openness, facilitate talent exchanges, and establish a community for talent cultivation.

In the new era of socialist modernization, China has been actively involved in reform and opening up for over four decades, increasingly participating in the global economy, politics, and international affairs. The growing inclusiveness of global citizenship in China is accompanied by a strong emphasis on national cultures and traditions, reflecting the reinforcement of national identity amidst extensive international engagement (Tse, 2011). In 2019, the Chinese government issued "An Outline for the Implementation of Civic Morality in the New Era". This outline promotes the active advocacy of core socialist values while comprehensively enhancing public morality, professional ethics, family virtues, and personal integrity. It emphasizes the continuous strengthening of education, practice, and institutional support to improve the moral quality of citizens, foster the all-round development of individuals, and cultivate a new generation capable of shouldering the significant task of national rejuvenation. Furthermore, several other educational policy documents have been issued to reinforce these ideological discourses. School curricula have also been reformed in response to globalization since the 21st century, aiming to develop students with broad knowledge, essential skills for lifelong learning, and global awareness, while nurturing a sense of national identity (Law, 2013).

In 2010, the "Outline of the National Plan for Medium and Long-Term Education Reform and Development (2010-2020)" underscored the significance of enhancing international understanding education, promoting intercultural communications, and fostering students' awareness of global issues and understanding of different cultures. Moreover, the Chinese MOE issued the "Core Competencies and Values for Chinese Students' Development" in 2016, which places citizenship education within a global context to cultivate Chinese students' global mindsets, international understanding, and engagement with diverse cultures, thus enabling them to address global and social challenges as global citizens (Li, 2021). Furthermore, the "Modernization of Chinese Education 2035", released by the Chinese government in 2019, presents fundamental concepts for advancing education modernization, such as prioritizing morality, promoting all-round development, and ensuring lifelong learning for all. It is one of the ten strategic tasks outlined in the document to continually create a new pattern of educational openness, strengthening cooperation with UNESCO, other international organizations, and multilateral organizations, etc. Besides, the Chinese government has consistently placed significant emphasis on the ideological and political education of young people and college students within the framework of Chinese socialist ideology. There has been a heightened focus on integrating ideological and political education throughout the entire teaching process. This includes aligning ideological and political theory courses with other subjects to create a synergistic effect. Consequently, the integration of ideological and political theories into all courses has been conducted to cultivate Chinese citizenship virtues through education, including in the field of ELT.

To this end, the importance of ideological and political education is increasingly prominent. As China's political, economic, cultural, scientific, and technological development accelerates, there is a growing need for China to have a greater presence on the international stage. These overarching economic and educational narratives have guided Chinese education towards a path of national planning. The various documents and socio-political initiatives aim to prepare students to be globally competitive and to become global citizens within the framework of socialism. The education has been encouraged to be more open to the world while taking China as the center and incorporating more elements specific to Chinese culture and current development (Law, 2013). Consequently, Chinese socialist values and Chinese culture are seen as crucial "soft power" tools for both domestic and global renewal to cultivate a strong sense of national identity among students rooted in Chinese socialist values (ibid.).

2.7 Summary of the Chapter

This chapter introduced the background and the concept and beliefs of global citizenship, followed by the beliefs and critiques of GCE and critical approaches to GCE. The introduction of cultural awareness and intercultural awareness as well as the global (intercultural) competence came next. Then the researcher described the GCE in China and Chinese national identities. The previous relevant studies include three subsections of GCE and English teaching & learning, GCE and textbook analysis, as well as focusing on the Chinese context. Moreover, some previous codings in textbooks analysis regarding GCE also have been reviewed to provide some enlightenment for the coding development in this study. For the metrolingualism issues in this chapter, the researcher introduced the concept, beliefs and pedagogical implications, as well as previous studies, followed by the introduction of some other relevant terms, such as ML, metrolingual citizenship and minority languages in Chinese context. Critical multicultural education and intercultural (global) sensitivity have been briefly introduced as well. Then the researcher further elaborated the concept of glocalization and its influence on ELT, and restated the intrinsic connections among some key terms that are involved in this study, that is, GCE and metrolingualism vs. ELT textbooks and curriculum. Next, Fairclough's three-dimensional framework and its application in ELT textbooks analysis were introduced briefly. Then, the grand narratives in the discursive field of China have been introduced. For the next chapter, methodology part will be expatiated.

CHAPTER 3
RESEARCH METHODOLOGY

This chapter is composed of five sections, including research design, research instruments and data collection, data analysis, trustworthiness and consistency. The summary of this chapter comes last. The section of research instruments and data collection contains three subsections, such as ELT textbooks, curriculum, overview and sampling of textbookscapes, and semi-structured interviews. The section of data analysis consists of five subsections, such as data analysis approaches, general data analysis procedures, data analysis of GCE in ELT textbooks, data analysis of textbookscapes in ELT textbooks, data analysis of GCE and metrolingualism in curriculum, and data analysis of semi-structured interviews.

3.1 Research Design

This study synthesizes two strands of qualitative data and quantitative data, and qualitative data are the prioritized strand. Qualitative data were gathered from the thematic descriptions of content analysis (Schreier, 2012) of both textual and visual contents regarding GCE and metrolingualism in ELT textbooks and curriculum, as well as interviews with primary school English teachers who have teaching experience of PEP and Yilin English textbooks. Content analysis is a more flexible and wider applicable as well as context-sensitive data analysis approach for systematically describing the meaning of qualitative material (Schreier, 2012), through which GCE and metrolingualism values can be scrutinized to a great extent.

The quantitative data in this study are regarded as the triangulation and supplementary to the qualitative data, which were collected by coding the content of ELT textbooks and counting the occurrence number or calculating the percentage of GCE and metrolingualism items according to representations of GCE and metrolingualism values in ELT textbooks. Moreover, quantitative data were gathered by counting the linguistic repertoire and the occurrence number of preferred codes in textbookscapes as well.

Thus, a qualitative approach with some quantitative elements is adopted in this study. Moreover, since most of the data analysis was carried out through written texts, visual images and interviews, the findings in this study were presented mainly in textual descriptions. Meanwhile, some numerical calculations are also included as the triangulation and supplementary to the qualitative findings, but they are not the main focus.

Being based on the theoretical frameworks for GCE of soft versus critical GCE (Andreotti, 2006) as well as Akkari and Maleq's framework (2020) for GCE, this study attempted to scrutinize the hidden ideologies embedded in ELT textbooks and curriculum and explore in what ways they adapt to the local, regional and global dimensions of citizenship in China. Additionally, Pennycook and Otsuji's (2015a) conceptual framework for metrolingualism was adopted to study metrolingualism issues. Firstly, this study scrutinized the metrolingual landscapes (MLs) in textbooks (referred to as "textbookscapes"), including LLs such as posters, public signs, etc., and MIs such as shopping and dining in canteens portrayed in textbooks. Secondly, the metrolingualism issues in the curriculum were examined as well.

Then, the researcher merged and compared both strands of qualitative data and quantitative data to abstract the holistic interpretation of GCE and metrolingualism values that are embedded in ELT textbooks and curriculum to answer the research question one. In order to answer the research question two, comparison studies were further made between different series of textbooks regarding GCE and metrolingualism that are represented. The research question three was answered through comparing different grade levels about the similarities and differences of GCE and metrolingualism that are represented in ELT textbooks. Then the researcher answered the research question four by analyzing teachers' interviews about their perceptions. Figure 3.1 shows the diagram of the qualitative approach design of this study.

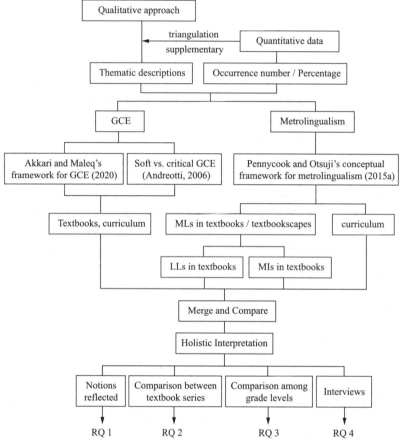

Figure 3.1　Diagram of the qualitative approach design

　　Besides, in order to achieve all the research purposes, this study collected various data including textual, visual and oral discourses from ELT textbooks and curriculum as well as interviews. Thus, the research instruments and the data collection will be elaborated in the following section.

3.2　Research Instruments and Data Collection

3.2.1　ELT textbooks

3.2.1.1　Selection and overview of textbooks

　　In 2001, English courses were introduced in primary schools in China, starting from the third grade. Since then, numerous publishing institutions have released several dozen English textbooks for primary schools, along with corresponding teaching references. Among these textbooks, those published by PEP and Yilin Press have gained significant popularity. Notably, PEP and Yilin Press are well-regarded publishing houses in the educational field in China, with a long-standing focus on research and development of textbooks for compulsory education.

The English textbooks selected for this study are specifically the ones published by PEP and Yilin Press for primary education in China. These textbooks cover four grades, starting from grade three and continuing up to grade six. Each grade consists of two volumes, resulting in a total of 16 textbook volumes. PEP textbooks were co-compiled by People's Education Press Ltd. and Lingo Learning Inc. from Canada, while Yilin textbooks were co-compiled by Yilin Press and Oxford University Press (China) Ltd. These textbook sets were published between 2012 and 2014 and comprise a total of 110 units, spanning a combined 1,118 pages of text.

There are five key reasons for selecting these two series of textbooks. Firstly, both PEP textbooks and Yilin textbooks were compiled and edited in accordance with the ECSCE. Secondly, these textbooks have received approval from the Chinese MOE. Thirdly, PEP and Yilin Press are highly regarded and widely popular publishers known for producing high-quality English textbooks for compulsory education. Their textbooks are utilized nationwide and carry significant influence. Notably, PEP is the most authorized publishing house for textbooks in China (Tse, 2011). Fourthly, the geographical distance between the two publishing houses, with PEP located in Beijing and Yilin Press in Nanjing, may provide a broader perspective and enhance the objectivity and reliability of examining the incorporation and distribution of GCE and metrolingualism within the textbooks. It also allows for comparative studies between these two series. Lastly, both PEP textbooks and Yilin textbooks were co-compiled by Chinese editors and native English-speaking editors. This may suggest the potential inclusion of Western paradigms in the textbooks, which warrants a critical examination of any hidden agendas.

3.2.1.2 Sampling of data regarding GCE in textbooks

To ensure that no relevant content pertaining to GCE in the textbooks was overlooked, the process of collecting sampling data for this study involved three procedures. Firstly, keeping the concept of GCE in mind, two researchers independently read through all the textbooks and selected samples that potentially contained GCE values. Secondly, the two researchers compared and discussed the selected GCE samples. In cases where they were unable to reach an agreement, a third researcher was consulted to discuss differing opinions and reach a consensus.

Lastly, after engaging in various discussions, the final sampling of data regarding GCE was determined.

It is important to note three selection principles that were applied in advance. Firstly, each scene within the textbooks was considered as one sample, even if it spanned two pages. On the other hand, multiple samples could be present on a single page. Secondly, considering that the textual content in primary ELT textbooks corresponds to visual images, both the text and its corresponding image were counted as one sample. Thirdly, the number of samples does not directly reflect the occurrence of GCE themes/subthemes, as a sample can be coded multiple times, generating multiple GCE themes/subthemes. Following these data collection procedures, PEP textbooks yielded 517 GCE samples, while Yilin textbooks provided 248 GCE samples, resulting in a total of 765 GCE samples.

3.2.2 Curriculum

3.2.2.1 Overview and components of the curriculum

The curriculum examined in this study was obtained from the national ECSCE. This curriculum was revised in 2011 by the Chinese MOE and published by Beijing Normal University Press. It consists of five components: Preface, Course Objectives, Grading Standards, Implementation Recommendations, and Appendix. The curriculum spans a total of 180 pages. According to the ECSCE, English courses are mandated to be taught from grade three of primary schools to grade nine of junior high schools (MOE, 2011). Table 3.1 presents a detailed overview of the curriculum's contents and components.

Table 3.1   Components of the curriculum

Section	Subsection	Pages
Preface	• Nature of the course • Basic concept of the course • Ideas of course design	pp.1-7
Course objectives	• The general objective • Grading objectives	pp.8-11
Grading standards	• Linguistic skills • Linguistic knowledge • Emotional attitudes • Learning strategies • Cultural awareness	pp.12-24

(to be continued)

Section	Subsection	Pages
Implementation recommendations	• Teaching suggestions • Evaluation suggestions • Suggestions on textbook compilation • Suggestions on development and utilization of curriculum resources	pp.25-44
Appendix	• List of phonetics items • List of grammar items • Vocabulary list • List of functional-notional items • List of topic items • Example of classroom teaching • Evaluation methods and cases • Reference suggestions for teaching skills • Classroom expressions	pp.45-180

3.2.2.2 Sampling of data in the curriculum

The general objective of the English course, as outlined in the ECSCE, aims to "assist students in developing preliminary comprehensive language competence, promoting mental development, and enhancing their overall humanistic qualities through English learning" (MOE, 2011, p.8). The curriculum is designed with five levels, aligning with the learning needs and cognitive characteristics of different age groups in compulsory education. For the purpose of this study, the focus lies on Level 2, which represents the requirements to be achieved by the end of Grade 6 in primary education. However, some aspects of Level 5, which pertains to the end of Grade 9 in junior high school education, may also be involved to a lesser extent.

The curriculum consists entirely of textual data, and for this study, the sampling selection primarily focuses on the first four sections, spanning from Page 1 to Page 44. Similar to the data collection procedures employed for GCE in textbooks, two researchers worked independently to thoroughly read and re-read the entire curriculum. They identified and underlined statements that potentially contained GCE and metrolingualism values. Subsequently, the two researchers compared and discussed these statements. In cases where consensus could not be reached, a third researcher was consulted to deliberate on differing opinions and establish a consensus. Following this, the researchers commenced the examination and coding of the data, adhering to the coding procedures outlined in this study, which will be elaborated upon in detail later.

3.2.3　Overview and sampling of textbookscapes

In this subsection, it is necessary to reiterate the three terms discussed in Chapter 2, namely ML, LL and MI. The interconnections between ML, LL, and MI, as well as the relationship between metrolingualism, ML, and textbookscapes, have already been extensively explained in Chapter 2. Therefore, the researcher will not restate them here. For the data collection of textbookscapes, the researcher focused on LLs in textbooks, which include posters, public signs, and other similar elements, as well as MIs involving activities like shopping and dining in canteens. Regarding the sampling of textbookscapes, it is important to note that one poster or one public sign was counted as one LL sample. Similarly, one shopping or dining activity was counted as one MI sample. Overall, there are a total of 155 samples of LLs and 24 samples of MIs across all textbooks.

3.2.4　Semi-structured interviews

3.2.4.1　Selection of participants

In order to answer the research question four, the researcher took a step further of textbooks analysis to see whether teachers aware of the existing GCE and metrolingualism embedded in those ELT materials. Semi-structured interviews were conducted with six English teachers who have teaching experience of either PEP textbooks or Yilin textbooks in primary schools from different parts of China through convenient or snowball sampling, and the number of participants who teach PEP textbooks is equal to the number of those who teach Yilin textbooks. Besides, the selection of the interviewees should not only take the convenient access into consideration, but also choose those "knowledgeable people" who are in the best position to offer in-depth information regarding their experience with ELT education and the textbooks at hand (Cohen et al., 2007). Thus, all participants selected for this study have more than 3 years of teaching experience. Moreover, convenient or snowball sampling could facilitate the speed and practicality of the study which is one of the purposeful sampling methods in the research.

By taking the above factors into consideration, six participants, who teach either PEP or Yilin textbooks from Grade 3 to Grade 6, were selected in order to help the researcher better understand the issues. The interviewees, aged between 25 and 40, have been teaching for three to seventeen years, with an average of 8.3 years of teaching experience. Among them, one has a junior college degree, four have bachelor's degrees, and one has a master's degree. Moreover, the schools where the interviewees teach are located in different provinces in China, including Henan,

Shandong, Hubei, Jiangsu, and one of them is the leader of the English teaching and research group in a primary school.

3.2.4.2 Validity of interview questions

The interview questions were compiled by the researcher based on the findings of ELT textbooks and curriculum analysis, as well as taking the reference of previous studies (Basarir, 2017; Goren & Yemini, 2017b). Then two specialists who hold a PhD degree were invited to help the researcher examine and polish the interview questions. After that, all the interview questions were piloted with five primary English teachers before doing the main interview. Furthermore, the researcher has made ongoing adjustments to the interview guides and questions during the process of interviews. Semi-structured interviews were conducted regarding some topics, such as teachers' awareness of GCE and metrolingualism in ELT, ELT implementation regarding GCE and metrolingualism, as well as challenges in ELT regarding GCE & metrolingualism. The guiding interview questions are shown in the Appendix C. Nevertheless, during the actual interview process, the sequence and the questioning manners of the predetermined questions may not be strictly followed, and some emerging questions may appear in order to elicit the data as much as possible through relaxed and comfortable conversations with teachers (Prabjandee, 2019).

3.2.4.3 Data collection procedures

The process of selecting and conducting interviews in this study followed several steps. Firstly, the researcher employed convenient or snowball sampling to identify qualified teachers who could participate in the interviews. Upon finding potential interviewees, the researcher approached them and asked for their consent to be interviewed. Secondly, semi-structured interviews were conducted with the participants who agreed to take part. The interviews were conducted in Chinese, which facilitated better understanding and enabled the interviewees to fully express themselves. Each interview had a duration of 30 to 50 minutes, totaling 246 minutes. Prior to recording the interviews, the researcher obtained the interviewees' agreement, and detailed notes were taken throughout the process. Thirdly, the researcher transcribed all the recorded interviews into written textual discourse using Chinese characters. During the transcription process, any unclear sections were clarified with the interviewees for accuracy. Further information regarding the participants and the duration of the interviews can be found in Table 3.2. To ensure the confidentiality of the interviewees' personal information, the names of the teachers have been replaced with the codes T1, T2, T3, T4, T5, and T6.

Table 3.2   Details about participants and interview duration

Interviewee	Years of teaching experience	Teaching textbooks	Teaching grades	Interview duration (approx.)
T1	11	PEP	Grades 4-6	30 mins
T2	7	Yilin	Grades 3-6	48 mins
T3	17	PEP	Grades 3-6	40 mins
T4	3	Yilin	Grades 3-4	42 mins
T5	4	Yilin	Grades 3-6	50 mins
T6	8	PEP	Grades 3-6	36 mins
Total				246 mins

3.2.4.4   Ethical considerations

Several ethical considerations were taken into account for the interviews conducted in this study. Firstly, all participants were provided with clear information about the purposes of this study, ensuring that they were fully informed before agreeing to participate voluntarily. Secondly, an information sheet for participants and an informed consent form were sent to the participants, asking them to sign and return the forms after reviewing and understanding the contents. Thirdly, the privacy and anonymity of the interviewees were respected throughout the study. They were assured that all collected data would be used solely for research purposes and that their personal information would be kept confidential. Importantly, the participants were informed that there were no foreseeable risks or dangers associated with their involvement and that they could withdraw from the study at any time without any negative consequences. Moreover, this study obtained permission from the Institutional Ethics Committee of a university to conduct the interviews, ensuring that the research adhered to the necessary ethical guidelines and regulations.

In order to analyze the collected data, this study adopted various data analysis approaches, it is necessary to further elaborate on how the researcher drew the findings through analyzing the data. Thus, data analysis will be the focus in the following section.

3.3   Data Analysis

3.3.1   Data analysis approaches

This study adopted content analysis (Schreier, 2012), Fairclough's three-dimensional framework of CDA (1995) and code preference analysis (Scollon & Scollon, 2003) to analyze the data, all of which worked together but with different priorities. Figure 3.2 shows the diagram of data analysis approaches employed in this study.

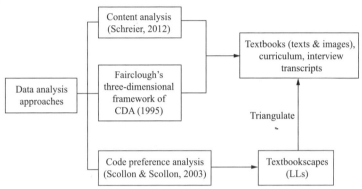

Figure 3.2   Diagram of data analysis approaches

The analysis was grounded in Schreier's qualitative content analysis (2012), since it is a more flexible and wider applicable as well as context-sensitive data analysis approach through which GCE and metrolingualism can be scrutinized to a great extent. Content analysis is a method for systematically describing the meaning of materials, and it is done by classifying materials as instances of the categories of a coding frame (Schreier, 2012). Thus, content analysis in this study was applied to all the texts and images in textbooks, curriculum, and interview transcripts.

The approach to CDA in this study employed Fairclough's three-dimensional framework (1995) to deconstruct the power relations and implicit ideologies regarding GCE and metrolingualism. Fairclough's CDA regards the relationship between language and society as internal dialectic, and the analysis of texts provides the study with a useful analytical tool, as discourse has been regarded as "(i) a language text, spoken or written, (ii) discourse practice (text production and text interpretation), (iii) sociocultural practice" (Fairclough, 1995, p.97). This method of discourse analysis contains linguistic description of the language text, interpretation of the relationship between the (productive and interpretative) discursive processes and the text, and explanation of the relationship between the discursive processes and the social processes (ibid.).

As has been elaborated in Chapter 2 that the text in this study includes the textual and visual contents in Chinese primary ELT textbooks and curriculum, and text analysis focuses on the descriptions of GCE and metrolingualism values in textbooks and curriculum. Discourse practice connects the discursive processes with the text to focus on the interpretations of GCE and metrolingualism values in textbooks and curriculum. Sociocultural practice associates the discursive processes with the social processes. In this study, the results of GCE and metrolingualism were explained by putting them in wider Chinese and global contexts. Thus, Fairclough's CDA was combined with content analysis to apply to all the texts and images in textbooks, curriculum, and interview transcripts as well.

Besides, Scollon and Scollon's (2003) code preference analysis is a common tool to analyze the preferred codes in LLs, which underlines that the preferred code is on the top, on the left, or in the center and the marginalized code is on the bottom, on the right, or on the margins. This analysis tool can help the researcher triangulate the results of content analysis and CDA regarding LLs, so the code preference analysis was applied to the LLs in textbookscapes.

3.3.2 General data analysis procedures

Qualitative content analysis is a major approach for data analysis in this study, being combined with CDA and code preference analysis. Coding is an important process in qualitative content analysis, which is to systematically categorize excerpts in the qualitative data in order to develop themes and patterns (Saldaña, 2016). Generally, the data analysis procedures can be elaborated in two phases.

Firstly, the researcher employed the coding system of open coding, axial coding, and selective coding, which was applied to all the texts and images in textbooks, curriculum, and interview transcripts to develop the themes regarding GCE and metrolingualism. Then, the preferred codes and marginalized codes were explored in LLs of textbookscapes through code preference analysis, which can be regarded as a triangulation method for the themes of metrolingualism.

For the second phase, Fairclough's three-dimensional framework of CDA was followed, including the linguistic descriptions of GCE and metrolingualism values in textbooks and curriculum (first dimension of text), interpretation of GCE and metrolingualism values in textbooks and curriculum (second dimension of discourse practice), and explanations of GCE and metrolingualism values as well as association of social effects regarding GCE and metrolingualism (third dimension of sociocultural practice). Figure 3.3 shows the diagram of general data analysis procedures.

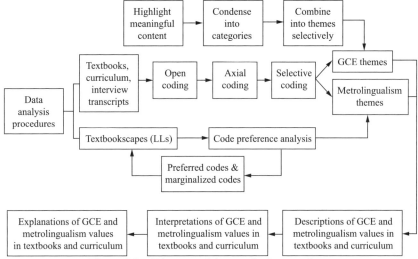

Figure 3.3   Diagram of data analysis procedures

In the following subsections, the researcher will go into further details on data analysis procedures for the coding based on the collected data and research questions in this study.

3.3.3   Data analysis of GCE in ELT textbooks

3.3.3.1   GCE coding procedures

As mentioned above, qualitative content analysis was adopted in this study, which is a method for systematically describing the meaning of qualitative material (Schreier, 2012). This can be done by classifying parts of the material as instances of the categories of a coding frame, while "coding" can be referred to a variety of different procedures, and coding in qualitative research is typically a conceptual device that opens up data in new ways and helps to create theory (ibid.). A coding frame is a way of structuring the material, a way of differentiating between different meanings in relation to the research questions, which consists of main categories or dimensions and a number of subcategories for each dimension which specify the meanings in the material with respect to the main categories (ibid.).

Generally, three strategies can be adopted to build a coding frame, which are a concept-driven strategy, a data-driven strategy, and combining concept-driven and data-driven strategies (ibid.). Concept-driven strategy can be based on theory, on prior research, on logic, on everyday knowledge, or on an interview guide, while data-driven strategy includes aggregation, subsumption, contrasting, and making use of open and selective coding adapted from grounded theory (ibid.). A typical combined strategy is to take important topics based on what is already known and turn them into major categories, and this first step would be the concept-driven part of the procedure. The main categories (also called "dimensions") of the coding frame are the aspects on which the researcher wants to focus during the analysis (ibid.). In the second step, subcategories can be created based on the materials to specify content on these topics, and this is the data-driven part of the strategy (ibid.).

In this study, the combined strategy was adopted, which is also the one that is most frequently used (ibid.). The concept-driven strategy in this study is based on the Akkari and Maleq's framework for GCE (2020), which suggests operationalizing GCE within three domains and each of these domains could be subdivided into a further subset of sub-domains (see Table 1.1). Those domains and subdomains can be regarded as the major categories during the concept-driven part. Moreover, since qualitative content analysis is also a highly flexible method, the coding frame should be tailored to the study material (Schreier, 2012). The data-driven strategy in this study includes the GCE themes and subthemes that were generated from the sampling of data in textbooks. Thus, GCE coding procedures in this study can be generally divided into two processes. Firstly, concept-driven coding was the starting point through coding in the GCE conceptual sense in mind deductively. Secondly, data-driven coding was processed through three steps, namely, open, axial, and selective coding, in order to let inductive themes and subthemes emerge from the data. In the following, GCE coding procedures in textbooks will be further elaborated.

During the concept-driven coding, two coders worked independently to categorize the GCE samples in textbooks into their corresponding GCE domains and sub-domains. It should be mentioned that there may be overlapping of samples in different domains and sub-domains, since one sample can be generated more than one GCE theme/subtheme. Those samples cannot fit into the predetermined GCE domains were categorized within the domain of emerging themes for GCE. Then the two coders met and discussed the disagreement, and the third coder was sometimes invited to take a consensus if the previous two coders could not reach agreement. Actually, the process of selecting samples can be regarded as an open coding to identify the relevant concepts. After reaching a consensus of the concept-driven coding, these two coders continued to do the data-driven coding.

Still, the two coders worked separately to examine and coded the data during the process of data-driven coding including three steps of open, axial, and selective coding. Firstly, the meaningful contents were highlighted and initial codes were identified in each GCE sample during the open coding stage; secondly, those initial codes were reexamined and identified the relationships among them, as well as successively condensed into categories during the axial coding stage; thirdly, the categories were combined into themes/subthemes by selectively choosing the ones related to the GCE domains or sub-domains they were categorized in during the concept-driven coding. The guiding principle applied to the coding of visual contents is, "What is the first and general impression I get about this visual content, and what details within it led me to that impression?" (Saldaña, 2016).

Besides, the occurrence number of themes and subthemes depends on how many times such themes/subthemes were coded, and the coded times were counted. As mentioned previously, one GCE sample in textbooks can be generated more than one theme/subtheme, so different themes/subthemes were coded separately and the occurrence number of each theme/subtheme was counted as once. After finishing all the steps in data-driven coding, the two coders met and discussed the tentative codings, and the third coder was sometimes invited to take a consensus. Then, the researcher refined the names and defined all the tentative themes and subthemes inductively. Finally, another coder and two experts were invited to help the researcher further polish the themes and subthemes as well as their definitions.

By following the above GCE coding procedures and the coding frame building strategy, the following subsection will be focused on the GCE coding frame and the definition for each theme or subtheme.

3.3.3.2   GCE coding frame

The process of building a coding frame can be broken down into several steps, including selecting, structuring, generating, defining, revising, and expanding (Schreier, 2012), which is a dynamic process. In order to help the researcher overcome any preconceptions and see more in the data (ibid.), two coders and two experts were invited to help the researcher further revise the coding frame during the study as well. Then the researcher made ongoing adjustments to the GCE coding frame during the study, so as to let more inductive themes as well as subthemes emerge from the data and attempt to cover the variation in the whole data as much as possible. The GCE coding frame contains 16 themes and 20 subthemes of GCE that were found in ELT textbooks. Table 3.3 shows the GCE coding frame for themes and subthemes embedded in textbooks.

Table 3.3　GCE coding frame for themes and subthemes embedded in textbooks

Domain	Sub-domain	Themes	Subthemes	Theme/Subtheme definition
Education for sustainable development	Education for development	Social development and progress	N/A	In this study, this theme refers to showing the development and progress of the society, especially the development and progress of science and technology.
		Omnipotent artificial intelligence	N/A	In this study, this theme shows the omnipotence of artificial intelligence in people's daily life.
	Environmental education	Environmental responsibility and sustainable development	N/A	In this study, this theme shows people's environmental awareness and environmental protection measures, etc.
		Harmonious coexistence of human-nature relations	N/A	In this study, this theme describes the images or related content of textbooks in which humans and nature coexist harmoniously.
Inter/multi-cultural education	Inclusive education	Harmonious coexistence of human-human relations	Kinship	In this study, this subtheme refers to showing love and care among family members as well as family-oriented activities.
			Friendship	In this study, this subtheme shows the friendship, sharing, and care among friends, etc.
			Empathy	In this study, this subtheme refers to showing compassion for the weak and the disadvantaged, etc.
			Tolerance	In this study, this subtheme refers to being tolerant of somebody or something that displeases you.

(to be continued)

94

Domain	Sub-domain	Themes	Subthemes	Theme/Subtheme definition
			Gratitude	In this study, this subtheme refers to a feeling of gratitude for somebody or something, such as gratitude for mother, gratitude for the hard-won life, etc.
		Globality	N/A	In this study, this theme usually shows an image of the whole world, displaying something similar or different around the world.
			Anglophone cultures	In this study, this subtheme refers to the cultures of Anglophone countries, including the cultural customs, festivals, diet cultures of North America, Australia, New Zealand, etc.
	Respect for diversity	Cultural diversity	Chinese cultures	In this study, this subtheme refers to the Chinese cultures or Chinese-style articles, including Chinese universal cultures and Chinese ethnic minority cultures.
			Global cultures	In this study, this subtheme refers to the culture that is widely spread in the world, no longer unique to a specific culture of a country, and usually refers to international festivals.
			Other cultures	In this study, this subtheme refers to some other cultures apart from Anglophone cultures and Chinese cultures.

(*to be continued*)

Domain	Sub-domain	Themes	Subthemes	Theme/Subtheme definition
Citizenship education	Civic and moral education	Civic virtues & morality	Civilized manners	In this study, this subtheme indicates that a person's behavior should conform to the norms of social etiquette, such as no littering, being courteous, etc.
			Rule compliance	In this study, this subtheme means that citizens should observe and obey social rules and laws, e.g. obeying traffics rules, following the school rules.
			Cooperation and solidarity	In this study, this subtheme refers to a team spirit in which people help and support each other in completing a task and overcome difficulties together.
			Diligence	In this study, this subtheme refers to a state of working hard, being not afraid of hardship, being steadfast work and study.
			Honesty	In this study, the theme of morality includes universal values such as honesty, integrity, braveness, kind-heartedness. The subtheme of honesty means being faithful, keeping promises, and being true to one's obligations, etc.
			Being helpful	In this study, this subtheme refers to the willingness to help others.

(to be continued)

Domain	Sub-domain	Themes	Subthemes	Theme/Subtheme definition
Emerging themes	N/A	World geography	Anglophone geography	In this study, this subtheme refers to the geography of Anglophone countries, including landmarks, places, regional characteristics and symbolic animals, etc. that unique to North America, Australia, New Zealand, etc.
			Chinese geography	In this study, this sub-theme refers to the land-marks, places, regional characteristics and symbolic animals, etc. that unique to China.
			Other geography	In this study, this sub-theme refers to the land-marks, places, regional characteristics and symbolic animals, etc. that unique to other countries that beyond Anglophone geography as well as Chinese geography.
		Healthy diet & lifestyle	N/A	In this study, this theme means that one should develop a healthy diet and lifestyle to keep physical fitness.
		Leisure lifestyle	N/A	In this study, this theme shows that the characters in textbooks relax themselves through some activities during non-working hours, e.g. picnics, playing games.

(*to be continued*)

Domain	Sub-domain	Themes	Subthemes	Theme/Subtheme definition
		Native-speakerism	Native-speakerism prestige & supremacy	In this study, this subtheme means that native-speakers are regarded as the authority of English teaching and the most ideal English teachers.
			Anti-native speakerism prestige	In this study, this subtheme refers to the phenomenon as opposed to the native-speakerism prestige, e.g. Textbooks show Chinese as English teachers.
		Career planning	N/A	In this study, this theme refers to people's dreams and plans for their future jobs.
		Commerciali-zation	N/A	Commercialization is the act of making profits. In this study, this theme shows that the characters in textbooks practice buying and selling of commodities or imitate buying and selling of commodities.
		Everyday philosophy	N/A	In this study, this theme includes some proverbs in daily life or some philosophical fables, e.g. learning by doing.
		Chinese educational principles	N/A	In this study, this theme refers to some content embedded with Chinese educational principles which advocate an all-round development for students in morality, intelligence, physical fitness, aesthetics, and labor, or some educational activities that reflect the Chinese educational policies, etc.

Besides, since the occurrence number of interactions among non-native speakers (NNS) and native speakers (NS) in textbooks was counted in Section 4.1.1, it is necessary to define two terms of "NS" and "NNS". NS in this study are defined as the characters from English-speaking countries in textbooks, such as the US, the UK, Canada, who usually have English names. Being constructed compared to NS, NNS in this study are defined as characters from non-English speaking countries in textbooks, and most of the NNS represented in textbooks are Chinese.

3.3.4　Data analysis of textbookscapes in ELT textbooks

3.3.4.1　Coding procedures for textbookscapes

As mentioned before, the data collection of textbookscapes includes LLs in textbooks such as posters, public signs in textbooks, and MIs containing the activities such as shopping and dining in canteens in textbooks. Thus, the data analysis of textbookscapes in ELT textbooks was also elaborated from these two aspects. Data-driven strategy is the prioritized one during the coding process for textbookscapes while keeping the conceptual framework for metrolingualism of this study in mind. Moreover, since each LL and MI sample can be regarded as an independent coding unit and cannot be further segmented, holistic coding was employed for coding the textbookscapes. Holistic coding is a kind of macro-level coding, which attempts to grasp basic themes or issues in the data by absorbing them as a whole rather than by analyzing them line by line (Saldaña, 2016). The themes for metrolingualism were generated from the sampling of textbookscapes. The coding procedures for textbookscapes are elaborated in following paragraphs, including the coding procedures of LLs in textbooks and the coding procedures of MIs in textbooks.

There are five steps for the coding procedures of LLs in textbooks. Firstly, LL samples in textbooks were identified and selected, which has already been elaborated in the data collection part. Secondly, the researcher grouped those LLs into two major categories and eight subcategories according to the linguistic repertoire in each LL sample, as well as counted the occurrence number of each subcategory of LLs. Thirdly, the researcher further calculated the proportion of each linguistic or non-linguistic code in LLs. Fourthly, the researcher analyzed the preferred code in each LL sample based on the framework of code preference analysis of this study, as well as calculated the occurrence number of the preferred code. Finally, the researcher meticulously read and reread those LL samples as well as the calculated numbers, and generated the tentative themes for LLs analysis in textbooks.

Besides, in order to ensure the reliability of the calculations, the researcher invited another coder to help reviewing all the counted numbers before generating the tentative themes. Then the researcher invited the two experts to help further polish the tentative themes. During the coding process of LLs in textbooks, the selection of LL samples can be regarded as the open coding stage, since the contents related to LLs in textbooks were identified; the axial coding stage was done during the second step above to group those LL samples into categories and subcategories; the selective coding stage was accomplished by generating the tentative themes for LLs analysis in textbooks. The calculation of numbers in Steps Two, Three, and Four above are the quantitative coding for triangulation purposes.

Similarly, the coding procedures of MIs in textbooks contain three steps. Firstly, those MI activities regarding shopping and dining in canteens in textbooks were identified and selected as MI samples during the open coding stage. Based on the conceptual framework of metrolingualism of this study, linguistic and spatial repertoires including linguistic repertoire and non-linguistic resources in each MI activity are regarded as the focus for MIs analysis in textbooks, since all those layered languages, tasks, practices and spaces combine together to produce spatial repertoires (Pennycook & Otsuji, 2015a). In this regard, the second step was focused on identifying those elements in all MI samples according to the categories of linguistic repertoire and non-linguistic resources. Lastly, the tentative themes for MIs analysis in textbooks were generated based on those categories. Still, another coder and two experts were invited to help examining the samples and polishing the tentative themes.

3.3.4.2 Revised coding frame for textbookscapes

By following the above procedures, a tentative coding frame was built for textbookscapes. On the other hand, building a coding frame is a dynamic process which can be further revised and expanded with the research progressing. The researcher made ongoing adjustments to the tentative coding frame for textbookscapes during the study to polish the names for those themes to be more succinct as well as easily understood. The coding frame for textbookscapes is illustrated below.

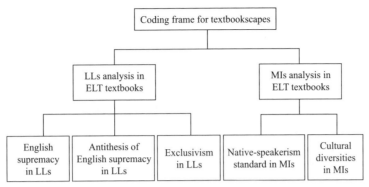

Figure 3.4   Coding frame for textbookscapes

3.3.5   Data analysis of GCE & metrolingualism in curriculum

3.3.5.1   Coding procedures

For data analysis of GCE and metrolingualism in the ELT curriculum, thematic analysis was adopted, which is a particular type of qualitative content analysis to focus on the themes mentioned in the materials (Schreier, 2012). Since the curriculum is all about textual statements, the data analysis is detailed from two aspects, statements regarding GCE in the curriculum and statements regarding metrolingualism in the curriculum. Still, data-driven coding was prioritized during the coding process to develop the themes regarding GCE and metrolingualism in the curriculum, three stages of coding system for open coding, axial coding and selective coding were still the focus. In the following paragraphs, the coding procedures regarding GCE and metrolingualism will be further elaborated.

As has been mentioned in the data collection part, the sampling of data in the curriculum was identified through two coders examining independently and discussing together all the statements in the curriculum, as well as categorizing the related statements into two groups including the statements regarding GCE and the statements regarding metrolingualism. Then these two groups of sampling data were coded successively. Since the coding procedures of the two groups of sampling data are similar, the researcher only specifies the coding procedures for the sampling data of GCE.

Generally, the coding procedures consist of three steps. Firstly, these two coders worked independently to examine and further identify the initial codes in the statements regarding GCE during the open coding stage; secondly, those initial codes were reexamined and identified the relationships among them, as well as successively condensed into categories during the axial coding stage; thirdly, the categories were combined into themes by selectively choosing the ones related to GCE concept. After developing the tentative themes, the two coders discussed with each other about the disagreement and revised the themes. Then the two experts were invited again to help the researcher further polish those themes. The development of themes regarding metrolingualism also follows the coding procedures described above, so it will not be restated here. The example of coding procedures for GCE & metrolingualism in the curriculum is shown in the Appendix D. The sampling of statements in the Appendix D are only a part of the sampling, not the whole sampling of data, the purpose is to show general coding procedures for GCE and metrolingualism in the curriculum.

By following the above coding procedures of GCE and metrolingualism in the curriculum, the coding frame was further developed in the next subsection.

3.3.5.2　Coding frame

Since the coding procedures have already been elaborated above including the initial codes, categories and themes, only code themes are presented here. Figure 3.5 shows a flat coding frame (Saldaña, 2016) for GCE and metrolingualism in the curriculum.

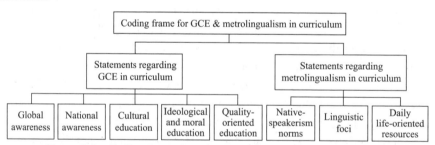

Figure 3.5　Coding frame for GCE & metrolingualism in curriculum

3.3.6　Data analysis of semi-structured interviews

3.3.6.1　Coding procedures

For data analysis of semi-structured interviews, thematic analysis was adopted. Concept-driven coding and data-driven coding were combined together to develop themes regarding teachers' perceptions toward GCE and metrolingualism. Concept-driven coding was based on the predetermined interview guide of this study to generate the code themes, including teachers' awareness of GCE & metrolingualism in ELT, ELT implementation regarding GCE & metrolingualism, and challenges in ELT regarding GCE and metrolingualism. Then, data-driven coding was conducted for interview transcripts to generate the categories. The data analysis procedures are further elaborated in following paragraphs step by step.

Generally, there are four steps for data analysis of teachers' interviews. Firstly, the researcher transcribed all the interview recordings into Chinese characters. Then, the researcher listened to the interview recordings again to further check the accuracy of the transcripts. Moreover, the notes that were taken during the interviews were further confirmed and fully expanded through listening to the recordings again. If there are some unclear parts during the transcription, the researcher would contact the interviewees again for confirmation.

Secondly, the researcher further analyzed the transcripts based on the predetermined themes developed through concept-driven coding, and let the categories emerge from all transcripts through data-driven coding of open coding, axial coding and selective coding. During this process, the researcher read and reread the whole transcripts meticulously, and identified the initial codes during the open coding stage; then the researcher reexamined the open codes and identified the relationships among them to generate categories; the researcher further combined the categories by selectively choosing the ones related to the predetermined themes.

Thirdly, the researcher translated the relevant extracts into English, and further revised the English names of those themes. Fourthly, in order to enhance the trustworthiness and consistency of this part of findings, another coder and the two experts were invited again to check the whole process of coding and the understandings of the extracts as well as the accuracy of the translation. Besides, in order to further elaborate how the interview findings were reached, an example of data-driven coding procedures for the transcripts is illustrated in Table 3.4.

Table 3.4　Example of data-driven coding procedures for the transcripts

Open coding	Axial coding	Selective coding
Initial codes	Categories	Themes
• Never heard of this concept • The whole world is like a community • Community with a Shared Future for Mankind • Globalized values • More inclusive and open	Conceptual understanding of GCE	Teachers' awareness of GCE & metrolingualism in ELT
• Teaching either British English or American English • Take British English or American English as a standard • Correct students' expressions	Awareness of linguistic inclusiveness in ELT	

(to be continued)

Open coding	Axial coding	Selective coding
Initial codes	Categories	Themes
• A little narrow regarding the cultural diversity	Awareness of critical multiculturalism in ELT	
• The awareness of global citizenship should be deeply rooted in everyone's hearts • English teachers also have a convenient condition in this respect • Should also provide timely guidance • All the subjects are interlinked	Awareness of roles of ELT teachers regarding GCE	
• Cultivate students' linguistic knowledge and skills as well as learning strategies • Without paying special attention to cultural awareness • Cultivate students' interest in English • Vocabulary memorization methods • Linguistic knowledge and skills	General implementation in ELT	
• Focus on Anglophone cultures • The differences between Chinese and Anglophone cultures • Cultures of non-English speaking countries have been rarely involved • British and American cultural customs are the main focus • Some other countries are rarely involved	Cultural foci in ELT	ELT implementation regarding GCE & metrolingualism
• Educate children a sense of family • The kinship among family members	Implementation of other GCE values in ELT	
• Cannot talk too much about something other than the textbooks in class • Mainly based on textbooks during the class	Textbook centralism	
• Only two English classes a week • 40 minutes for each class • Can't talk too much nonsense • Have to get to the point directly	Class time limit	Challenges in ELT regarding GCE & metrolingualism
• Teaching from the perspective of examination	Exam-oriented education	

(*to be continued*)

Open coding		Axial coding	Selective coding
Initial codes		Categories	Themes
• A challenge for teachers • Need to constantly improve professional ability and broaden horizons		Teacher training needed	
• From rural areas • Do not have a good language learning environment • English foundation may be weak		Educational disparity	
• They are primary school students • Just started learning English • May not be able to digest		Young age of primary school students	

3.3.6.2   Coding frame

Following the above data analysis procedures, the researcher made ongoing adjustments to the coding frame during the study. Table 3.5 shows the coding frame for interview transcripts in this study.

Table 3.5   Coding frame for interview transcripts

Code themes	Code categories
Teachers' awareness of GCE & metrolingualism in ELT	Conceptual understanding of GCE
	Awareness of linguistic inclusiveness in ELT
	Awareness of critical multiculturalism in ELT
	Awareness of roles of ELT teachers regarding GCE
ELT implementation regarding GCE & metrolingualism	General implementation in ELT
	Cultural foci in ELT
	Implementation of other GCE values in ELT
	Textbook centralism
Challenges in ELT regarding GCE & metrolingualism	Class time limit
	Exam-oriented education
	Teacher training needed
	Educational disparity
	Young age of primary school students

By following the above data analysis procedures, the findings for each RQ were answered. In order to enhance the trustworthiness and consistency of the findings of this study, some approaches were adopted, which will be elaborated in the following section.

3.4 Trustworthiness and Consistency

In a qualitative approach, validity and reliability have been translated into trustworthiness and consistency (Schreier, 2012). An instrument is considered trustworthy to the extent that it captures what it sets out to capture (ibid.). The trustworthiness in this study is focused on the trustworthiness of the coding frames, that is, the themes and categories can adequately represent the concepts under study. Consistency is assessed by comparing coding across persons (intersubjectivity) or over time (stability) (ibid.). In qualitative content analysis, a consistency check can be built into two procedures, that is, parts of the study materials are coded by another person, or parts of the materials are recoded by the researcher after approximately 10-14 days (ibid.). Besides, integrating intra-coding and inter-coding can also enhance the trustworthiness of the study. Moreover, another way to assess the trustworthiness is by expert evaluation (ibid.). In this light, the trustworthiness and consistency of this study are enhanced through the following procedures.

Two coders were invited, who are named as Coder A and Coder B for confidentiality. Coder A is a Chinese college English teacher with teaching experience for about seven years, who holds a master's degree and is a PhD candidate. Coder B is a Chinese primary school English teacher with teaching experience for about seven years as well, who also holds a master's degree. There are two reasons for selecting these two coders. Firstly, since the study materials of this study are Chinese primary ELT materials, primary school English teachers may have a better understanding of those materials, while college English teachers may have richer research experience. In this light, these two coders may help the researcher analyze the data more professionally and deeply. Secondly, they are friends of the researcher and were willing to help. Positive emotion is always the precondition to do research, which is also an emotional factor in selecting these two coders. Besides, two Chinese college English teachers with more than ten years of teaching experience were invited as experts, who hold PhD degrees and have rich research experience.

Before doing the data analysis, coding training was conducted by the researcher, including the research concern, theoretical framework, central research questions, goals of the study, and other major issues, as well as a demonstration of the coding process (Schreier, 2012). Besides, the researcher also introduced some major information to the two experts, including the research background, research purposes, research questions, theoretical frameworks, and some other research concerns. During the process of data analysis, the researcher was the main coder, participating in the whole process of coding all the data, and the other two coders took turns coding. Coder A was the main inter-coder of the researcher, since she may be more familiar with the process of data analysis, while Coder B sometimes intervened as the third party to resolve the disagreements.

As has been mentioned in the section of 3.2, the sampling of data regarding GCE in textbooks and the sampling of data in the curriculum were selected by the researcher and other two coders. Then the researcher and coder A worked separately to examine and code those sampling of data through the coding procedures of this study. After finishing the initial coding, these two coders met and discussed the coding results. If these two coders cannot reach agreement, Coder B was invited to discuss different opinions and took a consensus. In quantitative content analysis, reliability can be assessed by calculating the percentage or a coefficient of agreement (Schreier, 2012). This is useful for giving a summary impression of reliability, but has to be interpreted with the kind of material and the distribution of disagreements in mind (ibid.). In qualitative content analysis, discussion among coders can replace calculating a coefficient (ibid.). In this light, no coefficient of agreement is calculated, since discussions were made to resolve any disagreements.

After several rounds of discussion, the coding frames were built. Then the two experts were invited to examine the coding frames and offer some suggestions. The researcher further polished those themes and subthemes as well as the definitions in the coding frames according to the suggestions of the experts. Approximately 14 days later, the researcher recoded all the sampled data based on the revised coding frames and made further refinements. Besides, the building of coding frames in this study was based on the whole samplings of data, which could largely ensure the saturation of themes and categories. In this regard, the trustworthiness and consistency of the coding frames can be guaranteed to a great extent as well.

For the trustworthiness and consistency of the interview data analysis, the validity of the interview questions was checked by the two Chinese experts and piloted before conducting the semi-structured interviews in the main study. The quality of the interview data was maximized through rechecking the transcripts by the researcher and member checking for the unclear parts with the interviewees.

Moreover, the two coders and the two experts were invited again to check the whole process of coding and the researcher's understandings of the extracts as well as the accuracy of the translation.

Besides, triangulation and thick description were adopted to enhance the inference quality of this study as well. Tashakkori and Teddlie (2008) used the term "inference quality" to refer to the "quality of conclusions that are made on the basis of the findings in a study" (p.101) (as cited in Hashemi & Babaii, 2013). In this light, diversified data collection methods and data analysis approaches have contributed to the inference quality of this study, since the data were collected from textual, visual and oral discourses. Moreover, code preference analysis for LLs is another way to triangulate the results from content analysis combined with CDA. In order to ensure the accuracy of the calculations, the researcher invited another coder to help reviewing all the counted numbers. Moreover, Section 3.2 and Section 3.3 of this chapter have been elaborated in details regarding how the data were collected and how the results were reached.

3.5   Summary of the Chapter

This chapter introduced the research design of a qualitative approach in this study. Then, the researcher illustrated the research instruments and data collection by elaborating the selection and overview of the data as well as the procedures for sampling of the data, including ELT textbooks, curriculum, textbookscapes, and semi-structured interviews. Next, the validity of interview questions and the ethical considerations also have been detailed. For data analysis, the researcher further elaborated the data analysis approaches and the data analysis procedures, including the data analysis of GCE in ELT textbooks, data analysis of textbookscapes in ELT textbooks, data analysis of GCE and metrolingualism in curriculum, and data analysis of semi-structured interviews. Moreover, coding procedures and coding frames for each set of data have been illustrated as well. Next, the trustworthiness and consistency of this study have been expounded. By following the research methodology in this chapter, the findings of this study will be expatiated in the following chapter.

CHAPTER 4
RESULTS

There are six sections in this chapter, which answer all the four RQs. The first section answers the RQ 1, containing GCE embedded in ELT textbooks, textbookscapes analysis for metrolingualism in ELT textbooks, GCE & metrolingualism embedded in curriculum. The RQ 2 and the RQ 3 are answered in the second and the third sections regarding the similarities and differences. The RQ 4 is answered through three themes in the fifth section, including teachers' awareness of GCE & metrolingualism in ELT; ELT implementation regarding GCE & metrolingualism; challenges in ELT regarding GCE & metrolingualism. The summary of this chapter comes last.

4.1 GCE & Metrolingualism in Textbooks and Curriculum

In this section, the findings of RQ 1 are presented: In what ways do ELT textbooks and curriculum reflect the notions of GCE and metrolingualism for primary education in China? The following subsections will further elaborate the ways that the notions of GCE and metrolingualism are embedded in ELT textbooks through representing salient themes regarding GCE and metrolingualism.

4.1.1　GCE embedded in ELT textbooks

Using the coding frame presented in Table 3.3, the researcher calculated the occurrence frequency of each theme and subtheme in the collected data. Additionally, the proportions of these themes and subthemes in the textbooks were calculated. The statistical representation of GCE themes and subthemes in PEP textbooks and Yilin textbooks is presented in Table 4.1. This table includes the total occurrence number of themes and subthemes in both textbook series, which amounts to 770. Furthermore, Table 4.1 provides detailed data distributions across different grade levels and textbook series.

Table 4.1 provides an overview of the 31 themes/subthemes related to GCE found in ELT textbooks. In this study, the focus will be on the salient themes and subthemes, which are determined based on their occurrence numbers. According to Arbak (2005), the salient themes can be identified as the top three most frequently occurring themes based on the percentage of their occurrence numbers. In a previous study conducted by He & Buripakdi (2022), the top 20% of themes with the highest occurrence numbers were considered as salient themes. In this regard, the salient themes/subthemes in this study are as follows: Anglophone cultures (107), Chinese cultures (91), kinship (59), native-speakerism prestige & supremacy (55), Chinese geography (46), leisure lifestyle (44), Chinese educational principles (41). The numbers in brackets indicate the occurrence numbers of these themes and subthemes in the textbooks. The subsequent paragraphs will provide detailed elaboration on these salient themes and subthemes.

The subtheme of **Anglophone cultures** appears as a salient aspect that receives considerable attention in all textbooks, possibly overshadowing the rich diversity of cultures encompassed by GCE. It is observed that both textbook series primarily concentrate on introducing Anglophone festivals and dietary practices, potentially overlooking the incorporation of other diverse global cultures. Notably, Christmas and Halloween receive extensive coverage in these textbooks. For instance, on the Page 66 of PEP4V2, there is an illustration depicting John and Yang Ling visiting Mike's home for Christmas. The image portrays a Christmas tree, Mike's father dressed as Santa Claus, a table adorned with Christmas food like turkey, and people exchanging Merry Christmas greetings to celebrate the occasion. Similarly, there is an entire unit titled "At Christmas" in Yilin5V1, dedicated to introducing the Christmas Day celebration.

Table 4.1 Occurrence number of GCE themes and subthemes in PEP and Yilin textbooks

Themes	Sub-themes	Occurrence number in PEP3	Occurrence number in PEP4	Occurrence number in PEP5	Occurrence number in PEP6	Occurrence number in Yilin3	Occurrence number in Yilin4	Occurrence number in Yilin5	Occurrence number in Yilin6	Total number	Percentage (total number /770)
Social development and progress	N/A	0	0	0	3	0	0	0	1	4	0.52%
Omnipotent artificial intelligence	N/A	0	0	22	12	0	1	0	0	35	4.55%
Environmental responsibility and sustainable development	N/A	1	0	1	2	0	0	0	12	16	2.08%
Harmonious coexistence of human-nature relations	N/A	11	1	13	2	1	6	3	1	38	4.94%
Total in the domain of Education for sustainable development		12	1	36	19	1	7	3	14	93	12.08%

(to be continued)

111

Themes	Sub-themes	Occurrence number in PEP3	Occurrence number in PEP4	Occurrence number in PEP5	Occurrence number in PEP6	Occurrence number in Yilin3	Occurrence number in Yilin4	Occurrence number in Yilin5	Occurrence number in Yilin6	Total number	Percentage (total number /770)
Harmonious coexistence of human-human relations	Kinship	11	6	7	7	5	4	13	6	59	7.66%
	Friend-ship	2	3	1	5	1	1	2	1	16	2.08%
	Empathy	0	1	0	3	0	2	0	0	6	0.78%
	Tolerance	0	0	0	2	0	0	0	0	2	0.26%
	Gratitude	0	0	3	1	0	0	2	0	6	0.78%
Globality	N/A	0	3	0	0	0	0	0	0	3	0.39%
Cultural diversity	Anglo-phone cultures	27	17	17	5	3	6	18	14	107	13.9%
	Chinese cultures	7	12	26	13	3	4	16	10	91	11.82%
	Global cultures	3	0	8	0	2	0	4	3	20	2.6%
	Other cultures	0	0	1	0	0	0	0	0	1	0.13%
Total in the domain of Inter/multicultural education		50	42	63	36	14	17	55	34	311	40.39%

(to be continued)

Themes	Sub-themes	Occurrence number in PEP3	Occurrence number in PEP4	Occurrence number in PEP5	Occurrence number in PEP6	Occurrence number in Yilin3	Occurrence number in Yilin4	Occurrence number in Yilin5	Occurrence number in Yilin6	Total number	Percentage (total number/770)
	Civilized manners	3	2	6	0	2	0	0	8	21	2.73%
	Rule compliance	0	0	2	8	4	0	1	6	21	2.73%
Civic virtues & morality	Cooperation and solidarity	1	1	0	2	0	0	0	0	4	0.52%
	Diligence	0	0	2	1	0	0	0	1	4	0.52%
	Honesty	0	0	0	1	0	0	0	2	3	0.39%
	Being helpful	0	4	2	6	0	3	5	2	22	2.86%
Total in the domain of Citizenship education		4	7	12	18	6	3	6	19	75	9.74%
World geography	Anglophone geography	2	6	4	6	0	0	3	10	31	4.03%
	Chinese geography	6	8	7	5	1	2	4	13	46	5.97%
	Other geography	0	1	0	0	0	0	0	0	1	0.13%

(to be continued)

113

Themes	Sub-themes	Occurrence number in PEP3	Occurrence number in PEP4	Occurrence number in PEP5	Occurrence number in PEP6	Occurrence number in Yilin3	Occurrence number in Yilin4	Occurrence number in Yilin5	Occurrence number in Yilin6	Total number	Percentage (total number/770)
Healthy diet & lifestyle	N/A	4	4	4	0	0	3	4	4	23	2.99%
Leisure lifestyle	N/A	8	2	6	6	5	7	5	5	44	5.71%
Native-speakerism	Native-speakerism prestige & supremacy	18	7	22	4	1	0	3	0	55	7.14%
	Anti-native speakerism prestige	0	0	0	0	3	1	2	4	10	1.3%
Career planning	N/A	0	0	0	4	0	0	0	6	10	1.3%
Commercialization	N/A	3	13	1	1	0	8	0	0	26	3.38%
Everyday philosophy	N/A	1	0	2	1	0	0	0	0	4	0.52%
Chinese educational principles	N/A	0	11	22	4	0	3	0	1	41	5.32%
Total in the domain of Emerging themes		42	52	68	31	10	24	21	43	291	37.79%
Total		108	102	179	104	31	51	85	110	770	100%

Moreover, on Pages 78-79 of Yilin5V1, there is an illustration depicting a Caucasian family celebrating Christmas. The illustration introduces various customs associated with Christmas, such as sending gifts, decorating the Christmas tree, hanging stockings, and enjoying a meal with turkey and Christmas pudding. The high occurrence of Christmas in both textbook series is likely due to it being considered "the most important holiday in the UK". Similarly, the Chinese New Year is described as "the most important festival in China", and Thanksgiving is portrayed as "a very important holiday in the US" (as shown in the illustration on Page 83 of Yilin6V1). Furthermore, Halloween is another popular festival prominently featured in both textbook series. On Page 73 of Yilin5V2, there is an illustration and brief information about Halloween. Similarly, Page 33 of PEP3V1 shows an illustration depicting three children dressed in animal costumes, preparing to knock on someone's door. The presence of a pumpkin lantern hanging on the wall indicates that it is a Halloween night.

In addition to festivals, Western diet is another aspect of Anglophone cultures that appears frequently in both series of textbooks. For instance, on Page 48 of PEP3V1, there is an illustration showcasing a boy named Mike having breakfast with his mother. The food, as well as the presence of knives and forks on the table, align with Western eating habits. Similarly, Page 11 of Yilin5V1 presents an illustration featuring a Caucasian boy and a Chinese girl introducing coffee and tea. The images depict a Caucasian woman on the left making a cup of coffee, while a Chinese woman on the right is preparing tea. Furthermore, on Page 31 of Yilin6V2, there is an illustration highlighting the differences in breakfast preferences between Chinese and Western cultures.

The textbooks also frequently emphasize the subtheme of **Chinese cultures**. In Yilin6V1, there is an entire unit dedicated to the Chinese New Year, which is a significant festival in Chinese culture. This unit provides comprehensive coverage of various aspects related to this important celebration. On Pages 2-3 of Yilin6V1, there is an illustration depicting all the characters joyously celebrating the Chinese New Year. The image showcases typical Chinese New Year food, decorations, and other elements. For instance, Miss Li, Nancy, and Su Hai are shown making dumplings, Yang Ling is seen pasting "Fu" on the window, and Mr. Green is depicted hanging red lanterns on the eaves. In addition, the illustration captures the traditional ambiance of a Beijing courtyard house, further immersing the reader in the cultural context of the Chinese New Year. Furthermore, Yilin5V2 introduces a unit titled "Chinese Festivals", which provides insights into various other Chinese festivals. This unit highlights the diversity and richness of Chinese cultural traditions beyond the Chinese New Year.

Additionally, on Pages 68-69 of Yilin5V2, there is an illustration that focuses on four popular Chinese festivals. The Chinese New Year is introduced first, followed by the Dragon Boat Festival, the Mid-Autumn Festival, and the Double Ninth Festival (Chongyang Festival). The illustration showcases the activities and traditional foods associated with each festival, providing a glimpse into how people celebrate these occasions. Chinese cuisine is another prominent aspect within the subtheme of Chinese cultures. On Page 63 of Yilin5V2, there is an illustration presenting various Chinese dishes, including Beijing roast duck, squirrel fish, Chongqing hot pot, and Chinese pastries, etc. This highlights the rich and diverse culinary heritage of China.

Furthermore, the textbooks also touch upon the topic of birthdays, highlighting the differences between Chinese and Western birthday celebrations. Although there are similarities between them nowadays, traditional Chinese customs still exist when Chinese people celebrate their birthdays. On Page 78 of Yilin5V2, a dialogue between Su Yang and Su Hai reveals that they typically have a grand dinner with their family and enjoy noodles on their birthdays. Eating longevity noodles on Chinese birthdays is a traditional custom symbolizing longevity. Moreover, the textbooks incorporate other traditional Chinese cultures as well. For instance, on the Page 39 of PEP5V1, there is an illustration showcasing the playing of the pipa (a traditional Chinese musical instrument) and the practice of kung fu, providing glimpses into these traditional art forms.

The subtheme of **kinship** is also prominently featured in the textbooks, although it occurs less frequently compared to Chinese cultures. In PEP3V2, there is an entire unit dedicated to "My Family", which explores family-oriented activities and content. An illustration on Page 15 of PEP3V2 depicts a father, a mother, and their son. The image portrays the father and mother holding up their hands like a protective umbrella, symbolizing the nurturing and supportive environment in which their son grows up happily. Both the visual and textual content convey the theme of harmonious family affection. Similarly, another unit titled "Meet My Family" in PEP4V1 focuses on introducing one's family members. The same topic is also addressed in the Yilin series. For instance, Yilin3V1 contains a unit titled "My Family", which explores family-related content. On Page 63 of PEP4V1, John introduces his family members, including his mother, father, uncle, and aunt. Additionally, on Page 28 of Yilin3V1, there is a family song that sings, "Father, mother, brother, sister. They all love one another". The lyrics, accompanied by a happy family photo in the upper right corner, present a picture of a harmonious and loving family.

The subtheme of **native-speakerism prestige & supremacy** is indeed present in the textbooks, as it portrays native English speakers as English teachers and emphasizes their role in language instruction. In the PEP series, for example, Miss White is depicted as the English teacher and is identified as a native speaker. Furthermore, PEP textbooks often depict an international primary school setting with students from different countries and an all-English environment. On Page 4 of PEP3V2, there is an illustration where Miss White introduces two new students to the class. Amy, a girl from the UK, and Zhang Peng, a boy from Shandong province, China, are featured. The illustration implies that Amy, being from the UK, is a native English speaker. Similarly, on the Page 4 of PEP5V1, there is an illustration depicting two boys discussing their English teacher, Miss White, both of whom are portrayed as native speakers. Additionally, on Page 48 of Yilin5V1, there is a dialogue where Su Hai asks Mike about his father's occupation, and Mike responds that his father is an English teacher who is also a native speaker. It is important to note that while the textbooks may emphasize native-speakerism and the prestige associated with it, the fluidity and variations of Englishes spoken by non-native speakers should also be acknowledged and appreciated during communication.

Table 4.2 provides additional support for the subtheme of native-speakerism and the prominence of interactions between NNS and NS in the textbooks. The table illustrates that the majority of interactions portrayed in the textbooks occur between NNS and NS, while interactions among NNS make up the smallest proportion. This further reinforces the notion that native English speakers are often given greater emphasis and perceived as the ideal linguistic model within the context of English language learning. However, it is important to recognize that interactions among non-native speakers also play a significant role in language development and should be valued as an opportunity for linguistic growth and cultural exchange.

Table 4.2　Proportion of interactions in textbooks

Speakers	PEP	Yilin	Total number	Percentage (total number/750)
NNS-NS	284	113	397	52.93%
NS-NS	178	18	196	26.14%
NNS-NNS	30	127	157	20.93%
Total number			750	100%

*Note: 1. One conversation may involve both NS and NNS, and interactions may overlap.

　　　2. NNS stands for non-native speakers; NS stands for native speakers.

The subtheme of **Chinese geography** is frequently presented in the textbooks, and it often focuses on highlighting famous scenic spots, historic sites, and landmarks within China, while not exploring the diverse geography outside of China. This can contribute to a limited perspective on world geography. For instance, on Page 30 of Yilin6V1, there is a unit titled "Holiday Fun", which showcases various famous scenic spots in China, including the Great Wall, Summer Palace, Palace Museum, Tian'anmen Square, Shanghai Bund, and Shanghai Museum, etc. These illustrations and descriptions primarily highlight the beauty and significance of these Chinese landmarks. Similarly, on Page 25 of PEP4V2, there is an illustration depicting a weather reporter presenting the weather report, accompanied by a map of China showing the weather conditions in Beijing, Harbin, Lhasa, and Hong Kong. This further emphasizes the geographic focus on China within the textbooks. Additionally, on Page 53 of Yilin5V1, there is a mention of the time difference between China and the US, accompanied by images showing the landscapes of Shanghai and New York respectively. While this comparison highlights the time zones, it still maintains a focus on Chinese geography without providing a broader perspective on global landscapes. It is important to note that while the textbooks may primarily concentrate on Chinese geography, it is crucial to foster an understanding and appreciation of diverse world geography to promote a more comprehensive and inclusive educational experience.

The theme of **leisure lifestyle** in the textbooks portrays characters who prefer to engage in leisurely activities such as having picnics and enjoying fun-filled moments through playing games. On Pages 46-47 of PEP3V1, there is an illustration depicting a group of people having a picnic together. This image not only represents the theme of leisure lifestyle but also connects with the subtheme of kinship within the domain of inter/multicultural education. It showcases the importance of spending quality time with family and friends in a leisurely setting. In the Yilin series, the theme of leisure lifestyle is also consistently portrayed. Each volume often begins with an illustration featuring all the characters having fun together. For instance, on Pages 2-3 of Yilin3V2, there is an illustration showing the characters enjoying themselves at an amusement park. This image presents a vivid depiction of the characters engaging in leisure activities and experiencing joy and excitement together.

The theme of **Chinese educational principles** in the textbooks portrays the characters as versatile individuals who possess a wide range of skills and abilities. This reflects the emphasis on holistic development and a well-rounded education in Chinese educational principles, which promote the concept of quality education. For instance, on Page 42 of PEP5V1, there is an illustration depicting a girl who is capable of various activities, such as speaking both English and Chinese, singing English songs, dancing, swimming, cooking, and playing ping-pong. This portrayal highlights the importance of nurturing multiple talents and skills, aligning with the principles of quality education that aim to develop students in all aspects. Similarly, in the unit titled "What can you do?" in PEP5V1, almost all the children are depicted as versatile individuals who excel in various areas, including playing musical instruments like the pipa, practicing kung fu, playing basketball, drawing, and cooking, etc. This not only showcases the diversity of talents but also reflects the goal of quality education to foster a well-rounded development of students.

Furthermore, on Page 14 of PEP6V2, a dialogue presents Mike talking on the phone with his grandpa. Mike mentions watching children's shows on TV, but his grandpa inquires if he did anything else. When Mike shares that he cleaned his room and washed his clothes, his grandpa praises him as a "good boy". This conversation implies that children are expected to engage in household responsibilities and chores as a part of their education. It reflects the comprehensive approach of quality education, which encompasses not only academic learning but also moral values, life skills, and a sense of responsibility. These portrayals of versatile characters and the inclusion of various educational aspects, such as moral education, labor education, and the development of diverse skills, reflect the integration of quality education principles. The Chinese educational system emphasizes the importance of nurturing students' moral, intellectual, physical, and aesthetic qualities, fostering their all-round development.

The examples provided above highlight some salient themes and subthemes within ELT textbooks. However, to address the ways in which ELT textbooks reflect the notion of metrolingualism, the following subsection will delve into a textbookscapes analysis specifically related to metrolingualism in ELT textbooks.

4.1.2   Textbookscapes analysis for metrolingualism in ELT textbooks

In this section, textbookscapes in ELT textbooks were analyzed from two aspects, which are LLs analysis and MIs analysis. The sampling of textbookscapes contain 155 LLs and 24 MIs in all textbooks, which will be elaborated respectively in the following subsections.

4.1.2.1   Linguistic Landscapes analysis in ELT textbooks

Table 4.3 provides an overview of the linguistic repertoires of LLs presented in both series of textbooks, along with the percentage distribution of each LL category. The analysis considers various codes, including English code, Chinese code, visual codes (represented through images), and other linguistic codes. English code emerges as the dominant LL, constituting the highest proportion at 42.58%. Bilingual LLs that combine visual codes and English code account for 23.23% of the total LLs. Monolingual LLs of visual codes alone make up 14.84%, while monolingual LLs of Chinese represent 9.03%. Multilingual LLs that integrate visual codes, English code, and Chinese code amount to 4.52%. Bilingual LLs involving Chinese code and English code have a percentage of 3.87%, while bilingual LLs of visual codes and Chinese code have a smaller presence at 1.29%. Other linguistic codes, apart from the main languages and visual codes, have a limited share, accounting for only 0.65% of LLs. Figure 4.1 complements the information from Table 4.3 by illustrating the proportion of each code in the LLs of both textbook series. English code stands out, occupying the highest proportion at 54%. Visual codes, represented through images, make up 31.92% of the LLs, while Chinese accounts for 13.62%. There is only one additional code present in all LLs, constituting a mere 0.47% of the total. The subsequent paragraphs will elaborate on the different code themes identified in the coding frame for LLs analysis.

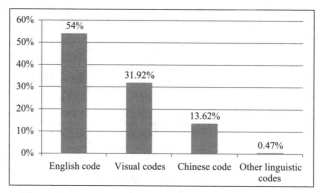

Figure 4.1   Proportion of each code in LLs of textbooks

English supremacy in LLs

English code is the most frequently used linguistic code among all LLs, and it also occurs as a monolingual LL most frequently. Even in bilingual or multilingual LLs, English code takes on the role of the preferred code. This preference for English code is evident in Table 4.4, which demonstrates that English code occurs far more frequently than any other code in preferred positions within bilingual and multilingual LLs.

Table 4.3 Linguistic repertoires of LLs and percentage in textbooks

Linguistic repertoire		Occurrence number in PEP3	Occurrence number in PEP4	Occurrence number in PEP5	Occurrence number in PEP6	Occurrence number in Yilin3	Occurrence number in Yilin4	Occurrence number in Yilin5	Occurrence number in Yilin6	Total number	Percentage (total number/155)
Monolingual LLs	English code	3	9	6	11	6	2	18	11	66	42.58%
	Visual codes	0	0	1	12	0	0	6	4	23	14.84%
	Chinese code	0	1	2	8	2	1	0	0	14	9.03%
	Other linguistic codes	0	0	1	0	0	0	0	0	1	0.65%
	Visual codes & English	0	1	10	9	1	2	7	6	36	23.23%
Bilingual & Multilingual LLs	Chinese & English	0	1	0	1	0	0	4	0	6	3.87%
	Visual codes & Chinese	0	0	0	0	0	0	0	2	2	1.29%
	Visual codes & English & Chinese	0	0	1	4	0	0	2	0	7	4.51%
Total		3	12	21	45	9	5	37	23	155	100%

Table 4.4   Code preference analysis of bilingual & multilingual LLs in textbooks

Code	English	Chinese	Visual codes
Occurrence number on preferred positions	27	9	15
Total	51		

*Note: Only bilingual and multilingual LLs are calculated.

For example, on Page 55 of PEP3V2, there are two instances of monolingual LLs that demonstrate the informative function through the use of English code. One LL depicts the name of a restaurant, which solely consists of the English word "Buffet". The other LL is a poster on the wall advertising a special offer, with the price marked in US dollars as "$8 each!". While these examples showcase the prevalence of English in delivering information, it is important to note that there are also instances in which the dominance of English code is challenged. These instances of antithesis to English supremacy within the LLs can be illustrated in the following paragraph.

Antithesis of English supremacy in LLs

Although monolingual LLs in English account for the largest proportion in the textbookscapes, there are still instances of monolingual LLs in Chinese that carry distinct Chinese cultural characteristics. These LLs often serve to convey Chinese cultural values and ideas. An example can be found on Page 18 of Yilin3V1, where a Chinese calligraphy painting is depicted on the classroom wall. It bears the inscription " 千里之行，始于足下 " (A journey of a thousand miles begins with a single step), taken from Lao Tzu's *Tao Te Ching*. This phrase encourages individuals to start small and work their way up, emphasizing the importance of perseverance and the potential for success even in challenging circumstances. These monolingual LLs in Chinese often encapsulate unique Chinese cultural elements that may be challenging to convey through other languages. Furthermore, there are LLs that rely solely on visual content without any textual information. For instance, an illustration on Page 58 of Yilin5V1 features a Caucasian boy who is Wang Bing's e-friend from the UK. The boy is depicted wearing a T-shirt adorned with the UK flag, which serves as a visual representation of his national identity. These examples highlight the use of monolingual LLs in Chinese to convey cultural values and the inclusion of LLs with visual content that communicates information without relying on text.

Exclusivism in LLs

The LLs found in textbooks primarily focus on linguistic codes in English and Chinese, with limited representation of other language codes. Interestingly, there is only one instance of LL that incorporates Spanish characters, as observed in PEP5V2. On Page 2 of PEP5V2, an illustration features a Spanish boy wearing a red T-shirt with the word "España" printed on it, which signifies his national identity. This example highlights the exclusive nature of LLs in textbooks, as they tend to prioritize the linguistic codes of English and Chinese while offering limited diversity in terms of other language codes.

In summary, English code emerges as the most preferred and frequently used code in LLs within both PEP and Yilin textbooks, followed by visual codes. On the other hand, Chinese is the least frequent code in LLs, while other linguistic codes are mostly excluded. Although there are some instances that challenge the dominance of English code in the textbooks, they are relatively few. Some of these instances aim to convey a discourse system unique to China. Therefore, English code not only serves informative functions within the LLs but also reinforces the supremacy of monolingualism within the textbookscapes. However, the textbooks do not address the inclusiveness of diverse metrolingual codes. The subsequent subsection will focus on the MIs concerning the analysis of textbookscapes for metrolingualism in ELT textbooks.

4.1.2.2 Metrolingual Interactions analysis in ELT textbooks

The coding procedures outlined in Chapter 3 offer a framework for analyzing code themes in MIs. In the subsequent paragraphs, the researcher will explore the code themes within MIs, focusing on linguistic repertoire and cultural repertoire. These two aspects provide insights into the language practices and cultural elements present in MIs. Linguistic repertoire refers to the range of languages used in MIs. It encompasses the languages employed for communication during activities such as shopping and dining in canteens. The analysis of linguistic repertoire in MIs sheds light on the language choices and interactions that take place within these everyday situations. On the other hand, cultural repertoire pertains to the cultural elements embedded within MIs. It involves the display of cultural practices, customs, and traditions that are relevant to activities like shopping and dining. Understanding the cultural repertoire in MIs provides insights into how language and culture intertwine in these everyday scenarios. Examining the linguistic repertoire and cultural repertoire in MIs could facilitates a deeper understanding of the language practices and cultural elements that shape these activities. This analysis contributes to a comprehensive exploration of the metrolingual aspects present in ELT textbooks.

Native-speakerism standard in MIs

It is notable that the textbooks predominantly feature British or American

English as the standard norm for all characters. This linguistic repertoire represents the sole language variety used in the MIs across the textbooks. An example can be found on Page 7 of PEP5V2, where an illustration accompanied by a dialogue depicts Sarah, a Caucasian girl, carrying a basket at a vegetable market to purchase vegetables. The interaction occurs between Sarah and a Chinese woman who is the seller. It is evident that both characters employ English following the standard of native-speakerism to communicate with each other. The vegetable stall displays common Chinese vegetables and fruits. The emphasis on the native-speakerism standard as the exclusive linguistic repertoire is apparent throughout the MIs in the textbooks. This approach may overlook the linguistic diversity and variations that exist within English-speaking communities and does not adequately reflect the multilingual and intercultural realities of language use in the real world.

Cultural diversities in MIs

In this code theme, the researcher primarily focused on the non-linguistic resources present in MIs, which revealed a combination of Chinese and Western cultures. An illustrative example can be seen on Pages 46-47 of PEP4V1, where characters of various backgrounds, including Chinese, Caucasians, and anthropomorphic animals, are depicted dining at an open-air restaurant. The counter displays a variety of common Chinese fruits and dishes, such as pears, apples, bananas, fish, salad, and noodles. Additionally, Western fast-food items like hamburgers and French fries are also showcased. The scene portrays people ordering food, with chopsticks, bowls, plates, and spoons placed on the left table. Interestingly, both Chinese food tools like chopsticks and Western food tools like knives and forks are present on the right table. This mix of utensils reflects the coexistence and integration of Chinese and Western culinary cultures within the MI activity. Another noteworthy detail is the menu held by Mike's mother, which is in English with the word "Menu" written at the top. Although the dishes listed below are not entirely clear, it suggests the Western dining practices in this particular context. Overall, this MI activity highlights the representation of a blend of Chinese and Western dietary cultures, showcasing the integration and coexistence of culinary elements from both traditions.

To summarize, the analysis of MIs in textbooks reveals that the textbooks predominantly adhere to the native-speakerism standard by featuring British or American English as the linguistic norm for all characters in MIs. However, this exclusive focus may fail to acknowledge the linguistic diversity and variations present within English-speaking communities, thereby neglecting the real-world multilingual and intercultural language use. Moreover, the non-linguistic resources in MIs showcase a combination of Chinese and Western cultures. This is evident through the presence of both Chinese and Western food tools, which highlight the coexistence and integration of culinary traditions. The incorporation of Chinese and Western elements within various everyday activities illustrates the cultural diversities represented in the non-linguistic resources of MIs. Thus, while the textbooks primarily reinforce the native-speakerism standard in linguistic repertoire, they do incorporate cultural diversities through the non-linguistic resources of MIs. To some extent, this integration of Chinese and Western elements adds richness to the portrayal of everyday activities in the textbooks.

Furthermore, to address the remaining part of RQ 1, the subsequent subsection will delve into the exploration of GCE and metrolingualism embedded in ECSCE.

4.1.3   GCE & metrolingualism embedded in curriculum

The curriculum outlines the overarching objective of the English course, which aims to "assist students in developing a preliminary comprehensive language competence, fostering mental development, and enhancing their overall humanistic qualities through English learning" (MOE, 2011, p.8). This objective is divided into five levels based on the learning needs and cognitive characteristics of different age groups during compulsory education. Level 2 corresponds to the requirements that should be attained by the end of Grade 6 for primary education, while Level 5 corresponds to the requirements for the end of Grade 9 for junior high school education. This study primarily focuses on the grading standards for Level 2. Furthermore, the comprehensive language competence contains five aspects, namely "linguistic skills, linguistic knowledge, emotional attitudes, learning strategies, and cultural awareness". These aspects contribute to the holistic development of students' language proficiency and cultural understanding within the English language curriculum.

Within this subsection, the researcher's attention is directed solely towards the statements pertaining to GCE and metrolingualism in the initial four parts of the curriculum. By carefully examining the descriptions provided in the curriculum, the subsequent paragraphs will provide detailed elaboration on the statements concerning GCE and metrolingualism.

4.1.3.1   Statements regarding GCE in curriculum

Global awareness

In the Preface of the curriculum, there are a total of five mentions emphasizing the significance of learning English in order to enhance global awareness, broaden international perspectives, and understand the diversity of the world. The following excerpts highlight the curriculum's statements on global awareness:

Excerpt 1: ...enhancing mutual understanding between China and the world (MOE, 2011, p.1).

Excerpt 2: ...improving the international competitiveness of the country and the international communication ability of the people (ibid., p.1).

Excerpt 3: ...better understand the world ...enhance their communication and understanding with teenagers from other countries (ibid., p.1).

Excerpt 4: ...to better adapt to the world multi-polarization, economic globalization and information technology in the future (ibid., p.1).

Excerpt 5: ...help students understand the diversity of the world ...enhance international understanding (MOE, 2011, p.2).

In these statements, English is acknowledged as both a tool and a bridge connecting China with the world. The curriculum explicitly states that the English course in compulsory education possesses dual attributes, serving instrumental and humanistic purposes (MOE, 2011). In the context of globalization, English is recognized as a crucial means for international communication and scientific and cultural exchanges (ibid.). Moreover, the objective of enhancing students' global awareness is closely linked to the principles of inclusive education and respect for diversity, as evident in Excerpts 1, 3, and 5. These excerpts aim to nurture an inclusive mindset among students, encouraging them to embrace the diverse global community. Excerpts 2 and 4 highlight how English proficiency can enhance the nation's international competitiveness and adaptability to economic globalization. Furthermore, the curriculum's diagram depicting the course objectives illustrates that the cultivation of students' global awareness is addressed within the aspect of "emotional attitudes" (MOE, 2011, p.9). This indicates that developing an open-minded and inclusive attitude towards global diversity is an integral part of the curriculum's approach to English education. Overall, the statements in the curriculum highlight the role of English as a tool for international communication and cultural exchange, while also emphasizing the importance of an inclusive mindset and respect for diversity in fostering students' global awareness.

The description of global awareness in the grading standards, particularly concerning emotional attitudes, may lack specificity. For instance, the curriculum states that students should gradually develop both national awareness and an international vision during the process of learning English (MOE, 2011). It also mentions the need to strengthen national awareness while expanding the international vision (ibid.). However, the specific methods or approaches to "form" and "expand" the "international vision" are not explicitly outlined in the curriculum. Furthermore, the curriculum states that at the Level 2 grading standard, students should demonstrate a willingness to engage with foreign cultures and enhance their national awareness (ibid.). At the Level 5 standard, students should have a deeper understanding of their own culture and a preliminary awareness of international understanding (ibid.). The curriculum recognizes the role of English as a tool for accessing global knowledge and perspectives, but it also underscores the significance of preserving and promoting Chinese culture and values, which will be elaborated in the following paragraphs.

National awareness

The curriculum places significant emphasis on enhancing students' Chinese cultural awareness and fostering patriotism. It highlights the importance of English education in deepening students' knowledge and appreciation of their own cultural heritage, while also nurturing a sense of patriotism. By integrating English learning with the exploration of Chinese, culture, the curriculum aims to foster a strong sense of cultural identity and pride among students.

Excerpt 1: ...spread Chinese culture, enhance their communication and understanding with teenagers from other countries... (MOE, 2011, p.1)

Excerpt 2: ...enhance patriotism, develop innovation ability... (ibid., p.2)

Excerpt 3: ...promote patriotism, form a sense of social responsibility and innovation, and improve humanistic quality (ibid., p.2).

The mentioned excerpts indicate that fostering students' patriotism is an important objective of English learning, which is also addressed within the "emotional attitudes" aspect of the "comprehensive language competence". Furthermore, the specific descriptions of emotional attitudes in the curriculum highlight national awareness, emphasizing the need to "form a national awareness", "strengthen the national awareness", and "have a deeper understanding of the culture of the motherland". These references underline the curriculum's objective to cultivate students' sense of national identity and pride. In terms of textbook compilation, the curriculum suggests that ELT textbooks should actively incorporate patriotic education, guiding students towards developing national self-esteem, self-confidence, and pride. This further emphasizes the integration of national awareness within the curriculum. Additionally, the curriculum hints at the importance of cultural education, which will be further explored in subsequent paragraphs.

Cultural education

The curriculum places significant emphasis on cultivating students' intercultural communication awareness and competence, as evidenced by its mention five times in the Preface. These statements highlight the curriculum's commitment to preparing students for effective communication and interaction in a multicultural and globalized society, aiming to foster intercultural understanding, respect for diverse perspectives, and develop practical intercultural communication skills.

Excerpt 1: ...cultivating talents with innovative ability and intercultural communication competence... (MOE, 2011, p.1)

Excerpt 2: ...develop the awareness and competence of intercultural communication... (ibid., p.1)

Excerpt 3: ...enrich life experience, form intercultural awareness... (ibid., p.2)

Excerpt 4: ...form intercultural awareness through experiencing the similarities and differences between Chinese and foreign cultures... (ibid., p.2)

Excerpt 5: ...promote the students' autonomous learning ability, thinking ability, intercultural awareness and the development of healthy personality (ibid., p.4).

The curriculum places great importance on cultivating students' intercultural communication awareness and competence as part of the comprehensive language competence. However, the grading standards may lack clarity in terms of how to foster these skills. The descriptions provided in the standards include being interested in and willing to learn about foreign cultures and customs at lower levels, being aware of cultural differences in language communication at a moderate level, and paying attention to similarities and differences between Chinese culture and foreign cultures at a higher level. However, it is not explicitly specified which cultures should be considered as "foreign cultures". This lack of clarity may require further clarification for effective implementation. Thus, the curriculum recognizes the significance of intercultural communication awareness and competence but would benefit from providing more precise guidance in this area.

The grading standards regarding "foreign cultures" in the curriculum tend to focus more on the cultures of Anglophone countries. The description of culture in foreign language teaching specifically refers to "the history, geography, local conditions, customs, traditional customs, lifestyles, norms of behavior, literature and art, and values of the countries where the target language originates" (MOE, 2011, p.23). Moreover, the term "English-speaking countries" is mentioned seven times in the specific descriptions of the grading standards related to cultural awareness. There are also specific items that highlight the importance of learning about the culture of these English-speaking countries, as outlined in the Appendix E, the grading standards of cultural awareness. These references suggest that the curriculum places particular emphasis on the cultures associated with English-speaking countries. It is important to note, however, that while these cultures may receive more attention, the curriculum should also strive to provide a balanced and comprehensive understanding of various cultures from around the world.

In ELT, the culture of English-speaking countries is often considered the primary target culture, encompassing various aspects and holding a prominent position compared to global culture. The curriculum provides detailed and specific descriptions of the culture of English-speaking countries. On the other hand, the description of global culture in the curriculum is relatively general, focusing on "knowing and understanding popular entertainment, sports activities, festivals, and celebrations around the world" (MOE, 2011, p.24). This suggests that the curriculum places less emphasis on global culture compared to the culture of English-speaking countries. Regarding the compilation of ELT materials, the curriculum suggests that they should "not only help students understand the essence of foreign cultures, including the similarities and differences between Chinese and foreign cultures, but also guide students in enhancing their ability to distinguish between cultures" (MOE, 2011, pp.23-24). Thus, it is essential to promote cultural understanding on a global scale.

To some extent, the curriculum's understanding of culture, as inferred from the statements, appears to be static and confined within certain boundaries. This perspective may overlook the dynamic nature, hybrid, and fluidity of cultures that emerge during intercultural communication in a global context. It is notable that the curriculum's emphasis on "foreign cultures" tends to prioritize cultures originating from English-speaking countries. Additionally, the discussion of the "differences and similarities between Chinese culture and foreign cultures" predominantly references Chinese culture and the cultures of English-speaking countries. This approach may not fully support the comprehensive development of students' intercultural communication competence. Furthermore, the curriculum integrates ideological and moral education into ELT, which will be further explained in subsequent paragraphs.

Ideological and moral education

The curriculum defines ELT as having both instrumental and humanistic attributes. Within the humanistic aspect, ideological and moral education is emphasized. It is stated that "ELT should contribute to the formation of students' correct outlook on life, values, and good humanistic qualities" (MOE, 2011, p.1). The curriculum aims to "foster students' good character, correct outlook on life, and values" (ibid., p.2). This aspect of education is classified within the curriculum as the cultivation of students' emotional attitudes. The curriculum highlights several aspects of emotional attitude development, including "the establishment of students' self-confidence, the development of willpower to overcome difficulties, the willingness to cooperate with others, and the cultivation of harmonious and healthy personalities" (ibid., p.20). These objectives reflect the curriculum's aim to not only impart language skills but also contribute to the holistic development of students by nurturing their emotional well-being, character, and values.

In addition, the curriculum emphasizes that "ELT materials are not only the main content and means of ELT, but also an important medium for students to carry out ideological and moral education" (MOE, 2011, p.40). This indicates that the compilation of ELT materials is guided by ideological considerations. Furthermore, the curriculum specifies that "ELT materials should actively incorporate elements of patriotism education, socialist core values, traditional Chinese virtues, and education for democracy, as well as the principles of the rule of law" (ibid., p.40). These guidelines reflect the incorporation of socialism with Chinese characteristics in the curriculum's approach to ideological and moral education. This emphasis is consistent with the inclusion of the theme of "civic virtues & morality" in textbooks.

In recent times, there has been a noticeable shift in the focus of ELT from a linguistic-centered approach to a quality-oriented education that aims to nurture students' comprehensive competence. This shift is reflected in the curriculum, which includes relevant statements pertaining to quality-oriented education. The curriculum acknowledges the importance of cultivating students' comprehensive competence and incorporates measures to achieve this goal. It emphasizes the development of students' language skills, critical thinking abilities, creativity, and cultural awareness. The curriculum recognizes that language learning is not solely about linguistic proficiency, but also about fostering a range of competencies to enable students to thrive in various contexts. By promoting a comprehensive approach to education, the curriculum aims to equip students with the necessary skills and abilities to navigate the challenges of the globalized world effectively.

Quality-oriented education

The curriculum places significant importance on quality-oriented education in ELT. It recognizes that "language learning holds value for students' overall development and aims to enhance their comprehensive humanistic qualities" (MOE, 2011, p.2). It is stated that "ELT can contribute to students' mental development by fostering an understanding of the diversity of the world, promoting intercultural awareness through the exploration of similarities and differences between Chinese and foreign cultures, enhancing international understanding, strengthening patriotism, and cultivating a sense of social responsibility and innovation" (ibid., p.2). By emphasizing these aspects, the curriculum seeks to provide students with a well-rounded education that goes beyond linguistic proficiency. It aims to foster students' personal growth, cultural awareness, global perspective, and a sense of responsibility towards society.

ELT can be considered as an integral part of interdisciplinary education, serving not only as a support for other subjects but also has the potential to integrate with them. The curriculum emphasizes the importance of "ELT in interpenetrating and connecting with other subjects to promote students' comprehensive development in cognitive ability, thinking ability, aesthetic ability, imagination, and creativity" (MOE, 2011, p.27). Through quality-oriented education, ELT not only enhances students' overall language competence but also focuses on developing their critical thinking skills. This approach aims to facilitate students' holistic development, aligning with the theme of "Chinese educational principles" in textbooks. By integrating ELT with other subjects, the curriculum seeks to create a synergistic learning environment that fosters students' cognitive abilities, cultivates their thinking skills, and supports their overall growth.

In conclusion, the curriculum emphasizes the importance of cultivating students' global awareness, although the specific methods and content for achieving this goal are not clearly outlined. It also highlights the significance of enhancing students' national awareness, including Chinese cultural confidence and patriotism, through ELT. While the curriculum does not provide explicit guidance on developing students' intercultural communication awareness and competence or specify which cultures should be included under the category of "foreign cultures". Additionally, the curriculum addresses the integration of ideological and moral education to foster students' civic virtues and morality within the framework of Chinese socialism. It also places great importance on quality-oriented education to facilitate students' comprehensive development. Moreover, the following subsection will delve into the metrolingualism-related content in the curriculum to explore its potential for facilitating GCE.

4.1.3.2 Statements regarding metrolingualism in curriculum

Native-speakerism norms

While the curriculum does not explicitly state that ELT should adhere strictly to the norms of native speakers, there is an inclination towards native-speakerism norms evident in the curriculum. The curriculum places particular emphasis on students' imitative practice, presenting language learning as a stimulus-response process and encouraging students to learn through continuous imitation. This approach can be observed in the following statements:

Excerpt 1: Willing to imitate and daring to express as well as having a certain perception of English during the process of learning (MOE, 2011, p.10).

Excerpt 2: Be able to imitate the speech according to the recordings (ibid., p.13).

Excerpt 3: Be able to write sentences by imitating examples (ibid., p.13).

Excerpt 4: Willing to explore the meaning of English and try to imitate it in one's daily life (ibid., p.20).

Excerpt 5: Perceiving and imitating the characteristics of English pronunciation (ibid., p.28).

Excerpt 6: In the initial stage of ELT, phonologic teaching should be mainly carried out by imitation. Teachers should provide students with plenty of opportunities to listen to sounds, repeat imitation and practice, and help students develop good pronunciation habits (ibid., p.45).

Additionally, the curriculum places significant emphasis on the accuracy of English usage, as well as the natural norms of pronunciation and intonation when speaking English. It highlights the importance of mastering correct language forms and patterns. For instance,

Excerpt 7: Be able to read the story or short passage correctly (ibid., p.14).

Excerpt 8: Be able to use uppercase and lowercase letters and common punctuation marks correctly (ibid., p.14).

Excerpt 9: Be able to use correct pronunciation and intonation in oral activities (ibid., p.16).

Excerpt 10: Be able to make the pronunciation and intonation natural and appropriate in oral activities (ibid., p.17).

Excerpt 11: Be able to pronounce 26 English letters correctly (ibid., p.18).

Excerpt 12: The pronunciation and intonation should be basically correct, natural and smooth (ibid., p.19).

Excerpt 13: Be able to recognize mistakes and correct them when using English (ibid., p.22).

Excerpt 14: Natural and standard pronunciation and intonation will lay a good foundation for effective oral communication (ibid., p.45).

Notwithstanding the curriculum mentions that "English has different accents such as British accent and American accent" (MOE, 2011, p.45), it does not explicitly address other varieties of English. Additionally, the curriculum states that "students should be exposed to different accents after mastering one accent" (ibid., p.45), implying the importance of first attaining proficiency in a "pure English" before encountering different varieties of World Englishes. Furthermore, the curriculum demonstrates an effort to move beyond the norms of native-speakerism by acknowledging the concepts of fluidity, emergence, and hybrid, which embrace an inclusive mindset towards the variation and "incorrectness" that may arise in students' English language learning. This approach recognizes the dynamic nature of language and encourages students to explore and experiment with different forms of expression. For instance, "Teachers should strive to create a harmonious classroom atmosphere, take an inclusive attitude towards students' mistakes during the process of language learning, and choose an appropriate opportunity and method to properly deal with them." (MOE, 2011, p.26)

Moreover, regarding phonological teaching, the curriculum adopts a broad socio-linguistic perspective by highlighting the importance of combining semantics with context and intonation with flow, rather than solely focusing on achieving monophonic accuracy (MOE, 2011). Those content indicate that teachers may temporarily tolerate students' linguistic mistakes but should identify an appropriate opportunity to address them properly. However, the curriculum does not provide explicit guidelines on how to address these mistakes or specify the criteria for determining what constitutes a "correct" or "appropriate" correction. The curriculum leaves room for interpretation and allows individual teachers to exercise their professional judgment in handling linguistic mistakes in a suitable manner.

The aforementioned points suggest that there is a tendency to adhere to native-speakerism norms when it comes to notions of "correct", "natural", "appropriate", "smooth", and "standard" English in the curriculum. However, it is important to note that the curriculum also recognizes the importance of language attributes in communication, emphasizing that the pursuit of monophonic accuracy alone should not be the sole focus. This indicates a consideration for language usage in real-world contexts. The curriculum's inclination towards native-speakerism norms aligns with the GCE subtheme of "native-speakerism prestige & supremacy" present in textbooks. This may lead to the assumption that ELT based on native-speakerism norms may lead to more intelligible communication. Moreover, the curriculum places significant emphasis on various linguistic aspects of ELT, including linguistic knowledge and linguistic skills. These aspects will be further illustrated in the following paragraphs.

Linguistic foci

The linguistic level of the curriculum encompasses linguistic knowledge and linguistic skills, which serve as the foundation for comprehensive language competence. It follows an "input-output" training model of language. Linguistic skills contain various abilities such as listening, speaking, reading, writing, and their comprehensive use. Listening and reading are the skills for understanding, while speaking and writing are the skills for expression (MOE, 2011). The grading standards for linguistic skills at level 2 are detailed in Appendix F. The grading standards for linguistic skills, particularly in the areas of "reading" and "writing", place some emphasis on adhering to native-speakerism norms by focusing on the correctness of these skills (refer to Appendix F for detailed grading standards). However, other items in the grading standards primarily prioritize language intelligibility and require students to produce appropriate output based on the given input. The curriculum does not explicitly specify the criteria for the input, which may inadvertently lead to an implicit reliance on native-speakerism norms mentioned in other sections of the curriculum. Linguistic knowledge encompasses various aspects such as pronunciation, vocabulary, grammar, and more. It is recognized as an essential component of comprehensive language competence and serves as a significant foundation for the development of linguistic skills (MOE, 2011). The grading standards for linguistic knowledge at Level 2 are provided in Appendix G.

While the grading standards for linguistic knowledge outline the expected output rules for students at Level 2, the curriculum does not explicitly specify the particular variety of English on which these rules are based (refer to Appendix G for details). However, it is likely that these rules are influenced by native-speakerism norms, as students are expected to "know" and "understand" them. Consequently, these statements within the linguistic level of the curriculum contribute to the previous theme of "native-speakerism norms" and the GCE subtheme of "native-speakerism prestige & supremacy" in textbooks. Regarding language function and topic, scanty clear guidance is provided on the specific language expression habits to be followed for English expressions related to various functions. Additionally, there is a lack of explicit instruction regarding the cultural customs that should be considered when addressing specific topics.

To align with the instrumental and humanistic aspects of English, the development of ELT materials should adhere to specific principles outlined in the curriculum. According to the curriculum guidelines, ELT materials should be closely connected to students' real-life experiences and aim to create an authentic learning environment as much as possible (MOE, 2011). This emphasis on authenticity will be further exemplified in the subsequent paragraphs.

Daily life-oriented resources

With a focus on developing students' comprehensive language competence in line with the instrumental and humanistic nature of English, the curriculum emphasizes the importance of presenting ELT content from a language use perspective. Consequently, the selection of ELT materials should be oriented towards real-life situations and serve practical purposes. The following excerpts provide examples of such statements, reflecting the curriculum's intention to ensure that ELT materials are relevant, meaningful, and applicable to students' everyday lives.

Excerpt 1: ...create as many opportunities as possible for students to use the language in real situations (MOE, 2011, p.4).

Excerpt 2: English courses should provide English learning resources close to students, close to life and close to times according to the needs of teaching and learning (ibid., p.4).

Excerpt 3: Teachers should create various contexts that are close to real life... (ibid., p.26).

Excerpt 4: The content and form of pedagogical practices should be close to the students' real life as well as in line with students' cognitive level and life experience; the pedagogical practices should be as close as possible to the actual use of language in real life... (ibid., p.27).

Excerpt 5: ...provide the context for students to observe, imitate, try and experience the authentic language so as to better reflect the authenticity and communicative features of ELT (ibid., p.30).

Excerpt 6: ELT materials should be authentic and typical, and the important language content should be with high repetition (ibid., p.40).

Excerpt 7: ...enable students to learn real, lively and practical English through different ways and in different forms, so as to experience and use the language directly (ibid., p.42).

The curriculum emphasizes the importance of presenting ELT content from a language use perspective and incorporating materials that are closely related to real-life situations, aiming for authenticity. The use of terms like "real situations", "close to life", and "authentic language" reflects the linkage between ELT and the concept of metrolingualism, which highlights the fluidity, emergence, and hybrid of language in daily life. However, there are some concerns regarding the interpretation of "authentic" and "real" situations and materials. It may need to further explicitly specify where these "authentic" and "real" situations should come from, and clarify whether they should be based on monolingualism, bilingualism, or multilingualism. This lack of explicit guidance raises questions about the language diversity regarding metrolingualism.

In summary, an analysis of the curriculum reveals that English language learning is perceived as an imitative practice, where students are encouraged to mimic native speakers. The curriculum emphasizes the importance of students acquiring linguistic knowledge and skills, while also following an "input-output" language learning model based on native-speakerism norms. Although the curriculum mentions the use of daily life-oriented resources, the statements associated with this approach still contain elements of native speakerism rather than a genuine metrolingual pedagogy. As a result, the statements regarding metrolingualism in the curriculum align with the analysis of textbooks, which also highlight similar themes.

In this section, the findings of RQ 1 have been addressed. A total of 16 themes and 20 subthemes were identified, occurring 770 times in ELT textbooks. Some salient themes and subthemes include Anglophone cultures (107), Chinese cultures (91), kinship (59), native-speakerism prestige & supremacy (55), Chinese geography (46), leisure lifestyle (44), and Chinese educational principles (41). Concerning the analysis of metrolingualism in ELT textbooks, the textbooks primarily focus on themes such as English supremacy, antithesis of English supremacy, exclusivism in LLs, native-speakerism standard, and cultural diversities in MIs. The curriculum analysis identified eight code themes related to GCE and metrolingualism, including global awareness, national awareness, cultural education, ideological and moral education, quality-oriented education, native-speakerism norms, linguistic foci, and daily life-oriented resources. The findings of RQ 1 suggest that ELT textbooks and the curriculum reflect the notions of GCE and metrolingualism by predominantly incorporating soft GCE-oriented themes and subthemes, while critical GCE perspectives are relatively scarce. The subsequent section will address RQ 2.

4.2 Similarities & Differences Between PEP and Yilin

This section focuses on examining the similarities and differences between PEP and Yilin textbooks concerning GCE and metrolingualism to address RQ 2: What are the similarities and differences of GCE and metrolingualism represented in ELT textbooks between PEP series and Yilin series for primary education in China? The findings are represented from two perspectives: similarities and differences in terms of GCE, and similarities and differences in terms of metrolingualism. Overall, the similarities between the two series outweigh the differences. However, there are discrepancies in the proportion of GCE themes between PEP and Yilin textbooks. Additionally, the extent to which metrolingualism themes are represented in the two series of textbooks varies. Further details will be provided in the following subsections.

4.2.1 Similarities & differences regarding GCE

As discussed in Section 4.1, there are a total of 16 themes and 20 subthemes related to GCE in ELT textbooks, with a cumulative occurrence of 770 instances. While the representation of these themes and subthemes is generally similar in both PEP and Yilin textbooks, there are variations in the proportion of each theme between the two series. A detailed comparison of the proportion of GCE themes and subthemes in PEP and Yilin textbooks can be found in Appendix H. In this subsection, selected samples of GCE content will be provided to illustrate the similarities and differences between the two series of textbooks in terms of GCE.

The comparison presented in Appendix H reveals that PEP textbooks encompass a relatively more diverse range of themes and subthemes compared to Yilin textbooks. PEP series includes a total of 30 themes/subthemes, whereas the Yilin series comprises 25 themes/subthemes. Figure 4.2 provides a visual comparison of the proportion of each GCE domain between the PEP and the Yilin series. In PEP textbooks, the domain of emerging themes stands out as the most salient, followed by the domains of inter/multicultural education and education for sustainable development. On the other hand, the domain of citizenship education ranks the least salient in PEP textbooks. In contrast, Yilin textbooks highlight the domain of inter/multicultural education as the most salient, followed by the domains of emerging themes and citizenship education. The domain of education for sustainable development is comparatively less emphasized in Yilin textbooks.

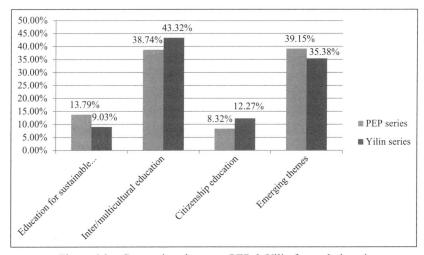

Figure 4.2   Comparison between PEP & Yilin for each domain

According to the detailed analysis in Appendix H, the salient themes and subthemes in PEP textbooks include Anglophone cultures (13.39%), Chinese cultures (11.76%), native-speakerism prestige & supremacy (10.34%), Chinese educational principles (7.51%), omnipotent artificial intelligence (6.9%), kinship (6.29%), etc. In comparison, the salient themes and subthemes in Yilin textbooks consist of Anglophone cultures (14.8%), Chinese cultures (11.91%), kinship (10.11%), leisure lifestyle (7.94%), Chinese geography (7.22%), etc. The numbers in parentheses represent the proportion of these themes and subthemes in the textbooks. Although there are similarities in the salient themes and subthemes found in both series of textbooks, there are also some differences. The following paragraphs will provide examples to further illustrate the variations in GCE themes between the two series of textbooks.

The subtheme of "native-speakerism prestige & supremacy" constitutes 10.34% in PEP textbooks and 1.44% in Yilin textbooks. This subtheme refers to the perception that "native speakers are regarded as the authority of English teaching and the most ideal English teachers…". The higher proportion of "native-speakerism prestige & supremacy" in PEP textbooks can be attributed to the presence of Miss White, a native English speaker, who serves as the English teacher throughout PEP series. Additionally, the entire PEP series revolves around Miss White and her students. In contrast, the English teacher in Yilin textbooks is portrayed as a Chinese individual named Miss Li, and the focus of the entire Yilin textbook series is primarily on Miss Li and her students. This difference in the portrayal of English teachers may explain why the subtheme of "anti-native speakerism prestige" accounts for 3.61% in Yilin textbooks but is absent from the PEP series.

Furthermore, the theme of "Chinese educational principles" has a higher proportion of 7.51% in PEP textbooks, while it accounts for 1.44% in Yilin textbooks. According to the GCE coding frame, "Chinese educational principles" emphasize the holistic development of students, encompassing moral, intellectual, physical, aesthetical and physical aspects. An illustration on Page 39 of PEP5V2 exemplifies this theme, where Sarah and John discuss the school calendar for April. The calendar displays various activities such as a swimming contest on April 1st, a math test on April 2nd, a Chinese test on April 3rd, an English test on April 4th, and a sports meet on April 5th. Moreover, "Chinese educational principles" encourage students to be cultivated versatility in various areas. Another instance is depicted on Page 39 of PEP5V1, where Miss White asks Mike about his talents. Mike responds by mentioning his ability to draw cartoons, and the picture shows other students demonstrating their talents, such as dancing, singing English songs, playing the pipa (a traditional Chinese musical instrument), practicing kung fu, and drawing cartoons. However, such content appears to be less prominent in Yilin textbooks.

The proportion of "omnipotent artificial intelligence" is significantly higher in PEP textbooks, possibly due to the presence of a robot character named Robin, who is a central figure and appears frequently throughout PEP series. In contrast, Yilin textbooks involve such content to a lesser extent. On Page 9 of PEP5V1, there is content showcasing Robin's introduction in Wu Yifan's diary. Robin is described as "short but strong", "really clever", "capable of speaking Chinese and English", "hard-working", "very helpful at home", and "strict". The visual content further emphasizes Robin's omnipotence, demonstrating abilities such as carrying multiple plates and bowls simultaneously, cooking, and even supervising Wu Yifan's homework. Furthermore, Robin is depicted as capable of caring for the sick and elderly. This portrayal suggests that Robin is indeed an all-powerful artificial intelligence robot that not only assists humans in various tasks but also coexists harmoniously with them.

Moreover, there are other content differences between PEP and Yilin textbooks that highlight distinctions between the two series. For instance, certain illustrations in PEP textbooks showcase ethnic minority cultures and regional characteristics. On Page 23 of PEP6V2, there are depictions of Turpan, including Mount Tianshan, a Mongolian yurt, grapes, Uyghur ethnic costumes, Xinjiang naan, and mutton kebabs. This content aims to introduce students to the cultural diversity within China. On Pages 12-13 of PEP4V2, there is a world map illustrating time differences in different countries and the living conditions of local people. Various national capitals across continents are marked on the map, such as London in Europe, Beijing in Asia, Cairo in Africa, New York in North America, Brasilia in South America, and Sydney in Oceania. This representation attempts to provide students with a preliminary understanding of global cultures and diversity.

Additionally, on Page 63 of PEP5V2, Sarah and Robin attend a world robot exhibition featuring robots from different countries, including Canada, Japan, Spain, China, and the United States. The cultural features of these robots, such as the maple leaf for Canada, Japanese kimonos and sushi, a Spanish guitar with "Spain" written in the background, a Chinese robot with a five-pointed star and the character " 武 " (Kung fu) written on a wall, and an American cowboy with a scarf resembling the Stars and Stripes and "USA" written on the wall, represent not only Anglophone and Chinese cultures but also other cultures, such as Japanese and Spanish. Moreover, PEP textbooks include content related to "world geography" beyond Anglophone and Chinese geography. On Page 22 of PEP4V2, an illustration depicts John's father in Singapore with the Merlion statue, a prominent landmark of Singapore, in the background. This introduces students to a different geographical location. Besides, PEP textbooks feature content related to the subtheme of "cooperation and solidarity", which is not present in the Yilin series. On Page 31 of PEP4V1, there is an illustration showing a group of animals working together to pull a large carrot. This content emphasizes the power of unity and collectivism.

In summary, while the GCE themes embedded in both PEP and Yilin textbooks are similar, there are notable differences in the proportion of each theme between the two series. PEP textbooks tend to have a greater diversity of themes compared to the Yilin series. These content differences between PEP and Yilin textbooks highlight disparities in their approaches to cultural diversity, global awareness, geography, and the theme of cooperation and solidarity, etc.

Besides, in order to further address the metrolingualism issues between PEP and Yilin, the similarities and differences regarding metrolingualism will be elaborated in the following subsection.

4.2.2　Similarities & differences regarding metrolingualism

Regarding the textbookscapes for metrolingualism issues, both LLs and MIs were analyzed in Subsection 4.1.2. In total, there are 155 LLs and 24 MIs across all the textbooks. PEP textbooks had a higher proportion of MIs, while Yilin textbooks had a higher percentage of LLs. Figure 4.3 illustrates the numerical differences of LLs and MIs between PEP and Yilin textbooks. The following paragraphs will provide a comparison analysis of LLs and MIs between PEP and Yilin respectively.

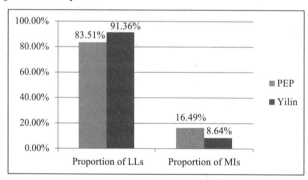

Figure 4.3　Comparison of LLs & MIs proportions between PEP & Yilin

Figure 4.4 displays the numeral comparison of linguistic repertoires of LLs and the percentage of each kind of LL between PEP and Yilin textbooks, which indicates that the English code as the monolingual LL has the highest proportion in both series of textbooks, and monolingual LLs occur more frequently than bilingual & multilingual LLs in both PEP and Yilin.

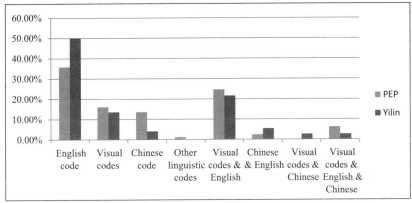

Figure 4.4   Comparison of Linguistic repertoires of LLs between PEP & Yilin

Moreover, Figure 4.5 further shows the comparison of proportion of each code in LLs between PEP and Yilin, which indicates that the English code is prevalent in all textbooks and it accounts for a higher proportion in Yilin.

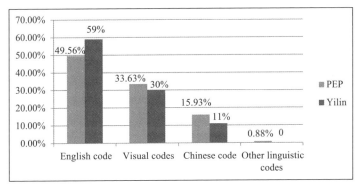

Figure 4.5   Comparison of proportion of each code in LLs between PEP & Yilin

While the occurrence of "other linguistic codes" is relatively rare in textbooks, it constitutes 0.88% of the content in PEP textbooks. However, it is completely excluded from the Yilin series. An example that highlights the inclusion of "other linguistic codes" can be found on Page 2 of PEP5V2. The illustration depicts a Spanish boy wearing a red T-shirt adorned with Spanish characters that spell "España", showcasing his national identity and adding a multilingual dimension to the textbook content.

In general, the proportion of Chinese code is not particularly high in both PEP and Yilin textbooks. However, PEP series exhibits a higher proportion of LLs with Chinese code compared to the Yilin series. In terms of LL diversity, PEP textbooks have a slightly more varied range of codes compared to Yilin textbooks. When analyzing LLs, it becomes evident that English serves a more informative function and embodies a sense of monolingualism supremacy across all the textbooks. Despite the inclusion of "other linguistic codes" in PEP textbooks, the prevalence of English code remains significant. Therefore, while there are differences in the presence of LLs, the similarities between PEP and Yilin textbooks outweigh the differences.

Furthermore, both PEP and Yilin textbooks adhere to native-speakerism norms of British or American English in all MIs. This includes aspects such as word spelling, pronunciation, grammar, pragmatics. Moreover, the MIs in both series of textbooks predominantly focus on Chinese and Anglophone cultures. This is further supported by the prevalence of GCE themes related to "Chinese cultures" and "Anglophone cultures" in both PEP and Yilin textbooks. These themes reflect the emphasis placed on these specific cultures within the educational materials. It is important to note that while the textbooks may prioritize these cultures, they may also include references or instances that introduce students to other cultures and promote intercultural understanding.

To conclude, the comparison analysis of metrolingualism issues in PEP and Yilin textbooks reveals several similarities. Both series of textbooks demonstrate the prominence of English code and prioritize it as the dominant linguistic code. The MIs in all textbooks follow the standard English norms of British or American English. Additionally, there is a predominant focus on Chinese and Anglophone cultures in the MIs across all textbooks. These findings highlight the shared characteristics and common themes in the representation of metrolingualism in both PEP and Yilin textbooks.

Furthermore, comparison analysis of similarities and differences among grade levels regarding GCE and metrolingualism will be elaborated in the following section to answer the RQ 3.

4.3 Similarities & Differences Among Grade Levels

In this section, the analysis aims to address RQ 3: What are the similarities and differences of GCE and metrolingualism represented in ELT textbooks of different grade levels for primary education in China? The examination reveals that GCE and metrolingualism themes are incorporated into each grade level to varying degrees. Additionally, distinct themes emerge as salient or excluded in different grades. The subsequent subsections will provide a detailed exploration of the similarities and differences in terms of GCE and metrolingualism respectively.

4.3.1 Similarities & differences regarding GCE

The analysis of similarities and differences among grade levels regarding GCE will continue to rely on quantitative data combined with qualitative analysis. The comparison of the proportion of GCE themes and subthemes among grades can be found in Appendix I. Additionally, Figure 4.6 provides a visual comparison among grade levels for each GCE domain. The analysis reveals that the domain of inter/multicultural education is the most salient in Grade 3 and Grade 5. On the other hand, the domain of emerging themes stands out as the most salient in Grade 4 and Grade 6. However, the domains of education for sustainable development and citizenship education occupy relatively lower proportions in all grade levels. Further qualitative analysis can be conducted to delve into the specific themes and subthemes within each domain, providing a more comprehensive understanding of the similarities and differences among grade levels regarding GCE representation.

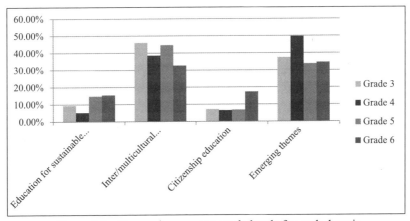

Figure 4.6   Comparison among grade levels for each domain

As detailed in Appendix I, the diversity of themes and subthemes in the textbooks exhibits a positive correlation with grade levels. The number of themes and subthemes increases as the grade level progresses. For instance, grade three contains 18 themes and subthemes, grade four has 20, grade five has 23, and grade six has 28. In grade three, some salient themes and subthemes include Anglophone cultures (21.58%), native-speakerism prestige & supremacy (13.67%), kinship (11.51%), and harmonious coexistence of human-nature relations (8.63%). Grade four highlights themes such as Anglophone cultures (15.03%), commercialization (13.73%), Chinese cultures (10.46%), and Chinese educational principles (9.15%). Grade five focuses on Chinese cultures (15.91%), Anglophone cultures (13.26%), native-speakerism prestige & supremacy (9.47%), Chinese educational principles (8.33%), and omnipotent artificial intelligence (8.33%). Grade 6 emphasizes themes such as Chinese cultures (10.75%), Anglophone cultures (8.88%), Chinese geography (8.41%), Anglophone geography (7.48%), environmental responsibility and sustainable development (6.54%), and rule compliance (6.54%). The numbers in brackets indicate the proportion of these themes and subthemes in the textbooks.

These findings emphasize the varying emphasis placed on different themes and subthemes across grade levels, as discussed in Section 4.1. To avoid redundancy, only a few examples will be provided here to further illustrate the comparison of GCE themes and subthemes among grade levels, particularly those that appear in one grade but are excluded from others (for detailed information, refer to Appendix I). For instance, the content on Page 57 of PEP6V1 presents an example of "tolerance", which is exclusively featured in Grade 6 and not included in other grade levels. In this illustration, Sarah is depicted as very angry, while her mother is shown smiling and advising her to "take a deep breath" and "count to ten" in order to alleviate her anger. This content aims to educate students about the importance of controlling negative emotions. By including such content, Grade 6 textbooks convey the message that students should learn to manage their negative feelings and practice tolerance towards others.

The theme of "career planning" is exclusive to Grade 6 textbooks, accounting for 4.67% of the content. This theme is not present in other grade levels, primarily due to the inclusion of a dedicated unit on "occupations" in PEP6V1. The content on Page 52 of PEP6V1 provides examples of different career choices based on individual interests and specialties. The passage highlights that individuals can pursue various careers according to their specific passions and talents. For instance, if one has a love for sports, they can consider becoming a coach, a sports reporter, or a physical education teacher. If someone possesses excellent typing skills, they may consider a career as a secretary. Additionally, if a student has an affinity for science, they can aspire to become a scientist. This content aims to introduce students to the concept of career planning and encourage them to reflect on their interests and aptitudes when considering future career paths. By providing concrete examples, the textbook seeks to broaden students' understanding of the diverse range of occupations available to them. The inclusion of such content in Grade 6 textbooks demonstrates a progressive approach to GCE, as it prepares students for future decision-making and fosters a sense of agency in their career development.

In Grade 4 textbooks, there is a higher percentage of content related to the theme of "commercialization", accounting for 13.73% of the overall material. This increased emphasis on commercialization is primarily attributed to the inclusion of unit topics such as "shopping" in Grade 4. In this study, the term "commercialization" is adopted to describe the depiction of commercial activities involving the characters in the textbooks. It encompasses scenarios where characters engage in buying and selling goods. For instance, an example on Page 61 of PEP4V2 portrays Sarah and John engaging in a role-play activity, imitating the process of buying and selling goods. This content serves to familiarize students with commercial transactions. By incorporating such content, the grade four textbooks aim to introduce students to the concept of commerce and its influence on society. It provides them with a practical understanding of economic systems and their relevance in daily life.

The subtheme of "honesty" is unique to Grade 6 textbooks, accounting for 1.4% of the content. This subtheme is not present in other grade levels, emphasizing its specific focus in Grade 6 curriculum. A short passage on Page 68 of PEP6V1 presents a story centered around the concept of honesty. In the story, a rich old businessman in a small town interacts with a factory worker, a coach, and a fisherman. The businessman gives each of them a seed as a test to determine who is the most honest. Only the fisherman proves to be truthful, and as a result, he is rewarded with the businessman's property. The main purpose of this short story is to educate students about the importance of honesty in all aspects of life. By showcasing the positive outcome for the fisherman, the story emphasizes the value of integrity and encourages students to adopt honesty as a guiding principle. Such content seeks to instill moral values and ethical behavior in students. The story serves as a means to convey the significance of honesty and its practical application in personal and social contexts.

The theme of "social development and progress" is exclusively featured in grade six textbooks, accounting for 1.87% of the content. This theme is not present in other grade levels, primarily due to the inclusion of the same unit topic, "Then and now", in both PEP and Yilin textbooks for Grade 6. Several illustrations on Page 41 of PEP6V2 demonstrate the concept of social development and progress by comparing people's living conditions in the past, present, and future. For instance, the illustrations depict that in the past, "cavemen didn't cook their meat", while in the present, "there are many things to help you cook". Furthermore, in the future, it is envisioned that "house robots" will be available to "cook, clean, and wash the dishes". These illustrations aim to highlight the changes and advancements that have occurred in society over time. By showcasing the progression of living conditions and technological innovations, the content fosters students' understanding of social development and encourages them to reflect on the potential future advancements.

In addition, the theme of "environmental responsibility and sustainable development" is more prominently featured in Grade 6 textbooks compared to other grade levels. This emphasis can be attributed to the presence of two units dedicated to environmental protection in Yilin textbooks for Grade 6. An illustration on Page 59 of Yilin6V1 depicts students engaging in a discussion on "how to keep the city clean". The illustration showcases various environmentally responsible actions, such as "taking the bus and the metro to school", "walking to school", "relocating some factories away from the city", "properly disposing of rubbish in bins", and "planting more trees". This content could raise students' awareness of environmental issues and encourage them to take responsibility for sustainable development. The illustration provides practical examples of actions that individuals can take to contribute to a cleaner and greener environment. The increased focus on the theme of "environmental responsibility and sustainable development" in Grade 6 textbooks aligns with the growing global concern for environmental issues. It aims to equip students with the knowledge and values necessary to become environmentally conscious citizens and advocates for a sustainable future.

In summary, the themes and subthemes discussed are present in each grade level to varying degrees, with some exclusions due to different unit topics. Moreover, the diversity of themes increases as students progress through primary education, with Grade 6 containing the widest range of themes and subthemes. These examples illustrate the intention to address age-appropriate topics and meet the developmental needs of students at different stages. It highlights the importance of considering the specific themes and subthemes included or excluded in each grade level, showcasing the nuanced progression of GCE themes throughout primary education to cater to students' developmental needs and educational objectives.

Furthermore, in order to delve deeper into the similarities and differences regarding metrolingualism issues embedded in different grade levels, a more detailed comparison analysis will be provided in the following subsection.

4.3.2　Similarities & differences regarding metrolingualism

Figure 4.7 displays the numerical differences of LLs and MIs across different grade levels in textbooks. The data reveals that grade six exhibits the highest proportion of LLs, while Grade 4 has the least proportion of LLs. Conversely, the percentage of MIs is highest in Grade 4 compared to other grades, largely due to unit topics such as "Shopping" and "At the snack bar" in Grade 4. Notably, Figure 4.7 indicates that Grade 6 does not feature any MIs. As the relevant examples have been previously illustrated in earlier sections and appendices, they will not be reiterated here. The subsequent paragraphs will provide a detailed comparison analysis of LLs and MIs among different grade levels, utilizing diagrams and textual descriptions.

Figure 4.8 presents a numerical comparison of linguistic repertoires of LLs and the proportion of each type of LL across different grade levels. The data reveals that monolingualism in English accounts for the highest proportion of LLs in all grades. Furthermore, the number of monolingual LLs surpasses that of bilingual and multilingual LLs in all grade levels.

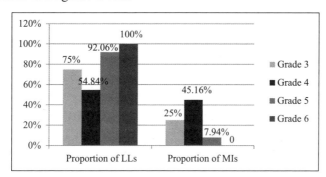

Figure 4.7   Comparison of LLs & MIs proportions among grade levels

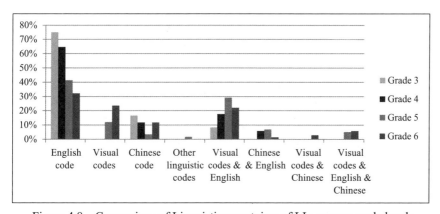

Figure 4.8   Comparison of Linguistic repertoires of LLs among grade levels

Figure 4.9 provides further insight by demonstrating that English is the most prevalent code, with the highest proportion among all LLs in every grade level.

Chinese code takes the secondary position in terms of popularity. The category of "other linguistic codes" is largely excluded from all grades, except for Grade 5, which includes a single instance of an "other linguistic code" on a T-shirt worn by a Spanish boy. This reinforces the prevalence of English as the dominant linguistic code across all grade levels. The above figures also reveal that the diversity of LL codes in Grade 5 and Grade 6 is generally broader compared to Grade 3 and Grade 4. This is likely due to the higher total number of LLs present in Grade 5 and Grade 6. Similarly, a greater variety of LL types are excluded from the lower grades, particularly bilingual and multilingual LLs. However, despite these differences, the similarities in LLs among different grade levels outweigh the variations, with the presence of English dominance evident across all grade levels.

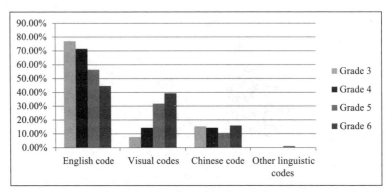

Figure 4.9   Comparison of proportion of each code in LLs among grade levels

Regarding the MIs, it is notable that there is a consistent adherence to native-speakerism standard norms across all grade levels. British or American English serves as the dominant standard in all MIs, with little variation among the grades. This suggests a preference for these English varieties as the linguistic benchmark in the illustrations. Moreover, a common trend observed across all grade levels is the predominant focus on Chinese and Anglophone cultures in the MIs. The illustrations predominantly depict scenarios and cultural elements related to these cultures. This emphasis on Chinese and Anglophone cultures reflects the curriculum's aim to familiarize students with their native culture and the English-speaking community. This finding is in line with the earlier comparison analysis between PEP and Yilin textbooks. While the MIs share these commonalities, it is important to note that they may also include some variations and unique cultural elements specific to each grade level. These variations might be attributed to the specific content and topics covered within the curriculum for each grade.

In conclusion, when considering metrolingualism issues in different grade levels, the similarities outweigh the differences. There is a noticeable increase in code diversity within LLs as grade levels progress. Monolingualism in English remains prevalent across all grades, with monolingual LLs outnumbering bilingual and multilingual LLs. English emerges as the most popular code, with the highest proportion in all LLs, followed by Chinese as the secondary code. Other linguistic codes are generally excluded from LLs, except for grade five where there is a single instance. The dominance of native-speakerism standard norms, as well as the focus on Chinese and Anglophone cultures, is evident throughout all grade levels. The next section will focus on the analysis of semi-structured interviews to explore teachers' perceptions to answer the RQ 4.

4.4 Teachers' Perceptions

In this section, the findings are represented to answer the RQ 4: What are teachers' perceptions toward GCE and metrolingualism in ELT textbooks and curriculum for primary education in China?, which are elaborated from three themes: teachers' awareness of GCE & metrolingualism in ELT, ELT implementation regarding GCE & metrolingualism, and challenges in ELT regarding GCE & metrolingualism. The subsequent subsections will provide a more elaboration on each of these themes.

4.4.1 Teachers' awareness of GCE & metrolingualism in ELT

Conceptual understanding of GCE

When questioned about teachers' understanding of GCE, all the participants acknowledged that the concept was largely unfamiliar to them, and they had not encountered it in their ELT practices. T1 and T4, however, associated GCE with globalization and believed that it aligns with the notion of "Community with a Shared Future for Mankind", considering the world as a collective community.

Extract 1 *T1: I have never heard of this concept... What I understand is that it may be a manifestation of economic globalization. Citizens should be cultivated to understand the differences in world cultures, civilizations, moral values, etc., so as to promote the development of globalization. This is my superficial understanding... However, the concept itself should be a more comprehensive and in-depth issue.*

Extract 2 *T4: I have never heard of this concept before. What I* *understand is that the whole world is like a community, and each country is a member of this community, just like the concept of "Community with a Shared Future for Mankind" proposed by President Xi.*

Moreover, both T5 and T2 made connections between GCE and ELT. T5 expressed the belief that ELT should embrace a more inclusive and open approach towards GCE. On the other hand, T2 placed more emphasis on Chinese education policies. Against the backdrop of quality-oriented education and the "double-reduction" policies in China, which aim to reduce student homework and off-campus training burden, T2 argued that the focus of ELT should shift from the traditional exam-oriented approach to fostering students' comprehensive development. This includes cultivating core literacy skills as well as promoting moral characters, intellectual development, physical fitness, aesthetic appreciation, and practical skills for students.

Extract 3 *T5: I haven't heard of this concept before, it may be more focused on globalized values, such as sustainable development. When it comes to English teaching, it may require the ELT to be more inclusive and open, and this is what I understand.*

Extract 4 *T2: I'm not familiar with this concept and I didn't come across it before. In terms of English teaching, it should focus on not only the linguistic knowledge and skills, but also the development of students' core literacy. Our government has been carrying out quality-oriented education and implementing the "double-reduction" policy, I think some traditional concepts, such as exam-oriented education or students being evaluated by scores, will be gradually changed. Everything is for the students to be able to grow up in a more comprehensive and healthy way and better adapt to the society in the future.*

T3 expressed a concern regarding the unequal economic development across the globe. She highlighted that children in extremely impoverished regions may not have equal access to education. It is important to note that education equity is not only a key objective of the Sustainable Development Goals (SDGs) outlined by the United Nations but also aligns with the overarching goals of GCE.

Extract 5 *T3: I'm quite unfamiliar with this concept, and my personal understanding is that children from all over the world have equal rights to receive education. However, there are still some poor areas of the world where children can't afford to eat, let alone study, for which learning may be a luxury.*

In summary, the concept of GCE appeared unfamiliar to all the teachers, and they expressed their individual understandings from various perspectives. Some teachers associated it with the process of globalization, perceiving the world as a collective community (Extracts 1, 2). Others discussed the implementation of GCE in ELT within the context of Chinese policies (Extracts 3, 4). Additionally, T3 viewed GCE through the lens of education equity on a global scale (Extract 5).

Awareness of linguistic inclusiveness in ELT

When discussing the topic of linguistic diversity in textbooks and ELT, T3 observed the presence of rigid stereotypes in linguistic portrayals. T3 noted that these portrayals might not fully capture the flexibility and emergency required for effective communication in people's everyday lives.

Extract 6 *T3: I think what you said is reasonable, since it is impossible for people to have a conversation with fixed sentence patterns as taught in textbooks in our daily life, and spoken language is very flexible and random in the real life. If we all follow the formal templates taught in textbooks to communicate, it will sound very rigid and inflexible...*

On the other hand, T1 expressed support for maintaining an English-only environment in both textbooks and ELT classes, despite agreeing that textbooks should be derived from real-life situations. T1 believed that the inclusion of other linguistic codes might hinder the learning process and suggested that focusing on English would create an immersive all-English environment for students. T1 emphasized the importance of prioritizing English language immersion in ELT.

Extract 7 *T1: Although we are all Chinese and our mother tongue is Chinese, those textbooks are designed to teach students to learn English, so they need to put students in an all-English environment... Meanwhile, I also agree with you that these daily activities in textbooks should be derived from life, but there should be an adjustment in different situations. If some other languages appear in the English textbooks, it may put the cart before the horse. We still need to put students in an English learning environment and make them feel closer to English. Thus, I think whether in English class or textbooks should be focused on the language that you are learning.*

Furthermore, other teachers supported the notion of an "English-only" policy, wherein British or American English is considered the "standard template". While T2 acknowledged the existence of other varieties of English, she maintained that it is crucial to provide primary school students with a standard template based on British or American English, as it serves as the foundation for English language learning. T6 shared similar concerns, expressing worry that the diversification of English teaching might pose difficulties for students in understanding the language.

Extract 8 *T2: In fact, I personally agree with what you said just now. However, for the primary education, especially for lower grade levels, I think it is very necessary to provide them with a standard template, otherwise they will not know how to say it. Then in the upper grade levels, they can be exposed to some other varieties of English. For the younger pupils, you have to be sure to tell them how to pronounce it in a certain way, and the variants can wait until they have mastered the basics.*

Extract 9 *T6: I think it is a little bit too broad in this aspect, since we are teaching either British English or American English during the class. However, if you tell the students that there exist other varieties of English, and people from different countries might pronounce it differently, they may not understand and easily get confused.*

In the similar vein, T5 expressed the belief that using such "less standard" English is the next best option. Now that she has the opportunity to expose students to more "standard English", she will continue focusing on British or American English in the future ELT practices.

Extract 10 *T5: On the other hand, I feel that when we are not sure about how to speak in a standard way, then we can choose another way to express it, as long as it can be understood by others. However, now that we have the opportunity to expose students to a more standard way of expression, I will still correct them and teach them to speak more standard English.*

Notwithstanding the majority of teachers advocating for British or American English as the standard in ELT, T4 expressed a different perspective. T4 emphasized the importance of broadening students' horizons and raising their awareness that English is not solely owned by English-speaking countries, but can be spoken by individuals from various nations. T4 suggested challenging the Anglophone culturalism in ELT. However, certain statements, such as "can speak English very well" and "in a systematic and correct way", indicate that T4 may still subconsciously view British or American English as the criterion for language proficiency.

Extract 11 *T4: In fact, English has been spoken in many other countries as well, and there are a lot of people who can speak English very well in non-English speaking countries. For example, a lot of Chinese people can speak English very well, too. Thus, teachers need to help students broaden their horizons and make them realize that foreign countries not only refer*

to British and American countries, but other countries beyond China
can be all called foreign countries…. Therefore, it doesn't mean that
the English spoken by British and Americans is good, while the English
spoken by African and Chinese is not good. As long as you express what
you want to say in a systematic and correct way, it is right.

To sum up, the teachers' overall awareness of linguistic inclusiveness in ELT
appears to be limited. While some teachers acknowledge the deviation of linguistics
in textbooks from everyday life, they still advocate for an "all-English environment"
in ELT (Extracts 6, 7). Additionally, British or American English is tacitly considered
the "standard template" in ELT, with a focus on providing primary school students
with this form of "standard English", while other varieties of English are stigmatized
(Extracts 8, 9, 10). However, there is also recognition among some teachers that
students should broaden their horizons to acknowledge English spoken in other
countries, while British or American English is still viewed as the criterion for
proficiency (Extract 11). Consequently, the teachers' awareness of linguistic diversity
in ELT may not be inclusive enough to challenge the notion of English ownership.

Awareness of critical multiculturalism in ELT

When mentioned about the cultural issues in textbooks, T3 acknowledged that
notwithstanding textbooks are diversified with Chinese and Anglophone cultures,
there may be still some limitations regarding the global cultures. She took them as
the starting point, while she gave just one example of Chinese and Western dining
habits in Extract 12. T5 also expressed her concern that the limitations of cultural
diversities in ELT may restrain children's mind. In the same time, T5 thought that
Anglophone cultures may be representative in English-speaking communities.
Therefore, T5 emphasized the responsibility of teachers to supplement the portrayal
of "non-representative" cultures in the classroom.

Extract 12 *T3: Regarding the cultural diversity that you are talking about,*
the textbooks might be a little narrow, but you can use them as a starting
point and then move on to other aspects. For example, people in Western
countries eat with knives and forks, and people in other places may not
have soup in the morning and evening like we do here, etc. So we should
not only let the children know about the differences between Chinese and
western life, but also expand to other places.

Extract 13 *T5: Textbooks lay more emphasis on the cultures of*
Western countries. In fact, I can't fully understand the so-called
"comprehensiveness" put forward by the textbook authors. They may
have only incorporated some representative contents into the textbooks,

and other contents may need teachers to make a supplementary. One of the limitations is that they may restrain children's minds, and the students will only come up with the UK, the US, etc. when mentions about English-speaking countries.

Similarly, T2 agreed that students should expand their horizons and gain exposure to diverse cultures worldwide. Nevertheless, T2 noted that there are limited opportunities to incorporate the cultures of non-English speaking countries into ELT courses, with a continued emphasis on the cultures of English-speaking countries. T2 suggested that students could be encouraged to independently explore and learn about these cultures through reading materials.

> **Extract 14** *T2: Yes, yes, there are more people speaking English in non-English speaking countries now, so we can encourage children to learn more about cultures around the world, after all, language itself doesn't exist in isolation, and it is the carrier of culture, but there are very few opportunities to be exposed to the cultures of non-English speaking countries during the class, which is still mainly concentrated in the culture of English countries. We can ask children to read more, and children will have more opportunities and channels to understand those cultures through reading. As long as they love to read and read more books, they will learn about those cultural issues, but not as much during the class...*

Additionally, T4 observed that the distinctive cultures are rarely featured. T4 expressed concern that including such content might be too intricate for primary school students.

> **Extract 15** *T4: We have learned the unit of Chinese Spring Festival, which involves how people in mainland China and Hong Kong celebrate the Spring Festival.*

However, T5 admitted that she had never considered this issue before. T6 believed that the limitations of the national curriculum can be supplemented through a school-based curriculum. T6 assumed that national textbooks should represent a popular and universal culture rather than specific cultures, and teachers can supplement local cultures to students during the teaching process. However, T6 may overlook the fact that cultural contact in daily communication is fluid and emergent, rather than fixed to a particular place.

> **Extract 16** *T5: I have never thought about the topic of minority cultures, but I have a concern that other courses do contain some content about it, so whether it is still necessary to include such content in our English classes.*

Extract 17 *T6: This question may involve the difference between a national curriculum and a school-based curriculum. What is represented in textbooks should be a kind of common cultural knowledge, and something special and specific can be supplemented by school-based courses. Since the situation of each region is different, different regions can make additional supplements to the textbooks according their local conditions. Take Henan (province) for example, we can supplement some traditional cultures of Henan to students. The national textbooks are unified across the country, so they may not be able to be so detailed and comprehensive, which requires school-based curriculum and teachers to supplement during the process of teaching.*

To conclude, teachers generally acknowledged that ELT courses may have a heavy focus on Anglophone cultures, potentially limiting students' perspectives. However, they tended to accept and conform to the transmission of such cultural hegemony (Extracts 12, 13). While T2 recognized the importance of expanding students' horizons, she deemed it unrealistic to incorporate such content into the ELT class (Extract 14). Teachers also expressed concerns about the necessity of including minority cultures in national textbooks (Extracts 15, 16, 17). Additionally, T6 believed that a school-based curriculum can supplement the limitations of national textbooks, but her statement may overlook the fluidity and emergent nature of cultural contact in people's daily lives (Extract 17). Therefore, there is a need for teachers to further enhance their awareness of critical multiculturalism, moving beyond mere recognition and celebration of cultural differences and addressing prejudice reduction as well.

Despite teachers generally perceiving GCE as a distant and lofty concept, with a lack of critical awareness of linguistic inclusiveness and multiculturalism in ELT, they still express a willingness to challenge hidden inequalities in ELT. Teachers recognize the need to continuously enhance their international awareness, broaden students' horizons, and promote Chinese cultural confidence. Furthermore, since 2016, the Chinese government has emphasized the integration of ideological and political education throughout all courses. Hence, it is essential to explore teachers' perceptions of their roles as ELT teachers in relation to GCE within this context. These perceptions will be further discussed in the following paragraphs.

Awareness of roles of ELT teachers regarding GCE

Consistently, all the teachers expressed support for the educational role of ELT, emphasizing that ELT teachers should actively take on the responsibility of promoting GCE. T1 suggested that while teachers of ideological and political courses or moral education courses may play a leading role in this regard, the ELT class should also provide an ideal space for fostering GCE.

Extract 18 *T1: In view of the current situation, I think the awareness of global citizenship should be deeply rooted in everyone's hearts. Although ideological and political course teachers or moral education course teachers play a leading role, English teachers also have a convenient condition in this respect and should also provide timely guidance.*

T2 further reinforced the notion that teachers of all subjects share the responsibility and obligation to go beyond mere intellectual teaching and integrate GCE into their respective subjects. T5 also emphasized the significance of fostering students' comprehensive competence and emotional sublimation in ELT practice.

Extract 19 *T2: In my opinion, all the subjects are interlinked and all for the better development of students. Thus, it cannot be said that you are the teacher of this subject then you only have the responsibility to teach the knowledge in this one subject. Language itself is to serve life and enable us to engage in various activities through using the language that we have learned... Language is needed in all areas of the society, and it is just a tool.*

Extract 20 *T5: As you said just now, English teachers of course also have the responsibility and duty in this regard. English course is not just to teach students to learn some linguistic knowledge, and the current educational environment is not simplified. For example, when we go out to attend high-quality classes, an excellent period of English class needs a theme throughout the whole process, which not only develops students' comprehensive competence, but also needs emotional sublimation.*

In the similar vein, T3 concurred that English teachers should incorporate ideological and political education into ELT. They both emphasized that they have been implementing this in their daily ELT practice. Particularly, under the background of ideological and political theories teaching in all courses that advocated by the Chinese government, T4 further highlighted the importance of "discipline education" and the "integration among subjects". These aspects can be considered as components of Chinese GCE.

Extract 21 *T3: I believe that English teachers also have the responsibility and obligation to carry out ideological education for students. I try to incorporate this kind of content into my teaching and make children aware of the correct ways to deal with things as well as help them build the right values.*

Extract 22 *T4: Now, under the background of ideological and political theories teaching in all courses, I have summed up a word that is "discipline education". Not only ideological and political course teachers and moral course teachers have the responsibility to carry out ideological and political education to students. In the English teaching, if we encounter a topic that is related to what I teach, we can also carry out an ideological and political education for students in the English class. Instead of saying that history course teachers only teach history and English teachers only teach linguistic knowledge, etc., there should be integration among subjects.*

To conclude, all teachers advocated the educational role of ELT and believed that English teachers also bear the responsibility as well as obligation to incorporate GCE into ELT practice. This is particularly important given the context of ideological and political theories being taught in all courses in China. Teachers of all subjects, including English teachers, should actively respond to this national policy and implement GCE within the framework of socialism with Chinese characteristics in ELT.

Furthermore, considering that the incorporation of GCE into ELT in the Chinese context may have certain Chinese characteristics, it is crucial to delve deeper into teachers' actual implementation of GCE and metrolingualism in ELT. This will be elaborated upon in the following subsection.

4.4.2 ELT implementation regarding GCE & metrolingualism

General implementation in ELT

When asked about their teaching priorities, most teachers stated that they tend to place greater emphasis on students' linguistic knowledge and skills. As T1 believed, she may not specifically focus on students' cultural awareness or emotional attitudes, but rather prioritize linguistic knowledge and skills, even though they are all required in the curriculum. Similarly, even under the backdrop of the "double-reduction" policy, T4 may also prioritize linguistic skills to help students achieve better results in exams.

Extract 23 *T1: As for the five aspects involved in the curriculum, I may pay more attention to the cultivation of students' linguistic knowledge and skills as well as learning strategies, without paying special attention to cultural awareness or emotional attitudes. Sometimes, if it is involved during the teaching, I may just make a simple extension for the students.*

Extract 24 *T4: I usually pay more attention to students' listening and* *speaking, since they seem did well in reading and writing from the feedback of their tests, but not very well in listening. Moreover, under the "double-reduction" policy, you cannot give students too much homework to do, so I ask the students to practice the speaking skill after school, so that they can master some important sentence patterns better at the same time.*

Besides, T2 and T6 also emphasized the importance of cultivating students' interest in English. T2 acknowledged that while cultivating interest is a primary task for lower-grade students, higher-grade students still need to focus on acquiring more linguistic knowledge and skills to excel in exams. Similarly, T6 believed that students in middle and higher grades should prioritize learning linguistic knowledge and engaging in more exercises to enhance their English proficiency. Therefore, although these teachers agree on the cultivation of students' interest, they also recognize that such cultivation is ultimately aimed at enhancing the learning of linguistic knowledge and skills, leading to improved English proficiency and better exam performance.

Extract 25 *T2: For students in the lower grade of primary school, I may focus more on cultivating students' interest in English. In the middle and senior grades, some vocabulary memorization methods and linguistic knowledge and skills may be more practiced. After all, they have to take exams.*

Extract 26 *T6: For the lower grade students, I will pay more attention to the cultivation of their interest, and let the children love to speak and express their ideas. In the middle grade, I will focus more on the vocabulary and grammar as well as some other linguistic knowledge. Then students in senior grade need to do a lot of exercises according to some test points, and repeatedly practice some important phrases and sentence structures, etc. Moreover, the teaching methods for each stage are also different, and gradually the students' English proficiencies will be improved.*

On the other hand, T5 stated that she had made some changes in her teaching, gradually shifting from the previous emphasis on linguistic knowledge and skills to the cultivation of students' emotional and cultural awareness. Additionally, she consciously integrates ideological values into her teaching practice. Thus T5's statements indicate that in-service teacher training may facilitate teachers to change their teaching ideas and pay more attention to something else rather than just being limited to some superficial knowledge in textbooks. Nevertheless, albeit the teaching direction of T5 maybe a bit different from that of other teachers, she still puts more emphasis on some common topics such as enhancing Chinese cultural confidence, family affection, friendship, rather than global issues, as evident in Extract 28.

Extract 27 *T5: In the past, I paid more attention to the teaching of linguistic knowledge and skills. In recent years, I have attended a lot of lectures, and I have been constantly summarizing and reflecting on myself as well. Now, I focus more on the education of students' emotional and cultural awareness, and I consciously intersperse some cultural and emotional awareness during the class.*

Extract 28 *T5: When I write teaching plans, I always think about what kind of emotional value this lesson has and what kind of ideological and moral education it can provide to children... How to improve their cultural confidence... How to get along with family and friends... How to get along better with people around you...*

To sum up, the teaching practices of most teachers primarily focus on linguistic knowledge and skills, and the cultivation of students' interest is aimed at promoting better learning outcomes in these areas, as well as improving their overall English proficiency to perform well in various exams (Extracts 23, 24, 25, 26). However, T5 differs from the other teachers as she places more emphasis on the education of students' emotional and cultural awareness, consciously incorporating these aspects into her teaching practice (Extract 27). Nevertheless, albeit T5 stated that she would like to move beyond textbooks, she may still prioritize common topics while ignoring students' critical literacy development and global issues (Extract 28).

Cultural foci in ELT

Generally, the foci of foreign cultural education in ELT tend to be on Anglophone cultures while ignoring other global cultures. Additionally, the intercultural communication is often assumed to be between Chinese and Western cultures. T1 and T4 contended that they may pay attention to the teaching of differences between Chinese and Western cultures to develop students' intercultural communicative competence.

Extract 29 *T1: In terms of foreign cultural education, I also mainly focus on cultures of English-speaking countries, and perhaps the most is to compare the differences between Chinese and Western cultures. However, cultures of non-English speaking countries have been rarely involved, and I may talk about some occasionally.*

Extract 30 *T4: There is a section named "Culture time" in each unit of the textbook, which mainly compares the differences between Chinese* *and Western cultures. I also pay more attention to this aspect and the development of students' intercultural communication competence.*

Similarly, T2 further expressed that Western cultures are the main focus in her teaching of foreign cultures, since they are dominant in textbooks. On the other hand, textbooks rarely involve other foreign cultures, so she assumed that those contents do not have to be in teaching. Thus, textbook centralism has been shown in T2's teaching practice.

Extract 31 *T2: Western cultures have been introduced more in terms of foreign cultural education, such as Christmas, Halloween, Thanksgiving Day, and British and American cultural customs are the main focus, while some other countries are rarely involved, which mainly depends on textbooks. For example, there is a unit in the textbook specifically about Australia, you will definitely introduce more about this country, and then there are a lot of introductions about the UK and the US as well. However, since other non-English speaking countries are seldom mentioned in textbooks, the related contents are rarely involved during the teaching practice.*

In contrast to the previous statements, T5 observed the limitations of foreign cultural education in terms of cultural representation. As a result, she advocated for expanding beyond the confines of textbooks during teaching practice. However, she also acknowledged that this expansion is not as extensive compared to Anglophone cultures.

Extract 32 *T5: Textbooks are more inclined to British or American cultures, but we teachers can intersperse some cultures of other countries in the class. For instance, I have extended some of the Korean cuisine to the students when we talked about food last time. There will be some expansion based on textbooks, but not much.*

Moreover, T6 highlighted the importance of extracurricular education. She mentioned an annual activity in her school that served as a platform for students to showcase their talents and broaden their extracurricular knowledge. However, T6 acknowledged that some participating countries in this activity still predominantly represented English-speaking cultures, and she believed that these cultural contents should be key points in ELT. Additionally, T6 emphasized the promotion of confidence in Chinese culture, indicating a focus on fostering a strong sense of cultural identity.

Extract 33 *T6: ... Not only exam-oriented education, other aspects will also be involved. For example, there is an activity held every year in* *our school called International Culture Festival. Thus, we not just stick to textbooks, and we also expand some contents beyond textbooks. This activity mainly focuses on introducing English speaking countries, such as Australia, the UK, the US, Canada. Since they are the key points, we want to let students learn more about them... However, since Chinese culture confidence has been advocated, we are gradually transitioning from the International Culture Festival to our Chinese culture.*

Additionally, T2 argued that minority cultures could be better introduced in Chinese course or other subjects rather than ELT. T2 also emphasized that patriotism education should be a top priority across all subjects. Besides, T4 mentioned the introduction of differences in diet culture between northern and southern China, suggesting the integration of local cultural elements into the teaching of English.

Extract 34 *T2: Cultures of some minorities may be introduced more in the Chinese course or other characteristic courses of the school. Then I will educate the students to love our country, love Chinese culture, and love our city, etc.*

Extract 35 *T4: We just talk about some big aspects, such as the differences in eating habits between the north and the south of China, etc. without elaborating on these contents.*

Furthermore, T6 highlighted another activity held in her school that aimed to introduce more about the local culture in Henan province. This activity not only encouraged students to expand their knowledge about the world but also emphasized the importance of preserving and inheriting local traditions and heritage. However, there is a question regarding the statement of "open eyes to the world", as it seems to be focused primarily on the Anglophone countries while excluding of the rest in the world.

Extract 36 *T6: Besides, we also organized another activity called Henan Festival to let the students know more about our hometown, including the history, culture and local customs of various cities in Henan province. The purpose of this activity is to ask the students not only to open their eyes to the world, but also to see the traditional culture around us.*

In brief, the focus of cultural education in ELT tends to revolve around Anglophone and Chinese cultures, while neglecting other cultures from around the world. There is an implicit assumption that the development of students' intercultural communicative competence may primarily focus on the cultural contact between Chinese and Anglophone cultures (Extracts 29, 30). Moreover, textbooks centralism has been contended by some teachers, which facilitates them to only pay more attention to the dominant content in textbooks (Extract 31). Although one teacher expressed a desire to expose students to other cultures beyond textbooks, there still appears to be a greater emphasis on Anglophone cultures (Extract 32). Additionally, while T6 mentioned activities in her school aimed at broadening students' horizons and fostering a better understanding of local culture, it is questionable that Anglophone culture is the focus in those activities while neglecting the rest of the world and the diversity of other cultures worldwide (Extracts 33, 36).

Implementation of other GCE values in ELT

Environmental protection emerged as another prominent topic frequently mentioned by teachers during the interviews. For instance, T4 engaged in discussions with students on how to protect the environment in their daily activities. T5 even connected this topic to the current issue of proper disposal of used masks. Both T4 and T5 emphasized the teaching of environmental awareness, as it is included in the textbook.

> **Extract 37** *T4: For example, we had a discussion about whether to use plastic bags, paper bags or cloth bags while shopping in the supermarket when we learn a unit about protecting the earth in the textbook. All these contents are integrated into the text... Besides, I also ask the students to experience by themselves, such as how they save water in their daily life and take action...*

> **Extract 38** *T5: Besides, I will also connect with some hot topics of the moment. There is a unit about the environment protection, for example. We need to wear masks during the Covid-19 pandemic, how to dispose of used masks, garbage sorting, etc. These are all environment-related topics. Diverge students' thinking as much as possible, so that they can output more.*

Besides, T2 and T3 also mentioned about the importance of emotional education for students. T2 focused on cultivating empathy in students towards children in impoverished areas, encouraging them to appreciate their own educational opportunities and work harder. On the other hand, T3 extended the topic of family affection to provide students with education on the importance of familial relationships. Both teachers recognized the significance of emotional education in shaping students' values and fostering positive social and familial connections.

> **Extract 39** *T2: Sometimes I will let the students know about the studying situation of children in other countries around the world. There are still some children in some very poor areas of the world may not have the opportunity to receive education, so I educate the students to cherish the*

current studying opportunity and study harder in the future.

Extract 40 *T3: For example, there is a unit about my family. I not only teach students to master some expressions of family members, but also educate children a sense of family, such as the love of parents for them, the kinship among family members, etc. which is an extension of emotion.*

In conclusion, several teachers provided teaching examples to raise students' awareness of environmental protection (Extracts 37, 38). Others emphasized the importance of emotional education in various aspects, such as empathy and kinship (Extracts 39, 40). These statements highlight the central role of textbooks in teaching practice, as teachers utilize them as a foundation for carrying out emotional education on relevant topics. However, it is notable that while these teaching contents have connections to GCE, teachers often gravitate towards general and common topics rather than addressing critical issues.

Textbook centralism

The teachers consistently emphasized that their teaching primarily revolves around the use of textbooks, with any additional content being considered as extensions of the textbook material. T3 acknowledged that due to time constraints during class, she mainly focused on textbook-based teaching and had limited opportunities to explore other topics. She encouraged students to pursue their interests outside of the classroom through alternative channels. Similarly, T6 advocated for students to explore additional knowledge beyond textbooks through extracurricular activities, while still acknowledging the importance of basing classroom teaching on the textbook material.

Extract 41 *T3: I cannot talk too much about something other than the textbooks in class, since the time in class is too limited, and I may talk about it with the children after class. Thus, I encourage students to read more, and they can read books or surf the Internet to learn about what they are interested in, but it is mainly focused on the textbooks during the class.*

Extract 42 *T6: It is still mainly based on textbooks during the class, and I may supplement with some daily life phrases. The students can learn more about other aspects through doing extra-curricular activities, but not much in the class.*

To summarize, the teaching practice of most teachers primarily focuses on enhancing students' linguistic knowledge and skills to improve their English proficiency. However, it is evident that the cultural education in ELT tends to revolve around Anglophone and Chinese cultures, with limited inclusion of cultures from other non-English speaking countries. The development of students' intercultural communicative competence is often assumed to be based on the cultural contact between China and the West. The prevalence of textbook centralism further reinforces the dominance of Chinese and Anglophone cultures in ELT. The teachers' statements also indicate a preference for general and common GCE topics, rather than addressing critical issues. Therefore, there is a pressing need for the cultivation of critical literacy among in-service teachers and the incorporation of critical multiculturalism education in ELT.

The interviewed statements highlight the prevailing trend of adopting a soft GCE pedagogy in ELT practices, which aligns with the representation found in textbooks. However, some teachers have expressed awareness of certain limitations in ELT, yet they still tend to adhere to existing stereotypes. Therefore, it is important to delve deeper into the specific concerns that teachers encounter in their teaching practice regarding GCE and metrolingualism. The following subsection will explore these challenges faced by teachers in ELT practices.

4.4.3　Challenges in ELT regarding GCE & metrolingualism

Class time limit

Teachers generally expressed that the constrained time allocated for each class hinders their ability to cover extensive additional content. T1 specifically mentioned that they prioritize the use of textbooks, resulting in limited inclusion of content beyond the textbook material during class. This is primarily due to the constraints imposed by the limited class time available. Similarly, T6 acknowledged the challenge of covering all content within the restricted class time, leading to prioritization of important exam-related material.

Extract 43 *T1: For another, there is a concern about the time and efficiency of the class. Now we mainly teach some linguistic knowledge and skills as well as learning strategies, etc. and cultural awareness will be simply penetrated into the texts. The teaching content is mainly based on textbooks. If teachers deliberately talk about something beyond textbooks during the class, teachers need to pay more time, and then the time in class may not be enough.*

Extract 44 *T6: The amount of time in class is also concerned, and sometimes it is difficult for us to involve many aspects in the class, since there is no time. Some of the key content about the exam needs to be strengthened practice, so the exam achievements of the students are still the priority.*

Exam-oriented education

Furthermore, the prevalence of exam-oriented education remains prominent in ELT. T5 argued that although there is a current push to reduce the academic burden, the focus on examinations still persists in actual teaching practice. T6 further supported this notion, stating that teaching is still confined within the framework of examinations, despite the call for quality-oriented education for students. As long as the examination system remains in place, achieving true quality-oriented education becomes challenging.

Extract 45 *T5: Although the exam-oriented education has been reduced now, it is still unavoidable to carry out teaching from the perspective of examination during the actual ELT practice. Thus, besides developing children's thinking and sublimating their emotions, we also need to teach them about the tests.*

Extract 46 *T6: Although we have always been advocating quality-oriented education, the college entrance examination system is still there, so our actual teaching is still largely confined to the framework of examinations, and there is little content that can be really expanded. Thus, I feel that the current teaching is still focused on exam-oriented education, not really achieving quality-oriented.*

Teacher training needed

Besides, T1 mentioned that teachers themselves need to continually enhance their own literacy and expand their horizons, as the concept of GCE is new to them and may seem disconnected from students' daily lives. Consequently, it becomes challenging for teachers to consciously and actively incorporate such aspects of content into their teaching practice. The statements from teachers highlight the crucial need for GCE training for both pre-service and in-service teachers. Such training would enable teachers to develop a deeper understanding of GCE and enhance their awareness in this area, ultimately facilitating their ability to effectively integrate GCE principles into their teaching.

Extract 47 *T1: GCE is so new to us that it will be more difficult to consciously integrate it into teaching practice. It is also quite distant from students' daily life... So it is quite difficult for teachers to consciously incorporate those contents into teaching practice.*

Educational disparity

Moreover, T1 observed that the wealth disparity among students can contribute to inequality in GCE. Children from economically disadvantaged families may have limited opportunities to engage with the cultures and local customs of other countries, which can hinder their development of GCE to some extent. T5 added that many of the children she teaches come from rural areas and have weak English foundations, making it challenging for them to absorb a large amount of content simultaneously. These factors highlight the importance of considering the diverse backgrounds and needs of students when implementing GCE in the classroom, and addressing the potential disparities that may exist in accessing GCE opportunities.

Extract 48 *T1: What's more, for students from families with better economic conditions, they will have more opportunities to get in touch with cultures and customs of different countries, and they will definitely have better GCE than those students who come from families with relatively poor economic conditions.*

Extract 49 *T5: Since most of the children I teach are from rural areas, they themselves do not have a good language learning environment, and their English foundation may be weak as well.*

Young age of primary school students

Another concern raised by teachers is whether it is appropriate to introduce such content to primary school students at a young age. This concern was expressed by both T3 and T4. They questioned whether the students' young age and developmental stage are suitable for engaging with GCE topics. This concern reflects the teachers' consideration for the students' cognitive abilities, maturity, and readiness to comprehend and engage with complex global issues. It indicates the need for careful consideration and age-appropriate approaches when incorporating GCE into the primary school curriculum.

Extract 50 *T3: ...Besides, they are still too young to accept too much teaching content.*

Extract 51 *T4: After all, they are primary school students who have just started learning English, and they may not be able to digest it if you talk too much.*

In conclusion, the statements from teachers in ELT practice reveal several concerns regarding GCE and metrolingualism. Teachers expressed limitations in extending beyond textbook content due to time constraints, making textbooks the primary focus in their teaching. Besides, the exam-oriented education system remains deeply ingrained even under the background of "double-reduction" policy and quality-oriented education. Consequently, exam-related content continues to dominate ELT practice. Moreover, teachers acknowledged that GCE is a new concept for them, making it challenging to actively incorporate it into their teaching. They also recognized the elitism implicit in GCE and expressed concerns about introducing GCE topics to primary school students due to their young age. However, it is important to note that GCE could provide a conceptual perspective and framework to highlight the basic functions of education and it runs through primary, secondary and higher education as well as into lifelong learning. Therefore, there is a pressing need for critical GCE training for both pre-service and in-service teachers to deepen their understanding of GCE and enhance their awareness in this area.

4.5　Summary of the Chapter

This chapter presented the findings of all the research questions, revealing the ways of GCE and metrolingualism embedding in textbooks and curriculum. It explored the similarities and differences between PEP and Yilin textbooks, as well as across different grade levels, regarding GCE and metrolingualism. Additionally, it provided insights into teachers' perceptions of these concepts. The subsequent chapter will delve deeper into a detailed discussion of these findings.

CHAPTER 5
DISCUSSION

In this chapter, discussion is represented, which includes four sections. The first section focuses on the discussion on RQ 1, and then followed by the section of the discussion on RQ 2 and RQ 3. The discussion on RQ 4 comes after that. For each section, the summary of the findings for each RQ is restated first, and then the discussion is elaborated. The summary of this chapter comes last.

5.1 Discussion on RQ 1

In this section, the findings of RQ 1 will be summarized first, and the discussion on GCE & metrolingualism in textbooks and curriculum will be followed.

5.1.1 Summary of RQ 1

In summary, the findings from RQ 1 reveal that ELT textbooks and curriculum predominantly reflect the concepts of GCE and metrolingualism through a soft GCE approach. Critical GCE perspectives are relatively scarce, as the focus lies on incorporating numerous themes and subthemes aligned with soft GCE principles. In total, there are 16 themes and 20 subthemes that occur a total of 770 times in relation to GCE within ELT textbooks. Salient themes and subthemes include Anglophone cultures (107), Chinese cultures (91), kinship (59), native-speakerism prestige and supremacy (55), Chinese geography (46), leisure lifestyle (44), Chinese educational principles (41), etc. The numbers in brackets indicate the occurrence numbers of these themes and subthemes in the textbooks.

The analysis of textbookscapes for metrolingualism in ELT textbooks was conducted from two perspectives: LLs analysis and MIs analysis. The findings were categorized into five main themes: English supremacy in LLs, antithesis of English supremacy in LLs, exclusivism in LLs, native-speakerism standard in MIs, cultural diversities in MIs. The research revealed that English code is the most favored and frequently used linguistic code in the textbooks. It serves not only informative functions in LLs but also reflects the prevalence of monolingualism in the textbookscapes, thus overshadowing other varieties of English. The dominance of English code in the LLs reinforces the notion of English supremacy, while the antithesis theme attempts to challenge this perspective. However, exclusivism in LLs implies a limited representation of diverse languages and cultures, potentially marginalizing non-English languages and speakers. Regarding the MIs, the native-speakerism standard is evident, emphasizing the idealization of a native English speaker in ELT. On the other hand, cultural diversities within MIs aim to incorporate various cultural elements, broadening students' understanding of different cultural perspectives. Overall, the findings highlight the prevalence of English code as the dominant and the need for a more inclusive and diverse representation of languages and cultures in ELT textbooks to promote metrolingualism.

Furthermore, the analysis of the curriculum revealed eight main themes regarding the integration of GCE and metrolingualism. These themes include global awareness, national awareness, cultural education, ideological and moral education, quality-oriented education, native-speakerism norms, linguistic foci, and daily life-oriented resources. The curriculum emphasizes the cultivation of students' global awareness, national awareness, and global competence. It integrates cultural awareness of English-speaking countries within the curriculum in terms of foreign cultures. Additionally, the curriculum addresses ideological and moral education, as well as quality-oriented education, aiming to instill values and promote overall educational excellence. Native-speakerism norms and linguistic foci are also prominent in the curriculum, emphasizing the importance of English language skills and the idealization of native English speakers. Moreover, the curriculum advocates for the use of daily life-oriented resources, connecting language learning to real-life contexts and experiences.

In the following subsection, a detailed discussion will be presented, focusing on the findings of RQ 1, which explored the ways GCE and metrolingualism are embedded in ELT textbooks and curriculum.

5.1.2　Discussion on GCE & metrolingualism in textbooks and curriculum

In this subsection, the focus is on the discussion of salient themes related to GCE and metrolingualism in textbooks and curriculum. The discussion includes interpretations of these themes, referencing previous studies, providing explanations for the findings, and making claims based on this study's analysis. To analyze the data, CDA was employed in this study. CDA is a "critical" approach that aims to uncover connections between textual attributes and social processes, such as ideologies and power relations (Fairclough, 1995). Additionally, critical GCE serves as another conceptual framework in this study, viewing GCE as a means to challenge and counteract the embedded hegemony (Andreotti, 2006). The findings of this study are interpreted and explained by connecting them to a broader Chinese social context. The analysis takes into consideration the age and educational level of the students, as well as the year of compilation of the textbooks. By employing CDA and critical GCE, this study provides a deeper understanding of the ways GCE and metrolingualism are represented in ELT textbooks and curriculum, shedding light on the ideologies and power relations that are present within them.

The research findings regarding GCE suggest that GCE themes are prominently featured in all the textbooks analyzed. However, it is important to acknowledge that these themes may present certain challenges when it comes to achieving complete inclusiveness. It is possible that the presence of utopian images in the textbooks inadvertently detracts attention from hidden ideologies and conflicts that exist in the real world. Furthermore, the textbooks tend to establish norms and ideals based on native English speakers and their communities. While this focus is understandable, it is important to consider that it may inadvertently marginalize other cultural perspectives and voices. Additionally, the representation of cultural diversity and world geography in the textbooks may unintentionally overlook countries from the outer and expanding circles, thereby neglecting their unique contributions and experiences. This limited representation of cultural diversity can potentially lead to a distorted understanding of cultural differences and a failure to address the complex issues that exist in the global society (Gay, 2015). Recognizing these limitations is crucial, and efforts should be made to foster a more comprehensive representation of cultural diversity and incorporate GCE themes in textbooks. It is important to address these issues and strive to provide a broader understanding of the world that encompasses a wide range of cultural perspectives and experiences.

Moreover, the analysis of the textbookscapes in relation to metrolingualism in both series of textbooks is consistent with the findings of GCE in the textbooks. It is worth highlighting that certain themes, such as the notion of "English supremacy in LLs" and "exclusivism in LLs", as well as "native-speakerism standard in MIs", resonate with the subtheme of "native-speakerism prestige & supremacy" found within the GCE discourse present in the textbooks. These themes could potentially lead to the influence of specific linguistic varieties and the prominence of certain linguistic norms in ELT. Additionally, the representation of Chinese and Western dietary cultures in the textbookscapes indicates the salience of "Chinese cultures" and "Anglophone cultures" throughout all the analyzed textbooks. The inclusion of themes like "anti-native speakerism prestige" and the "antithesis of English supremacy in LLs" adds a valuable layer of diversity to the textbooks, encompassing a broader range of languages and cultures. These themes contribute to a more inclusive representation of linguistic and cultural diversity within the educational materials.

What's more, certain statements within the curriculum pertaining to GCE and metrolingualism, such as "cultural education" and "native-speakerism norms", play a significant role in shaping the presence of the aforementioned GCE and metrolingualism themes found in textbooks. The curriculum serves as a guiding document, providing a solid foundation for the development of these textbooks. The inclusion of global awareness within ELT materials is focused on commonly shared global topics and Anglophone-oriented cultures. While there is room for improvement in terms of incorporating the influence of "glocalization" on both global and local communities. Moreover, the curriculum places emphasis on the integration of "daily life-oriented resources" in ELT, highlighting the importance of practical and relevant language use. This approach encourages students to engage with language in meaningful ways that relate to their everyday lives, contributing to their language proficiency and cultural understanding. However, it is worth noting that both series of textbooks tend to adhere to a "native-speakerism standard" and promote monolingualism in English code at the linguistic level. While this may be an area for further exploration and development, it is important to acknowledge the efforts made in creating comprehensive ELT materials that cater to the needs of language learners. The prevalence of monolingualism and the embedded norms of native-speakerism within textbooks and curriculum may inadvertently convey implicit messages regarding the perceived centrality or marginality of certain languages within societies (Shohamy, 2006). This observation highlights the importance of ongoing reflection and open dialogue to ensure that ELT materials continuously evolve to promote inclusivity and embrace the richness of linguistic diversity.

Besides, both series of textbooks demonstrate a certain alignment with the curriculum's emphasis on quality-oriented education, ideological and moral education, and patriotism education. This indicates a shared commitment to these important educational aspects. It can be observed that the textbooks reflect the principles of GCE and metrolingualism as outlined in the curriculum to some extent. The inclusion of harmonious themes promoting a cosmopolitan idealism is worth considering that an excessive focus on these themes may inadvertently limit students' critical thinking development. Striking a balance between nurturing a global perspective and encouraging independent analysis is crucial for their intellectual growth. Additionally, it is important to broaden students' horizons by acknowledging and incorporating the experiences and contributions of other regions of non-English speaking countries. Although English may not be directly associated with these regions, it is vital to recognize their geopolitical significance and foster a more inclusive perspective. Efforts should be made to ensure that the ELT materials provide a more comprehensive understanding of the global landscape, encompassing a diverse range of geopolitical interactions and promoting a broader awareness of different regions and cultures. By doing so, students will be better equipped to navigate the interconnected world and develop a more nuanced and inclusive worldview.

Indeed, learners have the opportunity to develop their knowledge, skills, values, and behaviors related to global citizenship to a certain extent through the inclusion of GCE themes in the textbooks. The moral values highlighted in the textbooks, such as "cooperation and solidarity", "diligence", "honesty", align with the advocated values in the curriculum. This finding is consistent with Puspitasari's study, which observed the presence of dominant moral values in textbooks that can facilitate the development of GCE (Puspitasari et al., 2021). However, it is important to acknowledge that the distribution of these themes throughout the textbooks is uneven. This observation aligns with previous studies that have highlighted the unbalanced representation of GCE themes in textbooks (Ait-Bouzid, 2020). It is crucial to ensure a more balanced and comprehensive coverage of GCE themes throughout the textbooks to provide learners with a holistic understanding of global citizenship and its associated values. Efforts should be made to provide learners with ample opportunities to engage with a wide range of GCE themes and values. By doing so, learners will be better equipped to develop a global mindset and contribute positively to their local and global communities.

The presence of metrolingualism in textbooks and curriculum highlights a similar observation made in previous studies, where cultures and English are portrayed as stable and static, disregarding the dynamic nature of language over time and distance. This representation does not align with the fluid, diverse, and flexible nature of cultures in lingua franca contexts, nor does it adequately address the diverse realities faced by students (Syrbe & Rose, 2016). The presence of native-speakerism in this study reflects findings from previous research, which suggest that it may contribute to learners being placed within an imaginary homogeneous discourse community (Xiong & Yuan, 2018). The belief in promoting "native" English as the ideal standard can pose challenges to internationalization efforts and hinder the development of GCE (Saarinen & Nikula, 2013; Cavanagh, 2017). It is also consistent with previous research that identifies the ideology of internationalization being associated with "Englishzation" (Botha, 2013; Piller & Cho, 2013; Botha, 2014). The findings regarding unified identities in this study align with previous research, which suggests a tendency towards a monolithic view of identity and an idealized, utopian image of the community (Yumarnamto et al., 2020; Babaii & Sheikhi, 2017). This observation underscores the need to acknowledge and represent a more diverse range of identities and communities, as well as to foster a more inclusive, dynamic, and flexible portrayal of language, cultures, and identities in order to better prepare students for a diverse and interconnected world.

Besides, the cultural representation observed in this study aligns with previous research that has highlighted the simplistic cultural depictions in textbooks. These depictions may not effectively facilitate the development of culture awareness and open-mindedness among students (Davidson & Liu, 2018). It is important to consider these findings in light of Zhu's study (2013), which found that the themes embedded in textbooks tend to focus more on international and national issues. The lack of emphasis on local complexities and realities may hinder students' understanding of living in a multiethnic society (Mansilla & Wilson, 2020). Additionally, the findings are consistent with previous research that emphasizes the importance of Chinese culture in citizenship education and the development of Chinese identity (Law, 2013). Recognizing and valuing the cultural heritage and diversity within China is crucial for fostering a sense of belonging and promoting a comprehensive understanding of citizenship. In light of these, it is important to provide a more nuanced and comprehensive portrayal of cultures, encompassing both local and global perspectives. Engaging students in the consideration of complexities and realities of living in a multiethnic society can further enhance their cultural awareness, open-mindedness, and social responsibility, fostering their development as global citizens.

Nevertheless, it is worth noting that the findings of this study differ from the perspectives put forth by some other researchers who have highlighted certain GCE themes (De La Caba & Atxurra, 2006; Ait-Bouzid, 2020). The absence of indigenous cultural representations in textbooks, as noted by Brown and Habegger-Conti's study (2017), is another aspect that does not align with the findings of this study. Additionally, it is worthy to note that the expectations placed on young citizens to undertake the mission of national revival and socialist modernization are highlighted. This demonstrates a strong commitment to national development and the cultivation of a collective identity among young citizens. By prioritizing these goals, there is an opportunity to instill a sense of responsibility and dedication in the younger generation, enabling them to actively contribute to the progress and prosperity of the nation. It is important to ensure that ELT materials address national aspirations and goals while also providing a comprehensive and inclusive portrayal of global citizenship. By striking a balance between these various aspects, we can better prepare young citizens to navigate the complexities of both local and global contexts while contributing positively to the society and broader world.

The findings of this study suggest that there is a focus on a soft approach to GCE in ELT, which aligns with the observations made in Ait-Bouzid's study (2020). It is worth noting the benefits of the soft GCE approach, which may promote a sense of harmony and unity among students, but it also should be acknowledged that this approach may offer limited opportunities for the development of critical thinking skills, potentially presenting a somewhat idealized notion of GCE (Woods & Kong, 2020). Furthermore, these findings reaffirm Basarir's research, which highlights the need for more comprehensive content on global issues in order to enhance learners' global awareness (Basarir, 2017). It is essential to strike a balance by incorporating opportunities for critical thinking, addressing global issues, and enabling students to develop their own perspectives. By integrating these elements into ELT, students can be empowered to become active participants in addressing global challenges, nurturing their critical thinking skills, and fostering an inclusive sense of global awareness.

With the deepening of "Reform and Opening up", there has been an increased emphasis on the openness of China's education system. In line with this, the Chinese government has implemented educational policies aimed at fostering students' global awareness and promoting international communication skills. These policies integrate moral concepts derived from Confucianism, along with principles of socialist modernization, into the curriculum and textbooks. In light of these considerations, it is evident that the curriculum upholds the importance of both global awareness and national awareness, recognizing the value of fostering an understanding of the world and a strong sense of national identity. Furthermore, the curriculum underscores the significance of "ideological and moral education", playing a pivotal role in imparting students with a solid ethical foundation that guides their actions and choices. By incorporating these values into the curriculum, China's educational system seeks to nurture well-rounded individuals who possess not only the necessary knowledge and skills but also a global perspective, a deep appreciation for their nation, and a strong moral compass.

Nowadays, it is important to acknowledge that English, to some extent, has been subject to market forces, leading to its commodification. Additionally, the proliferation of standardized English tests has further reinforced the influence of Anglophone cultures and their perceived superiority in English language learning. Consequently, themes related to "Anglophone cultures", "native-speakerism prestige & supremacy", and "Anglophone geography" often find their way into ELT. Within these ELT materials, there is a subtle emphasis on the cultural aspects associated with English-speaking countries, which can inadvertently reinforce certain stereotypes and perceptions. While the intention may be to expose students to different cultures and enhance their understanding of the English language, there is a need to ensure a balanced representation of diverse cultures and linguistic backgrounds. It is important for educators to approach these themes with sensitivity and inclusivity, fostering an appreciation for a wide range of cultures and languages beyond the dominance of Anglophone cultures. By incorporating a more diverse range of cultural references and highlighting the global nature of English language usage, ELT materials can contribute to nurturing a more inclusive and cosmopolitan perspective among students. Furthermore, promoting a broader understanding of English as a language of communication and fostering intercultural competence can help students navigate the complexities of the interconnected world. By embracing a more nuanced and inclusive approach to ELT, students could engage in global contexts confidently and effectively while preserving their own cultural heritage.

Throughout history, in China, there has been a longstanding appreciation for the values of harmony and family, which find their roots in the teachings of esteemed philosophers like Confucius and Mencius. These values have played a significant role in shaping the content of textbooks, where themes of kinship and harmonious thematic content as well as civic virtues are frequently emphasized. This emphasis reflects the enduring importance placed on fostering social cohesion and interpersonal relationships within Chinese society. In contemporary Chinese society, various concepts have been put forth to promote collective development, such as the "Community with a Shared Future for Mankind" and the "Belt and Road Initiative". These concepts serve as grand narratives that highlight the vision of a harmonious, unified, and friendly image. These narratives, when incorporated into textbooks, aim to inspire a sense of shared responsibility and cooperation among students, fostering a deep-rooted commitment to societal progress and global engagement. By recognizing the significance of these values and narratives in the educational context, those ELT materials contribute to cultivating a sense of unity, empathy, and collective well-being among students. The portrayal of harmonious ideals and the promotion of a shared future serve to nourish a sense of optimism, encouraging students to actively contribute to the betterment of society and the world at large.

In light of the evolving educational landscape, it is noteworthy to observe that GCE has undergone a recontextualization within ELT materials. This recontextualization is characterized by the prominence of sociopolitical ideology, embodying a perspective that places an expectation on the younger generation to actively contribute to the nation's revival and socialist modernization (Wu & Tse, 2023). Consequently, there exists an emphasis on the reinforcement of socialist civic education, with the aim of nurturing individuals who possess a profound sense of national pride while upholding the cherished values of traditional Chinese culture. Concurrently, students are encouraged to remain keenly attuned to the ever-evolving global education trends, thereby fostering a holistic perspective that aims to promote global consciousness rooted in fundamental socialist principles. It is worth highlighting that these educational objectives are thoughtfully aligned with the vision of developing a modern nation of China within the context of globalization (Wang, 2023).

For another, the emergence of nascent global citizenship sentiments (Davidson and Liu, 2018) and the concept of metrolingualism embedded in ELT may present challenges to achieving critical GCE. A critical examination of ELT and cultural instruction, as well as the objectives and approaches of GCE, are ongoing areas of exploration and development (Byram et al., 2017). Striving for a balanced position in these areas remains a complex task. Efforts to incorporate critical GCE into ELT and establish a comprehensive GCE curriculum, along with pedagogical approaches that embrace metrolingualism, pose significant challenges within compulsory education for ELT. The aim is to strike a balance between local positioning and global orientation, while navigating the process of "glocalization" (杨雪 , 2017). It is crucial to move beyond an idealized vision of GCE and work towards a realistic template that reflects the complexities of the real world (Woods and Kong, 2020).

In this context, it is important to provide teachers and students with ample space to cultivate critical literacy skills and empower them to be critical consumers and creators of educational materials, despite the pressures imposed by native-oriented standardized English testing. This allows for the emancipation of critical thinking abilities and encourages active engagement, fostering a deeper understanding and appreciation of diverse perspectives. By creating an environment that supports critical literacy development, educators can enable students to navigate the complexities of interconnected world nowadays, fostering their ability to think critically, analyze information, and contribute meaningfully to global conversations.

Furthermore, it is essential to consider another significant aspect in light of the previous discussion, particularly when examining ELT materials intended for primary school students who are generally under the age of 12. As outlined in Appendix B, the learning objectives for GCE at the primary level primarily focus on tasks such as "describing", "identifying", "recognizing", and "understanding" GCE-related topics. On the other hand, critical thinking and action towards these topics are primarily expected at the upper secondary level, where objectives include tasks such as "critically analyzing", "critically examining", and "critically assessing" (refer to Appendix B for further details). Considering this perspective, the inclusion of utopian images and common global topics in textbooks becomes more understandable for primary school students, as it allows them to recognize and appreciate a nascent global citizenship sentiment. After all, the cognitive abilities of primary students are still developing and may not yet be fully matured. Furthermore, it is worth noting that these ELT materials were compiled before UNESCO issued official documents on GCE. Consequently, the cosmopolitan idealism depicted in textbooks may reflect a certain understanding of GCE at the time of their creation and may also align with the prevailing global context during that period.

As far as the stage of knowledge is concerned, it is somewhat intriguing to observe that certain GCE themes have already found their way into those ELT materials, despite being compiled prior to the official issuance of GCE documents by UNESCO. However, it is important to note that the predominant focus in these materials leans towards soft GCE themes. It is worth acknowledging that this study does not aim to represent two extreme positions, either being overly "soft" or overly "critical", but rather seeks a balanced approach. The intention is to raise awareness among stakeholders about the diverse reality surrounding GCE, as the absence of criticality and cultural diversity in ELT may potentially create future issues and hinder intercultural understanding. It is crucial to recognize that the development of critical GCE thinking, which is expected at the upper secondary level, is a gradual process that cannot be achieved overnight. It begins with laying the foundation at the primary level. In this regard, this study argues that even primary ELT materials should provide ample opportunities to foster students' critical thinking skills. By integrating the diverse realities of the world to some extent, while striking a balance and incorporating elements of critical thinking and cultural diversity, primary ELT materials can adapt to the influence of "glocalization" on both global and local communities, thereby facilitating the gradual development of students' global awareness and intercultural competence. This approach nurtures a nuanced understanding of the world and cultivates open-minded and empathetic individuals who are equipped to navigate the complexities of the "glocalized" society.

Especially nowadays, it is increasingly evident that linguistic diasporas are primarily engaging in communication through online platforms, leading to the emergence of a more emergent and improvisational phenomenon of everyday multilingual and multicultural contact. Consequently, it becomes necessary to acknowledge everyday multilingualism and critical multiculturalism in educational materials, recognizing communication as a dynamic, goal-oriented network of diverse and differentiated communicative choices made by individual speakers when interacting with other individuals, rather than the rigid linguistics and cultures for accumulation of static and self-contained language and cultural systems (Matras, 2008). To effectively address this evolving landscape, traditional Second Language Acquisition (SLA) approach within ELT may require innovative adaptations. These adaptations would enable stakeholders to enhance their critical literacy in relation to both external and internal diversities, while simultaneously fostering a sense of Chinese "glocal" citizenship education. The following section will delve into a discussion on RQ 2 and RQ 3.

5.2   Discussion on RQ 2 & RQ 3

In this section, the findings of RQ 2 and RQ 3 will be summarized first, and the discussion on the similarities and differences will be followed.

5.2.1   Summary of RQ 2

Generally speaking, PEP textbooks and Yilin textbooks exhibit certain similarities and differences in terms of their salient themes and subthemes. PEP textbooks predominantly feature themes such as Anglophone cultures, Chinese cultures, native-speakerism prestige & supremacy, Chinese educational principles, omnipotent artificial intelligence, and kinship. These themes, represented as proportions in the textbooks, account for 13.39%, 11.76%, 10.34%, 7.51%, 6.9%, and 6.29% respectively. Similarly, Yilin textbooks also emphasize Anglophone cultures, Chinese cultures, kinship, leisure lifestyle, and Chinese geography, with proportions of 14.8%, 11.91%, 10.11%, 7.94%, and 7.22% respectively. While there are similarities in the salient themes and subthemes between PEP and Yilin textbooks, there are notable differences as well. PEP textbooks exhibit a greater diversity of themes compared to the Yilin series. These differences in content highlight disparities in their approaches to GCE. In terms of metrolingualism, it is evident that English supremacy is a prevailing aspect in all textbooks. However, there is a slight variation in the proportion of English code in LLs, with Yilin textbooks having a slightly higher representation compared to PEP. Furthermore, the inclusion of native-speakerism standard is prominent in both textbooks across various illustrations. The summary of findings for RQ 3 will be presented in the subsequent subsection.

5.2.2 Summary of RQ 3

The analysis of GCE themes across different grade levels reveals both similarities and differences. In grade three and grade five, the domain of inter/multicultural education stands out as the most prominent. Conversely, the domain of emerging themes takes center stage in Grade 4 and Grade 6. However, the domains of education for sustainable development and citizenship education have relatively lower proportions across all grade levels. There is a noticeable increase in the diversity of themes and subthemes as the grade level progresses. Grade 3 includes 18 themes and subthemes, Grade 4 has 20, Grade 5 has 23, and Grade 6 has 28. In Grade 3, salient themes and subthemes include Anglophone cultures (21.58%), native-speakerism prestige & supremacy (13.67%), kinship (11.51%), and harmonious coexistence of human-nature relations (8.63%). Grade 4 highlights themes such as Anglophone cultures (15.03%), commercialization (13.73%), Chinese cultures (10.46%), and Chinese educational principles (9.15%). Grade five focuses on Chinese cultures (15.91%), Anglophone cultures (13.26%), native-speakerism prestige & supremacy (9.47%), Chinese educational principles (8.33%), and omnipotent artificial intelligence (8.33%). Grade 6 emphasizes themes such as Chinese cultures (10.75%), Anglophone cultures (8.88%), Chinese geography (8.41%), Anglophone geography (7.48%), environmental responsibility and sustainable development (6.54%), and rule compliance (6.54%). The numbers in parentheses indicate the proportion of these themes and subthemes in the textbooks.

In terms of metrolingualism issues across different grades, there is an increasing diversity of codes in LLs as the grade level progresses. However, the prevalence of English monolingualism in LLs remains consistent across all grades, and the number of monolingual LLs outweighs the bilingual and multilingual LLs in each grade. Furthermore, English supremacy continues to prevail across all grade levels, and native-speakerism standard norms are dominant. The subsequent subsection will delve into discussion of the similarities and differences between the two series of textbooks, as well as the comparisons among various grade levels.

5.2.3 Discussion on similarities & differences

To gain a deeper understanding of the similarities and distinctions between PEP and Yilin textbooks, it is pertinent to mention two approaches, "One standard for one series of textbooks" (一纲一本) and "One standard for multiple series of textbooks" (一纲多本). The former policy, which was primarily in place prior to the "Reform and Opening up" of China, aimed to establish a unified national curriculum with a single set of textbooks implemented nationwide. However, acknowledging the vast expanse of the country and the varying economic development in different regions, the Chinese MOE recognized the need for flexibility in the curriculum to accommodate local conditions. In light of this, the compilation of primary and secondary school textbooks started to embrace a diversified approach while adhering to the fundamental requirements of the national curriculum. This approach, known as "One standard for multiple series of textbooks", allows for the customization of content based on local economic development and the specific educational needs of different regions (钟启泉 , 2009). By adopting such an approach, educational materials can be tailored to suit the requirements of local communities, fostering a more adaptive and inclusive educational environment.

Against this backdrop, it becomes apparent why the similarities between PEP and Yilin series outweigh the differences. Both sets of textbooks were developed based on the guiding national curriculum. Consequently, it is understandable that there are numerous unit topics that overlap and result in content similarities. PEP series comprises a total of 42 units, while the Yilin series consists of 64 units, with 15 units in each series sharing the same or similar topics. Despite the high degree of similarity in unit topics between the two series, there are still some differences attributable to the distinct publishers and regional considerations. The curriculum emphasizes the need for textbooks to account for regional differences and exhibit certain flexibility in content across different regions (MOE, 2011). Hence, it is pertinent to provide a brief introduction to the histories and characteristics of the regional locations of PEP and Yilin textbooks in order to gain a better understanding of the differences between these two series.

PEP, established in 1950, has a significant history as a prominent publishing house in China. Its primary focus lies in the compilation, editing, and publishing of textbooks for compulsory education, along with other educational books and teaching materials across various educational levels. In addition to its domestic endeavors, PEP has undertaken projects in collaboration with numerous international organizations such as UNESCO, UNICEF, and UNFPA. Further, PEP has formed partnerships with publishing houses in different countries, including the Longman Publishing Group of the UK, the Pan Pacific Publishing Company of Singapore, and the Lingo Media International Group of Canada, etc. Situated in Beijing, the capital city of China, PEP benefits from its location as a political, cultural, and international communication hub. Being a highly international metropolis, Beijing provides PEP with a broader international perspective and opportunities for engagement with international organizations and entities beyond national borders. These factors may help explain the enhanced thematic diversity and frequency found in PEP textbooks.

On the other hand, Yilin Press, founded in 1988, primarily focuses on the publication of foreign language books, foreign language teaching materials, and works of foreign literature. It has established itself as a renowned and influential publisher in China, particularly in the field of translation. While Yilin Press may have a more specialized focus, which covers a broader range of educational materials for compulsory education, its contributions to the promotion of world literature are noteworthy. Yilin Press is situated in Nanjing, the capital city of Jiangsu Province, which holds significance as a political, economic, and cultural center in southern China. While Beijing may have more international exposures, the geographical location of Nanjing still plays a vital role in shaping the cultural and intellectual landscape of the region. This context, combined with Yilin Press's expertise and dedication to foreign language publications, helps to foster a unique perspective in their textbooks. Therefore, considering the different historical backgrounds, geographical factors, and the specialized focus of Yilin Press, it is understandable that the themes in their textbooks may exhibit a specific emphasis and may be presented in a slightly different manner compared to the more diverse range of themes found in PEP textbooks.

Indeed, PEP possesses a long history compared to Yilin Press. During the time of "One standard for one series of textbooks", PEP played a pivotal role as the sole textbook publisher in China and has continued to maintain its position as a leading educational press in the country. This longstanding presence in the field of education has endowed PEP with a profound cultural foundation. Additionally, the location of PEP in Beijing holds significant importance beyond being the capital of China. Serving as a dynamic hub, Beijing attracts diverse cultures from both within the country and around the world. Being an international city, Beijing fosters an environment that embraces cultural hybrid. This inclusive atmosphere may elucidate why certain themes such as "globality", "other cultures", and "other geography" are more prominently explored within PEP textbooks. PEP's extensive history, deep cultural roots in education, and its location in Beijing, renowned for its cultural diversity, all contribute to its inclusive approach. Consequently, this may account for the presence of specific content in PEP textbooks that delves into global perspectives, other cultures, and diverse geographies.

Furthermore, as explored in Chapter 2, the prevailing discourses within China's educational landscape can significantly shape the content of textbooks. PEP, being the foremost education press in China, has likely been at the forefront of actively responding to the prevailing mainstream or status quo within the country. In doing so, PEP ensures that its textbooks align with the requirements set forth by national curriculum guidelines and reflect the influence of Chinese educational policies. Consequently, it is plausible that certain themes with emerging significance, such as "Chinese educational principles", are more prominently featured in PEP textbooks. This highlights PEP's commitment to meeting the demands of the national curriculum while staying attuned to the evolving educational landscape in China.

Additionally, it is worth noting that Beijing, being a modernized commercial metropolis, may exhibit a greater degree of commercialization compared to other regions. This may contribute to a higher proportion of content related to the theme of "commercialization" within PEP textbooks. It is important to recognize that commercialization has become increasingly prevalent in today's global culture, serving as a common reference point for participants involved in English language teaching and learning (Savski, 2022). Furthermore, the extensive historical background of PEP allows for a harmonious coexistence of Chinese traditional ideas and modern trends within their textbooks. This blend of traditional and contemporary influences adds depth and richness to the content presented in PEP textbooks.

Moreover, as discussed in Chapter 4, the presence of Robin, an all-powerful robot character, contributes to a notable emphasis on the theme of "omnipotent artificial intelligence" within PEP textbooks. This thematic focus not only reflects a vision for future technological advancements but also implies a perspective of global coexistence. In this regard, PEP may largely echo the grand narrative of building a powerful country in science and technology of China. On the other hand, it is important to acknowledge that PEP textbooks were compiled a decade ago when the concept of "artificial intelligence" depicted in the textbooks may have been more of a fantastical notion. It is remarkable to observe that, to some extent, the reality of "omnipotent artificial intelligence" has already materialized in certain contexts within China today. This observation highlights the forward-thinking nature of PEP in addressing technological advancements and their impact on society.

Indeed, the compilation of PEP textbooks may be influenced by a closer alignment with the grand narratives espoused by the Chinese government. By reflecting these narratives, PEP textbooks contribute to the broader vision and goals set forth by the government for the development. Being located in Beijing, a highly modern and technologically advanced city, PEP textbooks may be more adapted to the rapid advancements in science, technology, and innovation. The content of PEP textbooks may incorporate these advancements to equip students with the necessary knowledge and skills to thrive in a technologically driven society. Similarly, Yilin textbooks may adopt a more tailored approach in line with the specific developmental needs of Jiangsu province, with Nanjing as its capital. These textbooks may focus on subjects and themes that are particularly relevant to the region. Those localized approaches ensure that the educational materials resonate with the students' experiences, cultural heritage, and regional context.

Furthermore, to provide an explanation for the similarities and differences observed among the different grade levels, it is necessary to reference the ECSCE once again. Since the ECSCE serves as the national curriculum guiding the compilation of both sets of textbooks, it plays a crucial role in shaping their content. The nature, basic concepts, and overall objective of ELT as outlined in the curriculum are relevant and applicable across all grade levels of compulsory education. Consequently, the general direction of compiling textbooks for each grade follows a similar path. The overarching aim of ELT at each grade level is to facilitate the gradual development of students' comprehensive language competence, while also nurturing their overall humanistic qualities. This shared goal leads to a certain degree of consistency across different grade levels. As a result, it becomes understandable why certain themes are embedded within each grade level and why these similarities tend to outweigh the differences. By adhering to the principles and objectives outlined in the ECSCE, the textbooks strive to provide a cohesive and coherent learning experience for students throughout their compulsory education. This alignment ensures a smooth progression in students' language learning journey while fostering the cultivation of their holistic qualities.

Nonetheless, it is important to acknowledge that students of different ages possess distinct learning needs and cognitive characteristics. Recognizing this, the curriculum further subdivides the general objective into several grading goals that are tailored to cater to the specific learning needs and cognitive abilities of students at different grade levels. Within the entire stage of compulsory education, there are five grading goals, with two grading goals specifically designed for the primary education phase. This systematic approach portrayed by the ECSCE highlights its comprehensive and progressive nature as an English curriculum system. It takes into account the cultivation of students' comprehensive language competence and holistic humanistic qualities as the overarching objective. Simultaneously, it places emphasis on understanding the developmental requirements of students, thereby breaking down the general objective into grading goals that are suitable for the different age groups of learners. This approach ensures that the curriculum addresses the specific linguistic, cognitive, and emotional development of students at each stage of their compulsory education. Through providing a well-structured and age-appropriate curriculum, the ECSCE supports the gradual and systematic growth of students' overall personal development.

Additionally, the curriculum suggests that "the compilation of English textbooks should fully reflect the characteristics of different age groups and follow the principle of gradual transition from easy to difficult as well as from simple to complex..." (MOE, 2011, p.40). Consequently, it is understandable that themes and subthemes are represented in varying degrees in each grade level, with the diversity of themes increasing as students advance through the grades. Notably, Grade 6 tends to encompass the most diversified range of themes and subthemes. This can be attributed to the fact that Grade 6 marks the end of primary education, and students are preparing to transition into junior high school. As a result, the textbooks for Grade 6 may exhibit a greater level of content diversity compared to other grade levels. They strive to engage students and provide them with a well-rounded understanding of the English language and its cultural contexts. Such diversity could further enrich students' learning experiences and prepares them for the challenges and expanded curriculum they will encounter in their future education.

Admittedly, when conducting a comparative analysis of these two series of textbook, as well as examining each grade individually, it becomes evident that there are certain differences present. These differences can be attributed to various factors such as the historical background and geographical position of the publishing houses, as well as the specific requirements outlined by the national curriculum for each grade level. However, it is important to note that despite these differences, the overall similarities between the textbooks outweigh the variations observed. This phenomenon can be attributed to the guiding influence of the grand narratives of the state that shape the compilation of these textbooks. The alignment with these grand narratives ensures a certain degree of coherence and consistency across the series. Additionally, it is worth highlighting that despite the differences, all of these textbooks adhere to the same national curriculum, known as the "One standard", through which students across the country could be equipped with a comparable level of knowledge and skills. This unified approach allows for a standardized education system that promotes equal opportunities and a consistent learning experience for all students, regardless of their geographical location or the series of textbooks they utilize. Then the discussion on the RQ 4 will be elaborated in the following section.

5.3   Discussion on RQ 4

In this section, the findings of RQ 4 will be summarized first, and the discussion on teachers' perceptions will be followed.

5.3.1   Summary of RQ 4

Teachers' perceptions were examined within the framework of three themes: teachers' awareness of GCE & metrolingualism in ELT, ELT implementation regarding GCE & metrolingualism, and challenges in ELT regarding GCE & metrolingualism. Overall, it was evident that teachers acknowledged GCE as a relatively new concept, which seemed disconnected from students' everyday lives. Furthermore, teachers generally lacked sufficient awareness of linguistic inclusiveness, often implicitly considering British or American English as the "standard template" for students' English language learning. In terms of critical multiculturalism education within ELT, teachers demonstrated a potential lack of critical awareness when it came to intercultural sensitivity. On the other hand, teachers emphasized their role in integrating GCE into ELT within the context of socialism with Chinese characteristics. However, it was observed that traditional SLA methods still took precedence in the implementation of GCE and metrolingualism in ELT. This was evident through the emphasis on linguistic knowledge and skills, prioritization of British or American English variety, and a focus on Anglophone cultures, while inadvertently neglecting other cultures and languages from around the world. Moreover, teachers expressed concerns that pose potential barriers to the successful implementation of GCE and metrolingualism in ELT. These concerns included the constraints of limited class time, the deeply rooted concept of exam-oriented education, implicit elitism associated with GCE, as well as the young age of primary school students. These challenges, among others, may hinder the effective integration of GCE and metrolingualism into ELT.

The subsequent subsection will delve into a detailed discussion of teachers' perceptions, providing further insights into how teachers perceive GCE and metrolingualism within the context of ELT.

5.3.2 Discussion on teachers' perceptions

To some extent, the findings from the interviews align with the analysis of ELT materials, indicating a prevailing focus on soft GCE in teaching practices. It also highlights the teachers' limited awareness regarding critical GCE and metrolingualism, which may hinder the realization of true inclusiveness in GCE within ELT. Teachers' reflections reveal that GCE was a relatively new concept to them, despite unanimous agreement on the importance of integrating GCE into ELT. However, it is noteworthy that the specific topics related to GCE mentioned by teachers mostly revolved around common values such as patriotism, family ethics, and civilized manners, while overlooking sensitive global issues. In light of this, there appears to be an urgent need to provide ELT educators with pre-service and in-service training on effectively integrating critical GCE into their teaching practices. This study serves to further emphasize the gap that exists between educational policies and teaching implementation in classrooms. It sheds light on the necessity of bridging this gap by providing teachers with the necessary tools and knowledge to effectively incorporate critical GCE into their ELT instruction. By addressing this discrepancy, educational policies can be translated into practical teaching strategies that foster a more comprehensive and inclusive understanding of GCE among students.

Additionally, teachers have identified several challenges in implementing GCE and metrolingualism within ELT, shedding light on the prevailing issue that, despite educational policies aimed at reducing academic burdens, the ELT implementation still adheres to certain stereotypical expectations in practice. Teachers find themselves overwhelmed by various realistic demands, leaving little time or energy to expand the teaching content beyond the confines of the textbooks, let alone delving into critical GCE and metrolingualism within ELT. Furthermore, teachers' ELT practice may easily elide the discussion of how global linguistic hierarchies regarding ELT benefit only elite groups (Guilherme, 2007). It is imperative to address this concern by promoting a locality-conscious, socially and ecologically just education within ELT. This approach advocates for the development of a shared global identity, an appreciation for diversity, and respect for differences, etc. (ibid.). Educators could foster a learning environment that goes beyond the limitations of traditional teaching methods through advocating for a more inclusive and socially aware approach to ELT, encouraging students to critically examine the existing global linguistic hierarchies in ELT and empowering them to challenge and reshape these hierarchies for a more equitable and inclusive world. It is through such an approach that ELT can contribute to the development of inclusive global citizens who are committed to making a positive impact within their communities and beyond.

The interview results further indicate that teachers primarily focus on fostering students' intercultural communicative competence by centering their attention on Chinese and Anglophone cultures, while considering other cultures as additions. Their understanding of cultural education appears to align with the traditional multicultural perspective, which tends to view cultures as fixed, essentialist, and predetermined (Gillispie, 2011). This perspective is concerned with the transmission of the cultural heritage of the dominant society through the fixed system of knowledge and the perpetuation of the existing social order (Banks & Banks, 2016). However, this approach may raise questions regarding whether students' competence to deal with intercultural encounters in real-life situations can truly be cultivated, since the sociolinguistic reality nowadays is that students are more likely to engage in dynamic cultural communications rather than adhering to fixed cultural norms. Thus, it is important to recognize the flexible nature of cultures and the need to equip students with the skills and understanding to navigate these dynamic cultural interactions. Through fostering a more adaptable approach to cultural education within ELT, teachers can better prepare students for the complexities of intercultural encounters in the real world, encouraging them to explore multiple perspectives and develop the necessary skills and competencies to deal with the diverse and ever-changing sociolinguistic landscape they will encounter.

Besides, it is important to note that certain adjectives used by teachers, such as "correct" or "standard", to describe students' English learning tend to be indexed the inner circle English variety associated with middle class educated, often white, people from the global north (Jakubiak, 2020), while ignoring the fact that the prescribed norms such as grammar may vary in real intercultural communications. In this light, teachers' perceptions indicate a conflict between the emphasis on cultivating students' critical GCE and metrolingual communication and the dominant ideology of native speakerism as well as their idealized cultural and linguistic models. This reflects a tendency for teachers to take East-West intercultural communications for granted in classroom practice and display biases towards specific linguistic varieties and speakers' ethnicity. This pedagogical approach fails to facilitate a systematic critique of the Westernized ideology that pervades ELT, which may perpetuate the hegemony of certain groups and marginalize disadvantaged groups (Gillispie, 2011). Consequently, there is a need to challenge these biases and encourage a more inclusive and equitable approach to ELT that embraces a broader range of linguistic varieties and cultural perspectives to make ELT more culturally and Englishes diversified.

One possible explanation for this observation could be attributed to the intercultural understanding presented in ELT materials, which often equate intercultural communication encounters with native-English speakers. The ELT curriculum positions English within the context of globalization, informatization, and the polarization of the world (MOE, 2011), which provides a comprehensive list of functional-notional "can do" items for linguistic and communicative competence, which are considered essential for learners to navigate in the modern world (Xiong & Yuan, 2018). It could be possibly interpreted that the competence-based curriculum primarily focuses on equipping learners with linguistic knowledge and skills necessary for basic survival functions in the mainstream target culture, rather than delving into issues of monolingualism or multilingualism (ibid.). The emphasis lies on developing learners' competence to master the target language and become familiar with the lifestyle and culture associated with it. However, this emphasis on a monolingual and homogeneous identity within the target language community may be more imagined than reflective of the diverse realities of language use and cultural interplay (ibid.). Therefore, it could be beneficial to expand the scope of intercultural understanding beyond a narrow Anglophone perspective. By incorporating a more inclusive and diverse range of cultural experiences and perspectives within ELT, students can develop a broader understanding of intercultural communication that reflects the complex realities of the interconnected world. This approach would pave the way for a more comprehensive and fluid exploration of linguistic diversity and intercultural interactions within ELT.

However, teachers just performed passive followers of ELT materials, similar to a previous study in a Thai context that highlighted teachers' limited understanding of the national curriculum and their lack of creative implementation (Vibulphol et al., 2021). Additionally, previous research indicated that GCE is a relatively new paradigm in the field of ELT (Basarir, 2017; Porto, 2018; Boonsuk & Fang, 2021), which aligns with the findings of this study, suggesting that teachers generally lack knowledge about integrating GCE into ELT. The insufficient levels of knowledge, skills, attitudes, and actions exhibited by teachers regarding GCE and metrolingual education are also consistent with Glasgow and Paller's (2016) perspective on English as a symbol, as well as teachers' limited critical awareness. To address these challenges and promote a more effective integration of GCE and metrolingual education within ELT, it is crucial to provide teachers with opportunities for professional development and support. By enhancing teachers' understanding and awareness of critical GCE, they can be better equipped to critically analyze and adapt teaching materials to foster intercultural competence and metrolingual awareness among students.

In line with previous research, the perceptions of teachers in this study reinforce the notion that English teachers have a responsibility to move beyond a purely technical approach focused on linguistic skills and integrate GCE into ELT (Roux, 2019). However, despite their general support for GCE, teachers still encountered difficulties and challenges in implementing GCE within ELT, echoing the findings of Lee and Leung's study in the Chinese context (2006). These challenges expressed by teachers further align with the disparities identified in education by Li (2021). The persistence of native speakerism ideology as the dominant force in the field of ELT (Fang & Baker, 2017) hampers the critical perspective of multicultural education and alternative goals and approaches of critical GCE and metrolingualism-oriented pedagogy from gaining wider acceptance. This situation is similar to the context in Thailand, where the use of English is deeply rooted in a colonial structure that upholds the political and economic hegemony of Anglophone powers, in which participants' opinions were riddled with linguistic biases regarding "standard" English as superior to "non-standard" varieties of English (Buripakdi, 2014). To address these challenges, it is crucial to promote a greater understanding and awareness of the importance of GCE and metrolingualism within ELT. This includes challenging and deconstructing the native speakerism ideology, promoting linguistic diversity and inclusivity, and empowering teachers to adopt critical pedagogical approaches that foster intercultural understanding and respect for all linguistic varieties to serve the diverse needs and contexts of English language learners worldwide.

Besides, Osler and Starkey (2003) pointed out that citizenship education in the age of globalization has a threefold important task: to help the young live together in increasingly diverse local communities, in national communities that demand social solidarity and stability, and in an increasingly interconnected and interdependent world. In order to achieve these goals, the deeply ingrained traditional SLA norms may need to be challenged through teachers going beyond linguistic issues to develop students' critical spirit and comprehension of cultural differences to promote the understanding among all human beings (Xiong & Yuan, 2018). Moreover, it is easily to overlook such a problem that there may be big cultural differences among seemingly similar groups (diversity within diversity), and such intra-group differences within a cultural group are often as great as or greater than inter-group differences (LeRoux, 2002). In light of this, teachers should adopt a dynamic and flexible perspective, teaching content that represents cultures of different inter-groups and intra-groups, as well as encouraging students to look at issues in different ways to understand the complex web of intercultural relationships in the world today. It is essential for teachers to design their courses that are relevant to students' real-life communication needs with a focus on practicality and applicability to students' daily lives (Vibulphol et al., 2021). Teachers play a pivotal role in equipping students with the skills, attitudes, and knowledge necessary to navigate a diverse and interconnected world, fostering understanding, empathy, and respect among individuals from different cultures.

Critical multicultural education may need to be incorporated into ELT classrooms to challenge the stereotypical linguistic and cultural ideologies, and make the invisible taken-for-granted privilege visible, as well as amplify the space for voices from periphery (Kubota, 2018). By adopting a critical multicultural education framework, teachers can actively engage students in questioning and critically examining dominant cultural narratives and power structures. Additionally, intercultural communicative competence is the forming of intercultural sensitivity into behavior, while teachers' perceptions toward cultural foci implementation manifest the initial stages of the developmental model of intercultural sensitivity (Bennett, 1986). To foster critical intercultural communicative competence, both teachers and students need to move away from monocultural and monolingual norms prevalent in ELT practices and focus on the communicative practices of multicultural and multilingual speakers (Syrbe & Rose, 2016). Through the adoption of critical pedagogy, teachers and students are encouraged to become more inclusive toward diverse cultures and develop the competence to understand and value perspectives that differ from their own. This pedagogical approach promotes ELT classrooms to become transformative spaces that empower students to engage in meaningful intercultural interactions and develop their intercultural communicative competence in an everyday multilingual and multicultural community.

Indeed, it is important to strike a balance and avoid extremes when implementing a compromised approach that incorporates both "soft" and "critical" perspectives in ELT classrooms. It is not about completely abandoning one approach in favor of the other but rather about raising awareness of the diverse reality in the world and fostering critical literacy among students. Considering the young age of primary students, it is essential to be mindful of their cognitive development and the appropriateness of certain critical and sensitive issues. Teachers should provide guidance and gradually introduce students to deeper levels of critical literacy as they progress to upper secondary levels. In this way, students can gradually develop their critical intercultural awareness in a developmentally appropriate manner, since the absence of criticality and cultural complexity may cause future problems and obstacles to intercultural understanding (Risager, 2018). If students miss opportunities to deepen their critical intercultural awareness and critical literacy, some stereotypes and biased worldviews embedded in ELT may be further perpetuated in the future.

Actually, previous research has demonstrated that primary school students are not too young to gain knowledge about and interest in political and social matters in the world, and they should also be cultivated with an open attitude at an early age (Risager, 2018; Byram, 2008). Additionally, UNESCO (2015) has recognized the significance of GCE for primary school students and has set specific learning objectives for this age group (refer to Appendix B for more details). Given these findings and guidelines, it becomes even more crucial for teachers to create a learning environment that encourages primary school students to question, analyze, and critically engage with the cultural representations and assumptions present in ELT, as well as to empower students to develop a deeper understanding of cultural diversity, challenge stereotypes, and develop a sense of global citizenship. Through providing experiences that foster critical engagement and intercultural understanding, teachers could contribute to the holistic development of primary school students, preparing them to be active and responsible global citizens who are aware of the cultural complexities and societal issues in the world around them.

To this end, the analysis of the findings demonstrates the limitations of the current ELT in cultivating global citizenship sensitivity among students. It suggests that a reflective and dynamic environment, rather than simply imparting discrete and static cultural facts, is needed. However, effectively implementing a curriculum that maximizes critical GCE and metrolingualism awareness while demonstrating its perceived values may be challenging for ELT instructors. In light of these challenges, the current study emphasizes the need to reconsider the existing English education approach. It calls for an educational paradigm that allows students to engage with diverse and emergent languages and cultures at both global and local scales. Such an approach will enable young citizens to actively participate in the mission of national rejuvenation and socialist modernization while also incorporating critical "glocal" elements, empowering them to become Chinese "glocal" citizens. This transformation in ELT will play a significant role in developing a deeper sense of global citizenship among students and equipping them to contribute meaningfully to the society.

5.4   Summary of the Chapter

This chapter focuses on the discussion of the findings. It begins with a discussion of the findings related to RQ 1, which explores GCE and metrolingualism in textbooks and curriculum. Following that, the discussion delves into RQ 2 and RQ 3, examining the similarities and differences between PEP and Yilin textbooks, as well as variations across different grade levels. Finally, the discussion ends with an exploration of the teachers' perceptions in response to RQ 4. In the subsequent chapter, a conclusion section will be presented to further address the insights gained from this study and provide implications for the field.

CHAPTER 6
CONCLUSION

This chapter will be expounded from three sections, which are the summary of the findings, implications, and limitations of this study as well as recommendations for future studies.

6.1 Summary of the Findings

By utilizing a qualitative approach, this study explored the representation of GCE and metrolingualism within PEP and Yilin textbooks, as well as the ECSCE. Qualitative content analysis framework (Schreier, 2012), Fairclough's three-dimensional framework of CDA (1995), and code preference analysis (Scollon & Scollon, 2003) were employed to analyze the data. Theoretical frameworks such as soft versus critical GCE (Andreotti, 2006) as well as Akkari and Maleq's framework (2020) for GCE were used to address GCE-related issues, while Pennycook and Otsuji's (2015a) conceptual framework for metrolingualism was adopted to study metrolingualism-related issues. Additionally, semi-structured interviews were conducted with six primary school English teachers who taught either PEP or Yilin textbooks across Grades 3 to 6. Each participant was interviewed for 30 to 50 minutes, resulting in a total of 246 minutes of interview data. The findings presented in this study aim to address the following research questions:

(1) In what ways do ELT textbooks and curriculum reflect the notions of GCE and metrolingualism for primary education in China?

(2) What are the similarities and differences of GCE and metrolingualism represented in ELT textbooks between PEP series and Yilin series for primary education in China?

(3) What are the similarities and differences of GCE and metrolingualism represented in ELT textbooks of different grade levels for primary education in China?

(4) What are teachers' perceptions toward GCE and metrolingualism in ELT textbooks and curriculum for primary education in China?

The findings of RQ 1 shed light on the presence of GCE within ELT textbooks. They also encompass the analysis of textbookscapes to explore metrolingualism in ELT textbooks, as well as the examination of GCE and metrolingualism embedded in the curriculum. These findings reveal a predominant emphasis on soft GCE and a scarcity of critical GCE within the textbooks and curriculum. This is evident through the incorporation of numerous salient themes and subthemes aligned with soft GCE perspectives. In total, there are 16 themes and 20 subthemes related to GCE identified across all textbooks, with a cumulative occurrence of 770 instances. Among these, the most salient GCE domain is inter/multicultural education, followed by emerging themes, education for sustainable development, and citizenship education. Salient themes and subthemes include Anglophone cultures (107), Chinese cultures (91), kinship (59), native-speakerism prestige & supremacy (55), Chinese geography (46), leisure lifestyle (44), Chinese educational principles (41), etc.

Following that, a comprehensive analysis of textbookscapes was conducted to explore the representation of metrolingualism, encompassing both LLs and MIs, within the textbooks. The findings were categorized into five themes, each shedding light on different aspects. These themes include English supremacy in LLs, antithesis of English supremacy in LLs, exclusivism in LLs, native-speakerism standard in MIs, and cultural diversities in MIs. The findings further confirm the GCE-related results, highlighting that English remains the most prevalent and preferred code within the ELT materials. English code not only serves as an informative tool within the LLs but also perpetuates a sense of monolingualism supremacy in textbookscapes while ignoring other "Englishes". Additionally, Anglophone cultures are prominently featured in MIs, while cultural elements from the outer and expanding circles are noticeably absent from the overall portrayal. These findings emphasize the need for a more inclusive and dynamic approach that encompasses a wider range of linguistic and cultural diversities.

Regarding the examination of GCE and metrolingualism embedded in the curriculum, the findings were categorized into eight themes, namely global awareness, national awareness, cultural education, ideological and moral education, quality-oriented education, native-speakerism norms, linguistic foci, and daily life-oriented resources. Notwithstanding the curriculum emphasizes the importance of cultivating students' global awareness, the specific strategies and content for fostering this awareness may benefit from further clarity. In particular, the foreign cultural education embedded in the curriculum, which predominantly focuses on English-speaking countries, could benefit from a more critical multiculturalism pedagogy that embraces diverse perspectives. Furthermore, the curriculum also addresses ideological and moral education as well as quality-oriented education to develop civic virtues and morality among students within the framework of Chinese socialism. Moreover, it is worth noting that the native-speakerism norms inherent in the curriculum encourage students to learn English through emulating the "native" English, which may warrant a more inclusive approach that acknowledges the legitimacy of various English varieties and speakers. Lastly, the curriculum also highlights the importance of utilizing daily life-oriented resources for English language instruction. These findings could provide opportunities for reflection and potential enhancements to further promote GCE and metrolingualism within ELT.

The findings derived from RQ 2 and RQ 3 shed light on the similarities and differences pertaining to GCE and metrolingualism between PEP and Yilin textbooks, as well as across different grade levels. In general, the similarities between these textbooks outweigh the differences in terms of the salient GCE themes. These similarities can largely be attributed to the implementation "One standard for multiple series of textbooks" (一纲多本) and the grand narratives within the discursive field of China. Nevertheless, there are still some differences between PEP and Yilin textbook series, which are closely intertwined with the historical backgrounds and geographical positions of the respective publishing houses. The long-standing history of PEP series may give rise to a coexistence of Chinese traditional ideas and modern trends within its textbooks. Moreover, being based in Beijing and serving as a leading educational press in China, PEP textbooks may align more closely with the grand narratives and reflect the development of Beijing. Similarly, Yilin textbooks may be tailored to suit the specific context of Jiangsu province, with Nanjing as its capital. These contextual factors may contribute to the inclusion of more diverse themes within PEP textbooks. These insights highlight the nuanced variations between PEP and Yilin textbooks, stemming from their historical, geographical, and institutional contexts. Understanding these differences can facilitate a more comprehensive analysis of the GCE and metrolingualism embedded in these materials, and provide insights for ELT practices.

Moreover, the findings reveal that GCE themes and subthemes are incorporated into each grade level to varying degrees, and the diversity of these themes tends to increase as students progress to higher grades. Similarly, the diversity of codes within the LLs also expands with higher grade levels. However, it is important to note that native-speakerism standard and Anglophone cultures remain dominant across all grade levels. Recognizing that students of different ages possess distinct learning needs and cognitive characteristics; the curriculum takes this into account by breaking down the general objectives into specific grading goals. These grading goals are designed to align with the learning needs and cognitive characteristics of students at different grade levels. This differentiation in objectives may contribute to some variations observed among textbooks from different grades. By tailoring the curriculum to the specific requirements of students at different stages of their education, it seeks to provide a more targeted and effective learning experience. This approach acknowledges the importance of considering students' developmental stages and individual capacities, ultimately aiming to enhance the effectiveness of GCE and metrolingualism instruction within the ELT context.

The findings from RQ 4 primarily revolve around teachers' perceptions toward GCE and metrolingualism embedded in ELT materials, providing qualitative data that serves to reaffirm and elucidate the earlier analysis of textbooks and curriculum. These findings can be categorized into three main themes, namely, teachers' awareness of GCE and metrolingualism in ELT, ELT implementation regarding GCE and metrolingualism, and challenges in ELT regarding GCE and metrolingualism. In general, the findings indicate that GCE is a relatively new concept for the majority of teachers, and they perceive it as somewhat disconnected from students' daily lives. Furthermore, teachers generally exhibit a lack of awareness regarding linguistic inclusiveness, often tacitly considering British or American English as the "standard template". Consequently, the deeply entrenched native-speakerism ideology within ELT remains largely unchallenged in practice.

Despite professing their commitment to promoting Chinese GCE in ELT, teachers still tend to prioritize traditional SLA approaches. A concerning observation is that teachers often play a passive role as mere followers of prescribed teaching materials, lacking a profound and critical understanding of ELT and, by extension, inhibiting creative implementation. Additionally, some of the concerns expressed by teachers serve as obstacles to the effective implementation of GCE and metrolingualism within ELT. To some extent, the interview results align with the earlier analysis of ELT materials, highlighting the predominance of a soft approach of GCE in teaching practices. The limited awareness among teachers regarding critical GCE and metrolingualism poses a potential hindrance to achieving the real inclusivity in GCE within ELT. Therefore, it is important to recognize the complexities and the need for further professional development and support for teachers as well as enhance the potential for inclusive and transformative ELT practices through fostering a deeper understanding and encouraging critical engagement with GCE and metrolingualism.

The argument of this study, to some extent, echoes the grand narratives prevalent in the discursive field of China. These narratives encompass various dimensions, including social development, politics, economy, and culture, which provide a strong foundation for Chinese education to align with national planning. The primary objective is to cultivate and nurture the younger generation, empowering them to take on significant roles in achieving national rejuvenation. By integrating these grand narratives into the educational system, Chinese education demonstrates a remarkable commitment to the progress and revitalization of the nation. The teaching materials are designed to impart knowledge and skills that align with the broader goals and aspirations of the Chinese Dream. This holistic approach aims to instill a sense of purpose and responsibility in students, equipping them to contribute to the collective vision of a rejuvenated China. It is crucial to continuously refine the implementation of GCE and metrolingualism themes in ELT materials to foster a greater understanding and appreciation of different cultures and languages, and to empower students with the necessary skills to thrive in an interconnected world.

Furthermore, it is important to recognize that, in reality, teachers and students may encounter certain limitations and constraints that could impede the full development of critical GCE. These constraints may restrict the extent to which critical GCE can be fully realized. By acknowledging this, the potential gap that may exist between educational policies and their implementation in the classroom can be better understood. It is worth considering the possibility that there may exist areas for improvement in teachers' knowledge, skills, attitudes, and practices related to GCE and metrolingual education within the field of ELT. This raises a significant need to provide ELT teachers with comprehensive and ongoing professional development opportunities, both during their initial training and throughout their careers, to effectively integrate critical GCE and metrolingual pedagogy into their teaching practices. By providing teachers with the necessary support, resources, and training, an environment can be fostered to encourage the integration of critical GCE and metrolingual education within the ELT. This will enable teachers and students to navigate the complexities of a globalized world with increased cultural sensitivity and a broader understanding of diverse perspectives.

On the other hand, it is noteworthy that the GCE learning objectives for primary level education primarily focus on descriptive, identifying, recognizing, and understanding aspects of GCE-related topics. Given this emphasis, it is understandable that soft GCE themes embedded in ELT materials serve to provide primary school students with a nascent global citizenship sentiment. It is important to recognize that the development of critical GCE thinking, which becomes more prominent at the upper secondary level, is a gradual process that builds upon the foundation established during primary education. Furthermore, it is essential to acknowledge that primary school students are not too young to acquire knowledge about and gain interest in political and social matters around the world (Risager, 2018; Byram, 2008). They should be encouraged to cultivate an open attitude towards diverse perspectives. With this in mind, the aim of this study is to raise awareness among stakeholders about the diverse realities surrounding GCE. It is crucial to recognize that the absence of criticality and cultural diversity may potentially create future challenges and barriers to fostering intercultural understanding. Highlighting these concerns, this study seeks to foster an ELT that embraces criticality and cultural diversity, aiming to effectively address these potential issues and promote a more inclusive and globally aware mindset among learners.

To this end, this study suggests that teachers and students may benefit from greater opportunities to cultivate their critical literacy and assume the roles of consumers and creators of ELT materials. By doing so, they can enhance their global citizenship sensitivity and foster a critical multicultural mindset. This is essential for students to navigate and adapt to an everyday multilingual and multicultural community. Moreover, it encourages them to question the prevailing native speakerism and Anglophone cultures that embedded in ELT. By challenging these prevailing norms, students can actively engage with diverse and emerging linguistic and cultural phenomena on both global and local scales. This inclusive approach not only accommodates students' participation but also promotes the development of Chinese "glocal" citizens who are capable of navigating the complexities during the "glocalization". It is crucial to create an educational landscape that encourages students to embrace linguistic and cultural diversities while nurturing their competence to thrive in an increasingly interconnected and diverse world.

6.2　Implications

This study addressed the issues of GCE and metrolingualism in primary ELT textbooks and curriculum in the context of China through the new lens of soft vs. critical GCE. The findings may bear some theoretical and pedagogical as well as methodological implications.

Theoretically, this study explored the GCE and metrolingualism embedded in ELT textbooks and curriculum for primary education in China, the findings of which may have the potential to contribute to the expansion of the relevant theories of GCE in a nation-state and the feasibility of interdisciplinary implementation particularly at the initial stages of education. Additionally, it may also further extend the theoretical discourse of metrolingualism and "globalization from below", etc. Besides, this study could provide a new perspective on the integration of GCE and metrolingualism within ELT theory, laying a solid theoretical foundation for future research on critical multicultural education, intercultural sensitivity, everyday multilingualism, etc. Additionally, the introduction of some terms in this study, such as "glocal" citizenship, global citizenship sensitivity, may expand the theoretical terminology of GCE to some extent as well, enriching the understanding of these concepts. Moreover, the models proposed in this study may have theoretical implications for future research that aims to further explore the synergies between GCE and metrolingualism in ELT. To a certain extent, the findings of this study may contribute to the formulation of Chinese education policies, curriculum compilation, and textbook development, etc.

To be specific, it is worth noting that certain GCE themes have been identified in Chinese ELT textbooks and curriculum, indicating that GCE has been subtly incorporated into these materials even before the official UNESCO documents were published. However, it is important to acknowledge that this embedding may predominantly lean towards a "soft" orientation. Furthermore, this study introduces the concept of "textbookscapes" as a new kind of semiotic assemblage to better understand diverse semiotic resources in textbooks from a metrolingualism perspective. This concept offers an alternative lens through which to investigate metrolingualism-related issues in future studies, contributing to a deeper comprehension of this phenomenon. In terms of textbook compilation, this study conducts a comparative analysis between PEP and Yilin textbook series concerning GCE and metrolingualism. It is noteworthy that these two series of textbooks possess distinct strengths that can be mutually beneficial. By drawing upon each other's strengths, future textbook compilations can enhance the integration of GCE and metrolingualism, providing a more comprehensive and enriched learning experience for students.

Pedagogically, the findings of this study offer a foundation for further research and a growing understanding of how ELT can contribute to China's context-specific GCE and metrolingualism endeavors during the process of "glocalization". Building upon these findings, there are implications for education policy makers, ELT material designers, as well as English language teachers. Education policy makers could benefit from the findings by placing greater emphasis on fostering the development of critical GCE and implementing GCE as well as metrolingualism oriented ELT reforms, contributing to a more comprehensive and inclusive ELT. ELT material designers could consciously enhance the representation of linguistic and cultural diversities within teaching materials to make students be exposed to a broader range of perspectives and experiences, promoting intercultural understanding and appreciation. English language teachers, with a critical awareness of the GCE and metrolingualism embedded within ELT, play a crucial role in implementing these principles in the classroom. They can foster an inclusive worldview among students by encouraging them to critically engage with GCE themes and metrolingual practices. Additionally, teachers should strive to promote students' understanding and participation in a diverse society both locally and globally.

Besides, the GCE themes explored in this study can encourage teachers to pay more attention to the development of students' global citizenship in ELT. The critical analysis of these GCE and metrolingualism themes can also arouse teachers' critical awareness and reflection on their teaching practices, prompting them to make ELT more inclusive. Teachers may need to make necessary adjustments in terms of the incorporation of GCE content in their future teaching endeavors. The GCE guidance structure and learning objectives outlined by age/level of education in UNESCO's documents can provide general guidance for teachers in their instructional planning. Additionally, the comparative analysis of PEP and Yilin textbook series in this study may offer implications for textbook selection in different educational settings. Each series has its own focus and local considerations, so educators should broaden their perspectives and consider the merits of each series when making textbook choices. Moreover, the analysis of teachers' perceptions in this study sheds light on their actual implementation of GCE within ELT. This could provide insights for educators to reexamine the focus of teacher training programs, equipping teachers with the necessary knowledge and skills to effectively integrate GCE principles into their teaching practices.

However, it is important to note that metrolingualism primarily focuses on the languages within specific metrolingual communities. It is worth mentioning that this study primarily examines the portrayal of metrolingualism in ELT materials rather than authentic metrolingualism observed in cities. As a result, the pedagogical implications associated with metrolingualism, particularly in terms of specific types of linguistic diversity, may not be universally applicable to all communities in China. It is acknowledged that the concept of metrolingualism can be effectively integrated into education in certain locations; however, its relevance may vary for English learners in different contexts. In any case, the goal of this study is to raise awareness among stakeholders regarding the diverse realities present in the world, rather than suggesting that stakeholders should replicate the same form of metrolingualism in ELT. In this regard, the study provides an additional implication for future research to explore metrolingualism from various perspectives.

Methodologically, this study delved into the exploration of GCE and metrolingualism by examining textbooks, curriculum, and conducting interviews with teachers. The comprehensive explanation of the data collection and analysis procedures outlined in Chapter 3 holds implications for future research in this field. The coding frames developed in this study regarding GCE and metrolingualism can serve as a reference for future investigations. Furthermore, the guide for conducting semi-structured interviews can offer guidance for researchers in collecting data for future related studies. Of particular significance, the qualitative approach adopted in this study's design presents another implication for future research concerning the analysis of ELT materials in relation to GCE and metrolingualism. This approach offers an understanding of the subject matter and allows for a deeper exploration of the nuances and complexities inherent in GCE and metrolingualism within educational materials.

Last but not least, it is crucial to acknowledge that GCE cannot be approached with a one-size-fits-all mentality. Instead of imposing any foreign and rigid terminology, it may be more prudent to emphasize local engagement with the core values of global citizenship (Davidson & Liu, 2018). The traditional SLA embedded in ELT may require innovation to enable teachers and students to enhance their critical literacy pertaining to both external and internal diversities, while fostering Chinese "glocal" citizenship education. Refining ELT materials under the context of "glocalization" to make them more culturally and Englishes diversified may be the initial step to address the issue of the inclusive development of Chinese GCE. However, it is equally important to consider how teachers and learners critically utilize these materials to integrate their own language ideologies, cultural identities, and local language practices. This will enable them to decode and encode additional local and global ELT content, thereby further enhancing the inclusive nature of Chinese GCE.

6.3 Limitations and Recommendations

This study primarily focuses on the analysis of ELT materials, which involves the examination of representation and the deconstruction of ideologies. However, it is important to acknowledge that this study is very much exploratory, and there are some limitations that should be recognized. Firstly, the study only included ELT materials for primary education in China, making it challenging to generalize the findings to other contexts. Secondly, the examination of selected textbooks and curriculum restricts the ability to analyze the data diachronically over time. Thirdly, the study solely focuses on national textbooks and curriculum, without considering school-based textbooks and curriculums, limiting the exploration of specific local situations. Fourthly, the analysis of GCE and metrolingualism within textbooks and curriculum primarily adopts a macro perspective, potentially excluding certain micro-level details. Fifthly, the analysis of textbooks only considers textual and visual content, without including corresponding audio content, which may result in incomplete representation of the data. Lastly, it is important to note that the interview analysis relies on teachers' self-reported stories, which may not fully reflect their actual behaviors.

Considering the aforementioned limitations of this study, it is essential to provide recommendations for future research. These recommendations aim to enhance the scope and depth of analysis in the field of ELT. Firstly, future studies maybe more prudent to consider examining different educational levels and contexts to provide a more comprehensive understanding. This would enable researchers to explore the nuances and variations of GCE and metrolingualism across diverse educational settings. Secondly, conducting diachronic studies would be valuable in analyzing the longitudinal changes of GCE and metrolingualism within textbooks and curriculum. This approach would shed light on the evolution of these concepts over time. Thirdly, it is recommended that future research explores school-based textbooks and curriculums in addition to national materials. This would facilitate comparative analysis between different types of educational resources and provide a broader perspective on GCE and metrolingualism. Fourthly, researchers may consider employing other tools for micro-analysis of ELT materials, such as critical micro-semiotic analysis. This approach would allow for a more detailed examination of the subtle meanings embedded within the materials. Fifthly, future studies could also focus on analyzing GCE and metrolingualism within ELT audio-visual materials using multimodal discourse analysis. Furthermore, exploring the functions of tones and image-text relations in textbooks can provide valuable insights. Sixthly, it is recommended that future research includes the perspectives and stories of materials developers and other stakeholders. This would provide a more comprehensive and diverse range of data and viewpoints. Lastly, if feasible, observing real ELT classes would be beneficial to explore the actual behaviors of teachers and students in ELT practice. This would provide valuable insights into the implementation and impact of GCE and metrolingualism in real-world educational settings.

Despite the inevitable limitations of this study, it remains groundbreaking in terms of the new perspectives it offers and the sociocultural context it explores. It has laid a certain foundation for future studies in this field, providing valuable insights and opening up avenues for further research. While acknowledging the study's limitations, it is important to recognize the significance of its contributions. The study has introduced new perspectives and shed light on the intersection of GCE and metrolingualism within ELT. This approach has the potential to inspire future researchers to delve deeper into this field and explore additional dimensions. To some extent, this study has created a platform for researchers to build upon, allowing for the expansion and refinement of knowledge in this area.

Finally, it is necessary to mention that in light of the rapid advancement of science and technology, which constantly changes people's ways of living, learning, and working, posing new challenges to talent cultivation (MOE, 2022), the Chinese MOE issued the new edition of the ECSCE in 2022. Both the 2011 and 2022 editions of the ECSCE have provided comprehensive guidelines and a strategic framework for compulsory ELT over the past decade and for the future. It is worth noting that this study was conducted prior to the release of the 2022 edition of the ECSCE; therefore, the data utilized primarily originates from the 2011 edition. Nonetheless, subtle changes between the two editions offer invaluable insights for future diachronic research. The new curriculum exhibits an increased focus on global cultural education, demonstrating a greater variety of diverse, specific, and profound cultures from around the world. It places a growing emphasis on fostering cultural inclusivity in light of the impact of GCE. Notably, the new curriculum transcends an Anglophone cultural orientation and embraces a broader spectrum of global cultures, without singling out English-speaking countries. Furthermore, this shift is evident in the curriculum's emphasis on transcultural education and the cultivation of students' communicative competence within a multicultural world. It delves deeper into unraveling the intricacies of cultural interactions during transcultural communications. Moreover, cultivating students' sense of Community with a Shared Future for Mankind holds considerable prominence in the new curriculum. The explicit objective of nurturing students' global awareness and competence aligns harmoniously with the pursuit of global endeavors in the process of Chinese modernization. In light of this, future research can delve deeper into the study of the new ECSCE.

REFERENCES

[1] 白新杰. 我国少数民族语言濒危现象的生态学思考[J]. 广西民族研究, 2020, 156 (6)：128-135.

[2] 崔军, 汪霞. 塑造世界公民：麻省理工学院教育全球化的理念与策略[J]. 中国大学教学, 2010, (11)：91-93.

[3] 丁石庆. 论中国少数民族语言资源保护可持续精进路径[J]. 中央民族大学学报(哲学社会科学版), 2020, 47 (6)：167-173.

[4] 冯建军. 公民身份认同与学校公民教育[M]. 北京：人民出版社, 2014.

[5] 付宏. 从国家公民到世界公民：美国公民教育目标的转向[D]. 武汉：华中师范大学, 2011.

[6] 姜元涛. 世界公民教育思想研究[M]. 北京：科学出版社, 2015.

[7] 梁漱溟. 东西文化及其哲学[M]. 北京：商务印书馆, 2010.

[8] 芦雷. 美国"世界公民"教育的实施途径[J]. 教学与管理, 2010 (12)：77-80.

[9] 钱穆. 文化与教育[M]. 桂林：广西师范大学出版社, 2004.

[10] 宋强. 世界公民教育思潮研究[M]. 北京：中国社会科学出版社, 2018a.

[11] 宋强. 新时代"人类命运共同体"理念引领世界公民教育思潮的理路[J]. 教育学报, 2018b, 14 (3)：28-34.

[12] 肖礼全. 论中国英语教育的发展趋势[J]. 基础英语教育, 2006, 8 (6)：3-10.

[13] 杨婕. 义务教育阶段学校公民教育课程建构研究[D]. 大连：辽宁师范大学, 2016.

[14] 杨雪. 走向"世界公民"——论作为世界公民教育的外语教育[D]. 长春：东北师范大学, 2017.

[15] 张超. 加拿大中小学全球公民教育课程研究[D]. 哈尔滨：哈尔滨师范大学, 2020.

［16］钟启泉. 一纲多本：教育民主的诉求——我国教科书政策述评［J］. 教育发展研究，2009，4：1-6.

［17］Acar-Ciftci, Y. Critical multicultural education competencies scale: A scale development study[J]. *Journal of Education and Learning*, 2016, *5*(3): 51-63.

［18］Adler, N. J. *International Dimensions of Organizational Behavior*[M]. Mason: Thompson, 2008.

［19］Ahmad, M., & Shah, S. K. A critical discourse analysis of gender representations in the content of 5th grade English language textbook[J]. *International and Multidisciplinary Journal of Social Sciences*, 2019, *8*(1): 1-24.

［20］Ait-Bouzid, H. Exploring global citizenship as a cross-curricular theme in Moroccan ELT textbooks[J]. *Eurasian Journal of Applied Linguistics*, 2020, *6*(2): 229-242.

［21］Akkari, A., & Maleq, K. Rethinking global citizenship education: A critical perspective[M]// Akkari, A., & Maleq, K. (Eds.). *Global Citizenship Education: Critical and International Perspectives*. Bern: Springer, 2020: 205-217.

［22］Aktas, F., Pitts, K., Richards, J. C., & Silova, I. Institutionalizing global citizenship: A critical analysis of higher education programs and curricula[J]. *Journal of Studies in International Education*, 2016, *26*(1): 1-16.

［23］Alexander, J. *The Meanings of Social Life: A Cultural Sociology*[M]. Oxford: Oxford University Press, 2003.

［24］Almazova, N. I., Kostina, E. A., & Khalyapina, L. P. The new position of foreign language as education for global citizenship[J]. *Novosibirsk State Pedagogical University Bulletin*, 2016, *6*(4): 7-17.

［25］Amerian, M., & Esmaili, F. Language and gender: A critical discourse analysis on gender representation in a series of international ELT textbooks[J]. *International Journal of Research Studies in Education*, 2015, *4*(2): 3-12.

［26］Andreotti, V. Soft vs. critical global citizenship education[J]. *Policy and Practice: A Development Education Review*, 2006(3): 40-51.

［27］Andreotti, V., & Souza, L. (Towards) global citizenship education "otherwise" [M]// Andreotti, V., & Souza, L. (Eds.). *Postcolonial Perspectives on Global Citizenship Education*. New York and London: Routledge, 2012: 1-6.

［28］APCEIU. *Reconciliation, Peace and Global Citizenship Education: Pedagogy and Practice*[M]. Seoul: APCEIU, 2019.

［29］Appadurai, A. Grassroots globalization and the research imagination[M]// Appadurai, A. (Ed.). *Globalization*. Durham: Duke University Press, 2001: 1-21.

[30] Apple, M. W. *Official Knowledge: Democratic Knowledge in a Conservative Age (3rd ed.)*[M]. New York: Routledge, 2014.

[31] Arbak, Y. Dominant values of Turkish organizations: A contradictory phenomenon[J]. *Review of Social, Economic & Business Studies*, 2005, *5*(6): 69-88.

[32] Arnaut, K. Superdiversity: Elements of an emerging perspective[M]// Arnaut, K., Blommaert, J., Rampton, B., & Spotti, M. (Eds.). *Language and Superdiversity*. New York: Routledge, 2016: 49-70.

[33] Babaii, E, & Sheikhi, M. Traces of neoliberalism in English teaching materials: A critical discourse analysis[J]. *Critical Discourse Studies*, 2017, DOI: 10.1080/17405904.2017.1398671

[34] Baker, W. The cultures of English as a lingua franca[J]. *TESOL Quarterly*, 2009, *43*(4): 567-592.

[35] Baker, W. From cultural awareness to intercultural awareness: Culture in ELT[J]. *ELT Journal*, 2012, *66*(1): 62-70.

[36] Baker, W., & Fang, F. *From English Language Learners to Intercultural Citizens: Chinese Student Sojourners' Development of Intercultural Citizenship in ELT and EMI Programmes*[M]. London: British Council, 2019.

[37] Banks, J. A. Teaching for social justice, diversity, and citizenship in a global world[J]. *The Educational Forum*, 2004, *68*(4): 296-305.

[38] Banks, J. A., & Banks, C. A. M. *Multicultural Education: Issues and Perspectives (9th Edition)*[M]. Hoboken: Wiley, 2016.

[39] Basarir, F. Examining the perceptions of English instructors regarding the incorporation of global citizenship education into ELT[J]. *International Journal of Languages' Education and Teaching*, 2017, *5*(4): 409-425.

[40] Beacco, J., & Byram, M. *From Linguistic Diversity to Plurilingual Education: Guide for the Development of Language Education Policies in Europe (Main Version)*[M]. Strasbourg: Council of Europe, 2007.

[41] Bellamy, R. Citizenship beyond the nation state: The case of Europe[M]// O'Sullivan, N. (Ed.). *Political Theory in Transition*. London: Routledge, 2000: 91-112.

[42] Bennett, M. J. A developmental approach to training for intercultural sensitivity[J]. *International Journal of Intercultural Relations*, 1986(10): 179-196.

[43] Bennett, M. J. Developmental model of intercultural sensitivity[M]// Kim, Y. Y., & Semmler, K. L. M. (Eds.). *International Encyclopedia of Intercultural Communication*. Hoboken: John Wiley & Sons, 2017: 1-10.

［44］Ben-Rafael, E., Shohamy, E., Amara, M. H., & Trumper-Hecht, N. Linguistic landscape as symbolic construction of the public space: The case of Israel[J]. *International Journal of Multilingualism*, 2006, *3*(1): 7-30.

［45］Blackwood, R. J., Lanza, E., & Woldemariam, H. *Negotiating and Contesting Identities in Linguistic Landscapes*[M]. London: Bloomsbury Publishing, 2016.

［46］Block, D. Niche lingua francas: An ignored phenomenon[J]. *TESOL Quarterly*, 2007, *41*(3): 561-566.

［47］Block, D. Language education and globalization[M]// May, S., & Hornberger, N. H. (Eds.). *Encyclopedia of Language and Education, 2nd Edition, Volume 1: Language Policy and Political Issues in Education*. Bern: Springer, 2008: 31-43.

［48］Bodis, A. Integrating intercultural competence in course curricula in a tailored way[J]. *English Australia Journal*, 2020, *36*(1): 26-38.

［49］Boonsuk, Y., & Fang, F. Re-envisaging English medium instruction, intercultural citizenship development, and higher education in the context of studying abroad[J]. *Language and Education*, 2021, DOI:10.1080/09500782.2 021.1996595.

［50］Botha, W. English-medium instruction at a university in Macau: Policy and realities[J]. *World Englishes*, 2013, *32*(4): 461-475.

［51］Botha, W. English in China's universities today[J]. *English Today*, 2014, *30*(1): 3-10.

［52］Brown, C. W., & Habegger-Conti, J. Visual representations of indigenous cultures in Norwegian EFL textbooks[J]. *Nordic Journal of Modern Language Methodology*, 2017, *5*(1): 16-34.

［53］Brownlie, A. *Citizenship Education: The Global Dimension, Guidance for Key Stages 3 and 4*[M]. London: Development Education Association, 2001.

［54］Bryman, A. *The Disneyization of Society*[M]. London: SAGE, 2004.

［55］Buripakdi, A. Hegemonic English, standard Thai, and narratives of the subaltern in Thailand[M]// Liamputtong, P. (Ed.). *Contemporary Socio-Cultural and Political Perspectives in Thailand*. Dordrecht: Springer, 2014: 95-109.

［56］Byram, M. *Teaching and Assessing Intercultural Communicative Competence*[M]. Clevedon: Multilingual Matters, 1997.

［57］Byram, M. *From Foreign Language Education to Education for Intercultural Citizenship: Essays and Reflections*[M]. Britain: Cromwell Press, 2008.

［58］Byram, M., & Parmenter, L. Global citizenship[M]// Bennett, J. (Ed.). *The*

SAGE Encyclopedia of Intercultural Competence. Thousand Oaks: SAGE Publications, 2015: 347–350.

[59] Byram, M., Golubeva, I., Han, H., & Wagner, M. *From Principles to Practice in Education for Intercultural Citizenship*[M]. Bristol: Multilingual Matters, 2017.

[60] Calle Díaz, L. Citizenship education and the EFL standards: A critical reflection[J]. *Profile Issues in Teachers' Professional Development*, 2017, *19*(1): 155-168.

[61] Canagarajah, S. *Translingual Practice: Global Englishes and Cosmopolitan Relations*[M]. London: Routledge, 2013.

[62] Cao, Z. The idea and practice of language resources protection of China[J]. *Applied Linguistics*, 2019(4): 8-14.

[63] Caruana, V. Re-thinking global citizenship in higher education: From cosmopolitanism and international mobility to cosmopolitanism, resilience and resilient thinking[J]. *Higher Education Quarterly*, 2014(68): 85-104.

[64] Cavanagh, C. *The Role of English in Internationalisation and Global Citizenship Identity in South Korean Higher Education*[D]. Southampton: The University of Southampton, 2017.

[65] Cavanagh, C. The role of English in global citizenship[J]. *Journal of Global Citizenship & Equity Education*, 2020, *7*(1): 1-23.

[66] Cenoz, J., & Gorter, D. The linguistic landscape as an additional source of input in second language acquisition[J]. *IRAL*, 2008(46): 267-287.

[67] Chalak, A., & Ghasemi, B. A critical discourse analysis of four advanced ELT textbooks based on Fairclough's framework[J]. *Journal of Research in Applied Linguistics*, 2017, *8* (Special issue): 60-66.

[68] Chen, G. M., & Starosta, W. J. A review of the concept of intercultural sensitivity[J]. *Human Communication*, 1997(1): 1-16.

[69] Chen, G. M. The impact of intercultural sensitivity on ethnocentrism and intercultural communication apprehension[J]. *Intercultural Communication Studies*, 2010, *XIX*(1): 1-9.

[70] Chen, S. Advancing global citizenship education in Japan and China: An exploration and comparison of the national curricula[J]. *Citizenship Teaching and Learning*, 2020, *15*(3): 341-356.

[71] Choi, Y., & Kim, Y. Deconstructing neoliberalism in global citizenship discourses: An analysis of Korean social studies textbooks[J]. *Critical Studies in Education*, 2018, DOI: 10.1080/17508487.2018.1501718

[72] Chu, Y. Constructing *minzu*: The representation of *minzu* and *Zhonghua Minzu*

in Chinese elementary textbooks[J]. *Discourse: Studies in the Cultural Politics of Education*, 2018, *39*(6): 941-953.

[73] Cohen, L., Manion, L., & Morrison, K. *Research Methods in Education*[M]. London: Routledge, 2007.

[74] Cortazi, M., & Jin, L. Cultural mirrors: Materials and methods in the EFL classroom[M]// Hinkel, E. (Ed.). *Culture in Second Language Teaching*. Cambridge: Cambridge University Press, 1999: 196-219.

[75] Daghigh, A. J., Jan, J. M., & Kaur, S. Consumerism in Malaysian locally developed ELT textbooks[M]// Daghigh, A. J., Jan, J. M., & Kaur, S. (Eds.). *Neoliberalization of English: Language Policy in the Global South*. Bern: Springer, 2022: 137-150.

[76] Damiani, V. Introducing global citizenship education into classroom practice: A study on Italian 8th grade students[J]. *Center for Educational Policy Studies Journal*, 2018, *8*(3): 165-186.

[77] Davidson, R., & Liu, Y. Reaching the world outside cultural representation and perceptions of global citizenship in Japanese elementary school English textbooks[J]. *Language, Culture and Curriculum*, 2018, DOI: 10.1080/07908318.2018.1560460

[78] Davies, I., Ho, L. -C., Kiwan, D., Peck, C. L., Peterson, A., Sant, E., & Waghid, Y. *The Palgrave Handbook of Global Citizenship and Education*[M]. London: Palgrave Macmillan, 2018.

[79] Deardorff, D. K. Identification and assessment of intercultural competence as a student outcome of internationalization[J]. *Journal of Studies in International Education*, 2006, *10*(3): 241-266.

[80] Deardorff, D. K. *Promoting Understanding and Development of Intercultural Dialogue and Peace: A Comparative Analysis and Global Perspective of Regional Studies on Intercultural Competence*[M]. Report prepared for UNESCO Division of Cultural Policies and Intercultural Dialogue, Paris: UNESCO, 2013.

[81] De Costa, P. I. Constructing the global citizen: An ELF perspective[J]. *Journal of Asian Pacific Communication*, 2016, *26*(2): 238-259.

[82] De La Caba, M. & Atxurra, R. L. Democratic citizenship in textbooks in Spanish primary curriculum[J]. *Journal of Curriculum Studies*, 2006, *38*(2): 205-228.

[83] Delokarov, K. K. *Values of the Globalizing World*[M]. Moscow: Scientific Press Ltd., 2002.

[84] East, M. Moving towards "us-others" reciprocity: Implications of glocalisation

for language learning and intercultural communication[J]. *Language and Intercultural Communication*, 2008, *8*(3): 156-71.

[85] Ekanayake, K., Khatibi, A., & Azam, F. The impact of teacher education and English language education in fostering global citizenship education: A review of literature[J]. *International Journal of Advances in Scientific Research and Engineering*, 2020, *6*(7): 30-40.

[86] Erfani, S. M. The rationale for introducing "global issues" in English textbook development[J]. *Theory and Practice in Language Studies*, 2012, *2*(11): 2412-2416.

[87] Fairclough, N. *Language and Power*[M]. New York: Longman, 1989.

[88] Fairclough, N. *Discourse and Social Change*[M]. Cambridge: Polity Press, 1992.

[89] Fairclough, N. *Critical Discourse Analysis: The Critical Study of Language*[M]. London and New York: Longman, 1995.

[90] Fairclough, N. *Language and Power* (*2nd ed.*)[M]. London and New York: Routledge, 2001.

[91] Fairclough, N. *Analysing Discourse: Textual Analysis for Social Research*[M]. London: Routledge, 2003.

[92] Fang, F. Glocalization, English as a Lingua Franca and ELT: Reconceptualizing identity and models for ELT in China[M]// Yazan, B., & Rudolph, N. (Eds.). *Criticality, Teacher Identity, and (In)equity in English Language Teaching*. Bern: Springer, 2018: 23-40.

[93] Fang, F., & Baker, W. "A more inclusive mind towards the world": English language teaching and study abroad in China from intercultural citizenship and English as a lingua[J]. *Language Teaching Research*, 2017(9): 1-17.

[94] Fang, F., & Elyas, T. Promoting teacher professionalism in language education from the perspective of critical intercultural literacy[J]. *Intercultural Communication Education*, 2021, *4*(2): 177-190.

[95] Fang, F., & Jiang, L. Critical investigation of intercultural communication instruction: Building mainland Chinese university students' critical language awareness and intercultural literacy[M]// Reynolds, B. L., & Teng, M. F. (Eds.). *English Literacy Instruction for Chinese Speakers*. London: Palgrave Macmillan, 2019: 211-227.

[96] Fang, F., Yuan, L., Xu, H., & Wang X. Global Englishes and translanguaging in textbook design and curriculum development for universities in the Greater Bay Area of China[J]. *Asian-Pacific Journal of Second and Foreign Language Education*, 2022, *35*(7): 1-16.

[97] Fantini, A., & Tirmizi, A. Exploring and assessing intercultural competence[EB/OL]. (2006-01-01) [2022-10-21]. http://digitalcollections.sit. edu/worldlearning_publications/1

[98] Feng, W. D. Infusing moral education into English language teaching: An ontogenetic analysis of social values in EFL textbooks in Hong Kong[J]. *Discourse: Studies in the Cultural Politics of Education*, 2019, *40*(4): 458-473.

[99] Ferrari, J. R. *Critical Multicultural Education for Social Action*[D]. Colorado: University of Northern Colorado, 2010.

[100] Galloway, N., & Rose, H. *Introducing Global Englishes*[M]. London: Routledge, 2015.

[101] Gaudelli, W. *Global Citizenship Education: Everyday Transcendence*[M]. New York: Routledge, 2016.

[102] Gay, G. Teaching to and through cultural diversity[J]. *Curriculum Inquiry*, 2015, *43*(1): 48-70.

[103] Gebregeorgis, M. Y. Gender construction through textbooks: The case of an Ethiopian primary school English textbook[J]. *Africa Education Review*, 2016, *13*(3-4): 119-140.

[104] Gillispie, D. H. Curriculum & schooling: Multiculturalism, critical multiculturalism and critical pedagogy[J]. *The South Shore Journal*, 2011(4): 1-10.

[105] Glasgow, G. P., & Paller, D. L. English language education policy in Japan: At a crossroads[M]// Kirkpatrick, R. (Ed.). *English Language Education Policy in Asia*. Dordrecht: Springer, 2016: 153-180.

[106] Goren, H., & Yemini, M. Global citizenship education redefined—A systematic review of empirical studies on global citizenship education[J]. *International Journal of Educational Research*, 2017a(82): 170-183.

[107] Goren, H., & Yemini, M. The global citizenship education gap: Teacher perceptions of the relationship between global citizenship education and students' socio-economic status[J]. *Teaching and Teacher Education*, 2017b(67): 9-22.

[108] Gorter, D. Foreword: Signposts in the linguistic landscape[M]// Hélot, C., Barni, M., Janssens, R., & Bagna, C. (Eds.). *Linguistic Landscapes, Multilingualism and Social Change*. Frankfurt am Main: Peter Lang, 2012: 9-12.

[109] Gorter, D., & Cenoz, J. Linguistic landscapes inside multilingual schools[M]// Spolsky, B., Inbar-Lourie, O., & Tannenbaum, M. (Eds.). *Challenges for Language Education and Policy*. New York: Routledge, 2015: 151-169.

[110] Gray, J. (1998). *False Dawn*[M]. London: Granta Books.

[111] Gudykunst, W. B., & Kim, Y. Y. *Communicating with Strangers: An Approach to Intercultural Communication*[M]. New York: McGraw-Hill, 2002.

[112] Guilherme, M. *Critical Citizens for an Intercultural World: Foreign Language Education as Cultural Politics*[M]. Clevedon: Multilingual Matters, 2002.

[113] Guilherme, M. English as a global language and education for cosmopolitan citizenship[J]. *Language and Intercultural Communication*, 2007, 7(1): 72-90.

[114] Gürsoy, E., & Sali, P. A language course within the scheme of socially responsible teaching: ELT trainees' expectations[J]. *Journal of Educational and Social Research*, 2014, 4(2): 355-365.

[115] Hammer, M. R. Intercultural competence development[M]// Bennett, J. (Ed.). *The SAGE Encyclopedia of Intercultural Competence*. Thousand Oaks: SAGE Publications, 2015: 483-485.

[116] Han, H., Song, L., Jing, H., & Zhao, Y. Exploring perceptions of intercultural citizenship among English learners in Chinese universities[M]// Byram, M., Golubeva, I., Han, H., & Wagner, M. (Eds.). *From Principles to Practice in Education for Intercultural Citizenship*. Bristol: Multilingual Matters, 2017: 25-44.

[117] He, F., Qi, X., & Oxford University Press (China) LTD. English Textbook Writing Committee. *English 3* (Vol. 1) [M]. Nanjing: Yilin Press, 2012.

[118] He, F., Qi, X., & Oxford University Press (China) LTD. English Textbook Writing Committee. *English 3* (Vol. 2) [M]. Nanjing: Yilin Press, 2012.

[119] He, F., Qi, X., & Oxford University Press (China) LTD. English Textbook Writing Committee. *English 4* (Vol. 1) [M]. Nanjing: Yilin Press, 2013.

[120] He, F., Qi, X., & Oxford University Press (China) LTD. English Textbook Writing Committee. *English 4* (Vol. 2) [M]. Nanjing: Yilin Press, 2013.

[121] He, F., Qi, X., & Oxford University Press (China) LTD. English Textbook Writing Committee. *English 5* (Vol. 1) [M]. Nanjing: Yilin Press, 2014.

[122] He, F., Qi, X., & Oxford University Press (China) LTD. English Textbook Writing Committee. *English 5* (Vol. 2) [M]. Nanjing: Yilin Press, 2014.

[123] He, F., Qi, X., & Oxford University Press (China) LTD. English Textbook Writing Committee. *English 6* (Vol. 1) [M]. Nanjing: Yilin Press, 2013.

[124] He, F., Qi, X., & Oxford University Press (China) LTD. English Textbook Writing Committee. *English 6* (Vol. 2) [M]. Nanjing: Yilin Press, 2014.

[125] He, J. *A Critical Discourse Analysis of Values Embedded in Chinese College English Listening and Speaking Textbooks: The Perspectives of Neoliberalism*

and Unequal Englishes Frameworks[D]. Nakhon Ratchasima: Suranaree University of Technology, 2021.

[126] He, J., & Buripakdi, A. Neoliberal values embedded in a Chinese college English textbook[J]. *Humanities, Arts and Social Sciences Studies*, 2022, *22*(1): 143-154.

[127] Henderson, H., & Ikeda, D. *Planetary Citizenship: Your Values, Beliefs and Actions Can Shape a Sustainable World*[M]. Santa Monica: Middleway Press, 2004.

[128] Hashemi, M. R., & Babaii, E. Mixed methods research: Toward new research designs in applied linguistics[J]. *The Modern Language Journal*, 2013, *97*(4): 828-852.

[129] Ho, L. -C. Conceptions of global citizenship education in East and Southeast Asia[M]// Davies, I., Ho, L. -C., Kiwan, D., Peck, C. L., Peterson, A., Sant, E., & Waghid, Y. (Eds.). *The Palgrave Handbook of Global Citizenship and Education*. London: Palgrave Macmillan, 2018: 83-96.

[130] Hosack, I. Foreign language teaching for global citizenship[J]. *Policy Science*, 2011, *18*(3): 125-140.

[131] Hu, G., & McKay, S. English language education in East Asia: Some recent developments[J]. *Journal of Multilingual and Multicultural Development*, 2012(33): 345-362.

[132] Jaffe, A. Introduction: The sociolinguistics of stance[M]// Jaffe, A. (Ed.). *Stance: Sociolinguistic Perspective*. New York: Oxford University Press, 2009: 3-28.

[133] Jaffe, A. Multilingual citizenship and minority languages[M]// Martin-Jones, M., Blackledge, A. & Greese, A. (Eds.). *The Routledge Handbook of Multilingualism*. London and New York: Routledge, 2012: 83-99.

[134] Jakubiak, C. "English is out there—you have to get with the program": Linguistic instrumentalism, global citizenship education, and English-language voluntourism[J]. *Anthropology & Education*, 2020, *51*(2): 212-232.

[135] Jaworski, A. Metrolingual art: Multilingualism and heteroglossia[J]. *International Journal of Bilingualism*, 2014, *18*(2): 134-158.

[136] Jefferess, D. Global citizenship and the cultural politics of benevolence[J]. *Critical Literacy: Theories and Practices*, 2008, *2*(1): 27-36.

[137] Jenkins, H. *Fans, Bloggers, and Gamers: Exploring Participatory Culture* [M]. New York: New York University Press, 2006.

[138] Jensen, D. Grand narrative[M]// Given, L. M. (Ed.). *The SAGE Encyclopedia of Qualitative Research Methods*. Los Angeles: SAGE, 2008: 372-373.

[139] Kelly, A. V. *The Curriculum: Theory and Practice*[M]. London: Paul Chapman Publishing, 1989.

[140] Kerkhoff, S. N. Designing global futures: A mixed methods study to develop and validate the teaching for global readiness scale[J]. *Teaching and Teacher Education*, 2017(65): 91-106.

[141] Khondker, H. H. Globalisation to glocalization: A conceptual exploration[J]. *Intellectual Discourse*, 2005, *13*(2): 181-199.

[142] Kubota, R. Unpacking research and practice in world Englishes and second language acquisition[J]. *World Englishes*, 2018, *37*(1): 93-105.

[143] Landry, R., & Bourhis, R. Linguistic landscape and ethnolinguistic vitality: An empirical study[J]. *Journal of Language and Social Psychology*, 1997(16): 23-49.

[144] Law, W. -W. Citizenship, citizenship education, and the state in China in a global age[J]. *Cambridge Journal of Education*, 2006, *36*(4): 597-628.

[145] Law, W. -W. *Citizenship and Citizenship Education in a Global Age: Politics, Policies, and Practices in China*[M]. New York: Peter Lang Publishing, 2011.

[146] Law, W. -W. Globalization, national identity, and citizenship education: China's search for modernization and a modern Chinese citizenry[J]. *Frontiers of Education in China*, 2013, *8*(4): 596-627.

[147] Lee, W. O., & Leung, S. W. Global citizenship education in Hong Kong and Shanghai secondary schools: Ideals, realities and expectation[J]. *Citizenship Teaching and Learning*, 2006, *2*(2): 68-84.

[148] LeRoux, J. Effective educators are culturally competent communicators[J]. *Intercultural Education*, 2002, *13*(1): 37-48.

[149] Li, C. Perpetuating student inequality? The discrepancy and disparity of global citizenship education in Chinese rural & urban schools[J]. *Asia Pacific Education Review*, 2021, DOI: https://doi.org/10.1007/s12564-021-09708-7

[150] Liu, H., & Fang, F. Towards a Global Englishes-aware national English curriculum of China[J]. *ELT Journal*, 2022, *76*(1): 88-98.

[151] Liu, L., Zhou, B., Ma, J., Zhou, J., & Bewick, F. *English 5* (PEP) (Vol. 1) [M]. Beijing: People's Education Press, 2014.

[152] Liu, L., Zhou, B., Ma, J., Zhou, J., & Bewick, F. *English 5* (PEP) (Vol. 2) [M]. Beijing: People's Education Press, 2014.

[153] Liu, M., & Wang, L. The theory and practice of global citizenship education in Korean international school in Beijing[J]. *Comparative Education Review*, 2014(8): 82-92.

[154] Lourenço, M. From caterpillars to butterflies: Exploring pre-service teachers'

transformations while navigating global citizenship education[J]. *Frontiers in Education*, 2021, DOI: 10.3389/feduc.2021.651250

[155] Ma, J., Liu, L., Zhou, J., Zhou, B., Bewick, F., & Andersen, C. (2013). *English 4* (PEP) (Vol. 1)[M]. Beijing: People's Education Press.

[156] Ma, J., Liu, L., Zhou, J., Bewick, F., & Andersen, C. *English 4* (PEP) (Vol. 2) [M]. Beijing: People's Education Press, 2013.

[157] Ma, J., Zhou, J., Liu, L., & Bewick, F. *English 6* (PEP) (Vol. 2)[M]. Beijing: People's Education Press, 2014.

[158] Mahboob, A. The power of language in textbooks: Shaping futures, shaping identities[J]. *Asian English*, 2017, DOI: 10.1080/13488678.2017.1341080

[159] Maher, J. Metroethnicity, language, and the principle of Cool[J]. *International Journal of the Sociology of Language*, 2005(11): 83-102.

[160] Mansilla, V. B., & Wilson. D. What is global competence, and what might it look like in Chinese schools?[J]. *Journal of Research in International Education*, 2020, *19*(1): 3-22.

[161] Massey, D. *For Space*[M]. London: SAGE, 2005.

[162] Mathews, G., & Vega, C. A. Introduction: What is globalization from below?[M]// Mathews, G., Ribeiro, G. L., & Vega, C. A. (Eds.). *Globalization from Below: The World's Other Economy*. London: Routledge, 2012: 1-15.

[163] Matras, Y. Defining "Everyday Multilingualism"[M]//*Everyday Multilingualism*. Austrian Commission for UNESCO, 2008(June): 13-15.

[164] May, S., & Sleeter, C. E. *Critical Multiculturalism: Theory and Praxis*[M]. New York: Routeledge, 2010.

[165] Mehta, S. R. Introduction: Framing studies in glocalization[M]// Mehta, S. R. (Ed.). *Language and Literature in a Glocal World*. Singapore: Springer, 2018: 1-11.

[166] Mensel, L. V., Vandenbroucke, M., & Blackwood, A. R. Linguistic landscapes[M]// Garcia, O., Flores, N., & Spotti, M. (Eds.). *The Oxford Handbook of Language and Society*. New York: Oxford University Press, 2017: 423-449.

[167] MOE. *National English Curriculum Standards for Compulsory Education*[M]. Beijing: Beijing Normal University Publishing Group, 2011.

[168] MOE. *National English Curriculum Standards for Compulsory Education*[M]. Beijing: Beijing Normal University Publishing Group, 2022.

[169] Nasser, R., & Nasser, I. Textbooks as a vehicle for segregation and domination: State efforts to shape Palestinian Israelis' identities as citizens[J]. *Journal of Curriculum Studies*, 2008, *40*(5): 627–650.

[170] OECD. *PISA: Preparing Our Youth for an Inclusive and Sustainable World: The OECD PISA Global Competence Framework*[M]. Paris: OECD, 2018.

[171] Omidvar, R., & Sukumar, B. The effects of global education in the English language conversation classroom[J]. *English Language Teaching*, 2013, *6*(7): 151-157.

[172] Osler, A., & Starkey, H. Learning for cosmopolitan citizenship: Theoretical debates and young people's experiences[J]. *Educational Review*, 2003, *55*(3): 243-254.

[173] Osler, A., & Starkey, H. *Citizenship and Language Learning: International Perspectives*[M]. Stoke-on-Trent: British Council and Trentham Books, 2005.

[174] Osler, A., & Starkey, H. Extending the theory and practice of education for cosmopolitan citizenship[J]. *Educational Review*, 2018, *70*(1): 31-40.

[175] Otsuji, E., & Pennycook, A. Metrolingualism: Fixity, fluidity and language in flux[J]. *International Journal of Multilingualism*, 2010(7): 240-254.

[176] Otsuji, E., & Pennycook, A. Social inclusion and metrolingual practices[J]. *International Journal of Bilingual Education and Bilingualism*, 2011, *14*(4): 413-426.

[177] Otsuji, E., & Pennycook, A. Unremarkable hybridities and metrolingual practices[M]// Rubdy, R., & Alsagoff, L. (Eds.). *The Global-Local Interface and Hybridity: Exploring Language and Identity*. Bristol: Multilingual Matters, 2013: 83-99.

[178] Oxfam. *Education for Global Citizenship: A Guide for Schools*[M]. London: Oxfam, 2015.

[179] Pais, A., & Costa, M. An ideology critique of global citizenship education[J]. *Critical Studies in Education*, 2017(4): 1-16.

[180] Park, J.-Y. English as pure potential[J]. *Journal of Multilingual and Multicultural Development*, 2016, *37*(5): 453-466.

[181] Parmenter, L. Power and place in the discourse of global citizenship education[J]. *Globalisation, Societies and Education*, 2011, *9*(3-4): 367-380.

[182] Peck, A., & Stroud, C. Skinscapes[J]. *Linguistic Landscape: An International Journal*, 2015, *1*(1/2): 133-151.

[183] Pennycook, A. *Global Englishes and Transcultural Flows*[M]. London: Routledge, 2007.

[184] Pennycook, A. Linguistic landscapes and the transgressive semiotics of graffiti[M]// Shohamy, E., & Gorter, D. (Eds.). *Linguistic Landscape: Expanding the Scenery*. New York: Routledge, 2009: 302-312.

[185] Pennycook, A. Spatial narrations: Graffscapes and city souls[M]// Jaworski,

A., & Thurlow, C. (Eds.). *Semiotic Landscapes: Language, Image, Space.* London: Continuum, 2010: 137-150.

[186] Pennycook, A. *Language Mobility: Unexpected Places*[M]. Bristol: Multilingual Matters, 2012.

[187] Pennycook, A. Language policies, language ideologies and local language practices[M]// Wee, L., Goh, R. B. H., & Lim, L. (Eds.). *The Politics of English: South Asia, Southeast Asia and the Asian Pacific.* New York: John Benjamins Publishing Company. 2013: 1-18.

[188] Pennycook, A. Translanguaging and semiotic assemblages[J]. *International Journal of Multilingualism*, 2017, DOI: 10.1080/14790718.2017.1315810

[189] Pennycook, A., & Otsuji, E. Market lingos and metrolingua francas[J]. *International Multilingual Research Journal*, 2014a, *8*(4): 255-270.

[190] Pennycook, A., & Otsuji, E. Metrolingual multitasking and spatial repertoires: "Pizza mo two minutes coming"[J]. *Journal of Sociolinguistics*, 2014b, *18*(2): 161-184.

[191] Pennycook, A., & Otsuji, E. *Metrolingualism: Language in the City*[M]. London: Routledge, 2015a.

[192] Pennycook, A., & Otsuji, E. Making scents of the landscape[J]. *Linguistic Landscape*, 2015b, *1*(3): 191-212.

[193] Pennycook, A., & Otsuji, E. Lingoing, language labels and metrolingual practices[J]. *Applied Linguistics Review*, 2016, *7*(3): 259-277.

[194] Pennycook, A., & Otsuji, E. Fish, phone cards and semiotic assemblages in two Bangladeshi shops in Sydney and Tokyo[J]. *Social Semiotics*, 2017, *27*(4): 434-450.

[195] Pennycook, A., & Otsuji, E. Mundane metrolingualism[J]. *International Journal of Multilingualism*, 2019, *16*(2): 175-186.

[196] Piller, I., & Cho, J. -H. Neoliberalism as a language policy[J]. *Language in Society*, 2013, *42*(1): 23-44.

[197] Porto, M. Does education for intercultural citizenship lead to language learning?[J]. *Language, Culture and Curriculum*, 2018, DOI: 10.1080/07908318.2017.1421642

[198] Prabjandee, D. Becoming English teachers in Thailand: Student teacher identity development during teaching practicum[J]. *Issues in Educational Research*, 2019, *29*(4): 1277-1294.

[199] Pramata, H., & Yuliati. Global education in English classroom: Integrating global issues into English language teaching[J]. *International Journal of Social Science and Humanity*, 2016, *6*(9): 719-722.

[200] Preisler, B. Functions and forms of English in a European EFL country[M]// Bex, T., & Watts, R. (Eds.). *Standard English: The Widening Debate*. London: Routledge, 1999: 239-267.

[201] Puspitasari, D., Widodo, H. P., Widyaningrum, L., Allamnakhrah, A., & Lestariyana, R. P. D. How do primary school English textbooks teach moral values? A critical discourse analysis[J]. *Studies in Education Evaluation*, 2021(70): 1-11.

[202] Qi, H., & Shen, D. Chinese traditional world citizenship thoughts and its impact on the cultivation of Chinese world citizenship awareness[J]. *Citizenship Studies*, 2015, DOI: 10.1080/13621025.2015.1006580

[203] Rahim, H. A., & Manan, S. A. Towards transformative English language education: Evolving glocalization in textbooks used in Malaysia[M]// Cortazzi, M., & Jin, L. (Eds.). *Researching Cultures of Learning: International Perspectives on Language Learning and Education*. London: Palgrave Macmillan, 2013: 155-175.

[204] Rashidi, N., & Ghaedsharafi, S. An investigation into the culture and social actors representation in Summit series ELT textbooks within van Leeuwen's 1996 framework[J]. *SAGE Open*, 2015, 5(1): 1-10.

[205] Reidel, M., & Beck, S. A. Forcing the world to fit pre-existing prejudices: Why and how global education has failed in the State of Georgia[J]. *Journal of Research in Curriculum & Instruction*, 2016, 20(3): 196-207.

[206] Reimers, F. Educating for global competency[M]// Cohen, J. E., & Malin, M. B. (Eds.). *International Perspectives on the Goals of Universal Basic and Secondary Education*. New York: Routledge, 2009: 183-202.

[207] Reynolds, R., MacQueen, S., & Ferguson-Patrick, K. Educating for global citizenship: Australia as a case study[J]. *International Journal of Development Education and Global Learning*, 2019, 11(1): 103-119.

[208] Ribeiro, G. L. Globalization from below and the non-hegemonic world-system[M]// Mathews, G., Ribeiro, G. L., & Vega, C. A. (Eds.). *Globalization from Below: The World's Other Economy*. London: Routledge, 2012: 221-235.

[209] Risager, K. *Representations of the World in Language Textbooks*[M]. Bristol: Multilingual Matters, 2018.

[210] Ritzer, G. *The McDonaldization of Society*[M]. Thousand Oaks: Pine Forge, 2000.

[211] Rizvi, F. Internationalization of curriculum: A critical perspective[M]// Hayden, M., Levy, J., & Thompson, J. (Eds.). *Research in International*

Education. London: SAGE, 2007: 391-403.

[212] Rizvi, F. Towards cosmopolitan learning[J]. *Discourse: Studies in the Cultural Politics of Education*, 2009, *30*(3): 253-268.

[213] Robertson, R. Glocalization: Time-space and homogeneity-heterogeneity[M]// Featherstone, M., Lash, S., & Robertson, R. (Eds.). *Global Modernities*. London: SAGE, 1995: 25-44.

[214] Roudometof, V. Nationalism, globalization and glocalization[J]. *Thesis Eleven*, 2014, *122*(1): 18-33.

[215] Roudometof, V. *Glocalization: A Critical Introduction*[M]. London and New York: Routledge, 2016.

[216] Roux, R. Perspectives on global citizenship education of Mexican university English language teachers[J]. *Teaching, Researching, and Citizenship*, 2019(17): 139-145.

[217] Saarinen, T., & Nikula, T. Implicit policy, invisible language: Policies and practices of international degree programmes in Finnish higher education[M]// Doiz, A., Lasagabaster, D., & Sierra, J. M. (Eds.). *English-Medium Instruction at Universities: Global Challenges*. Bristol: Multilingual Matters, 2013: 131-150.

[218] Saldaña, J. *The Coding Manual for Qualitative Researchers*[M]. London: SAGE, 2016.

[219] Sali, P., & Gürsoy, E. Evaluation of a language course within the framework of socially responsible teaching[J]. *ELT Research Journal*, 2014, *3*(3): 140-152.

[220] Salimi, E. A., & Safarzadeh, M. M. A model and questionnaire of language education glocalization in Iran[J]. *International Journal of Instruction*, 2019, *12*(1): 1639-1652.

[221] Samadikhah, M., & Shahrokhi, M. A critical discourse analysis of ELT materials in gender representation: A comparison of Summit and Top Notch[J]. *English Language Teaching*, 2015, *8*(1): 121-133.

[222] Savski, K. Consumerism as lingua franca in ELT? Ideologies in a Thai textbook series[M]// Daghigh, A. J., Jan, J. M., & Kaur, S. (Eds.). *Neoliberalization of English: Language Policy in the Global South*. Bern: Springer, 2022: 91-104.

[223] Schreier, M. *Qualitative Content Analysis in Practice*[M]. London: SAGE, 2012.

[224] Scollon, R., & Scollon, S. W. *Discourses in Place: Language in the Material World*[M]. London: Routledge, 2003.

[225] Serrano, J. R. ELT and citizenship: Basic principles to raise social awareness through language teaching[J]. *HOW*, 2008, *15*(1): 63-82.

[226] Shi, X. The glocalization of English: A Chinese case study[J]. *Journal of Developing Societies*, 2013, *29*(2): 89-122.

[227] Shohamy, E. *Language Policy: Hidden Agendas and New Approaches*[M]. New York: Routledge, 2006.

[228] Shohamy, E. LL research as expanding language and language policy[J]. *Linguistic Landscape*, 2015, *1* (1/2): 152-171.

[229] Sleeter, C. Critical multicultural curriculum and the standards movement[J]. *English Teaching: Practice and Critique*, 2004, *3*(2): 122-138.

[230] Song, H. Deconstruction of cultural dominance in Korean EFL textbooks[J]. *Intercultural Education*, 2013, *24*(4): 382-390.

[231] Starkey, H. Human rights, cosmopolitanism and utopias: Implications for citizenship education[J]. *Cambridge Journal of Education*, 2012, *42*(1): 21-35.

[232] Stroud, C., & Heugh, K. Language rights and linguistic citizenship[M]// Freeland, J., & Patrick, D. (Eds.). *Language Rights and Language Survival: Sociolinguistic and Sociocultural Perspective*. Manchester and Northampton: St. Jerome Publishing, 2004: 191-218.

[233] Subroto, A. R., Jazadi, I., & Mahyuni. Socio-economic representations in English language textbooks used in regional Indonesia[J]. *Asian EFL Journal*, 2019, *21*(25): 121-142.

[234] Sultan, A., & Hameed, A. From global to glocal: An investigation of Pakistan military academy students' perspective on cultural aspects in English language pedagogy[J]. *Pakistan Journal of Distance and Online Learning*, 2020, *6*(1): 65-83.

[235] Syrbe, M., & Rose, H. An evaluation of the global orientation of English textbooks in Germany[J]. *Innovation in Language Learning and Teaching*, 2016, DOI: 10.1080/17501229.2015.1120736

[236] Troyer, R. A. English in the Thai linguistic netscape[J]. *World Englishes*, 2012, *31*(1): 93-112.

[237] Taylor, S. V., & Sobel, D. Addressing the discontinuity of students' and teachers' diversity: A preliminary study of preservice teachers' beliefs and perceived skills[J]. *Teaching and Teacher Education*, 2001, *17*(4): 487-503.

[238] Tse, T. K. Creating good citizens in China: Comparing Grade 7-9 school textbooks, 1997-2005[J]. *Journal of Moral Education*, 2011, *40*(2): 161-180.

[239] UN. Sustainable development goals: 17 goals to transform our world [EB/OL].

(2016-01-01) [2021-09-01]. https://www.un.org/sustainabledevelopment/blog/2015/12/sustainable-development-goals-kick-off-with-start-of-new-year/.

[240] UNESCO. *Intercultural Competences: Conceptual and Operational Framework*[M]. Paris: UNESCO, 2013.

[241] UNESCO. *Global Citizenship Education: Preparing Learners for the Challenges of the 21st Century*[M]. Paris: UNESCO, 2014.

[242] UNESCO. *Global Citizenship Education: Topics and Learning Objectives*[M]. Paris: UNESCO, 2015.

[243] UNESCO. *Global Citizenship Education: Taking it Local*[M]. Paris: UNESCO, 2018.

[244] Vibulphol, J., Prabjandee, D., Chantharattana, M., & Bupphachuen, P. English teachers' understanding of Thailand basic education core curriculum[J]. *English Language Teaching*, 2021, *14*(11): 128-143.

[245] Wang, L. Possibility of educating 'global citizens' through a Chinese national school curriculum[J]. *Asia Pacific Journal of Education*, 2023, DOI:10.1080/02188791.2023.2186224

[246] Wang, C., & Hoffman, D. M. Are WE the world? A critical reflection on selfhood and global citizenship education[J]. *Education Policy Analysis Archives*, 2016, *24*(56): 1-22.

[247] Wang, W. Teaching English as an international language in China: Investigating university teachers' and students' attitudes towards China English[J]. *System*, 2015(53): 60-72.

[248] Wattanavorakijkul, N. Measuring intercultural sensitivity of Thai university students: Impact of their participation in the US summer work travel program[J]. *rEFLections*, 2020, *27*(1): 81-102.

[249] Weale, A. Citizenship beyond borders[M]// Moran, M., & Vogel, U. (Eds.). *The Frontiers of Citizenship*. London: Palgrave Macmillan, 1991: 155-165.

[250] Williams, K. Language learning: Its moral and civic remit[J]. *Pedagogy, Culture and Society*, 2017(25): 59-71.

[251] Woods, O., & Kong, L. The spatial subversions of global citizenship education: Negotiating imagined inclusions and everyday exclusions in international schools in China[J]. *Geoforum*, 2020(112): 139-147.

[252] Wu, M. M. Second language teaching for global citizenship[J]. *Globalisation, Societies and Education*, 2019(11): 1-12.

[253] Wu, X., & Tse, T. K. "Chinese core, global trend": A critical discourse analysis of Chinese civics teachers' perceptions on global citizenship

education[J]. *Asia Pacific Journal of Education*, 2023, DOI: 10.1080/02188791.2023.2218059

[254] Xiong, T., & Yuan, Z. "It was because I could speak English that I got the job": Neoliberal discourse in a Chinese English textbook series[J]. *Journal of Language, Identity & Education*, 2018, *17*(2): 103-117.

[255] Yao, X. Metrolingualism in online linguistic landscapes[J]. *International Journal of Multilingualism*, 2021. DOI: 10.1080/14790718.2021.1887197

[256] Yumarnamto, M., Widyaningrum, A. Y., & Prijambodo, V. L. Identity and imagined communities in English textbooks illustrations[J]. *LEARN Journal*, 2020, *13*(2): 354-368.

[257] Zhang, Y., Ni, Z., Dong, J., & Li, J. Constructing the global diversity or reproducing the orientalist gaze: Evaluating identity options and cultural elements in an English intercultural communication textbook[J]. *English Language Teaching*, 2022, *15*(1): 130-143.

[258] Zhou, J., Ma, J., Liu, L., & Bewick, F. *English 6* (PEP) (Vol. 1)[M]. Beijing: People's Education Press, 2013.

[259] Zhou, J., Ma, J., Liu, L., Gong, Y., Wu, Y., Li, J., Zhou, X., Bewick, F., Booth, D., Booth, J., Broad, K., & Peterson, S. *English 3* (PEP) (Vol. 1)[M]. Beijing: People's Education Press, 2012.

[260] Zhou, J., Ma, J., Liu, L., Gong, Y., Wu, Y., & Bewick, F. *English 3* (PEP) (Vol. 2)[M]. Beijing: People's Education Press, 2012.

[261] Zhu, J. *Citizenship Education and Foreign Language Teaching: Deconstructing the Concept of Good Citizenship Embedded in Foreign Language Curricula in China and America*[D]. Logan: Utah State University, 2013.

[262] Zhu, H., Li, W., & Lyons, A. Polish shop(ping) as Translanguaging Space[J]. *Social Semiotics*, 2017, *27*(4): 411-433.

APPENDIX A

Table 1   Structure of GCE guidance (UNESCO, 2015, p.29)

Domains of learning		
Cognitive	Socio-emotional	Behavioral
Key learning outcomes		
• Learners acquire knowledge and understanding of local, national and global issues and the interconnectedness and interdependency of different countries and populations • Learners develop skills for critical thinking and analysis	• Learners experience a sense of belonging to a common humanity, sharing values and responsibilities, based on human rights • Learners develop attitudes of empathy, solidarity and respect for differences and diversity	• Learners act effectively and responsibly at local, national and global levels for a more peaceful and sustainable world • Learners develop motivation and willingness to take necessary actions
Key learning attributes		
Informed and critically literate • Know about local, national and global issues, governance systems and structures • Understand the interdependence and connections of global and local concerns • Develop skills for critical inquiry and analysis	Socially connected and respectful of diversity • Cultivate and manage identities, relationships and feeling of belongingness • Share values and responsibilities based on human rights • Develop attitudes to appreciate and respect differences and diversity	Ethically responsible and engaged • Enact appropriate skills, values, beliefs and attitudes • Demonstrate personal and social responsibility for a peaceful and sustainable world • Develop motivation and willingness to care for the common good

(to be continued)

Domains of learning		
Cognitive	Socio-emotional	Behavioral
Topics		
1. Local, national and global systems and structures 2. Issues affecting interaction and connectedness of communities at local, national and global levels 3. Underlying assumptions and power dynamics	4. Different levels of identity 5. Different communities people belong to and how these are connected 6. Difference and respect for diversity	7. Actions that can be taken individually and collectively 8. Ethically responsible behavior 9. Getting engaged and taking action
Learning objectives by age/level of education (see details in Appendix B)		
Pre-primary/ lower primary (5-9 years)	Upper primary (9-12 years)	Lower secondary (12-15 years)	Upper secondary (15-18+years)

APPENDIX B

Table 2   GCE learning objectives by age/level of education
(UNESCO, 2015, p.31)

Topics	Learning objectives			
	Pre-primary & lower primary (5-9 years)	Upper primary (9-12 years)	Lower secondary (12-15 years)	Upper secondary (15-18+ years)
1. Local, national and global systems and structures	Describe how the local environment is organized and how it relates to the wider world, and introduce the concept of citizenship	Identify governance structures, decision-making processes and dimensions of citizenship	Discuss how global governance structures interact with national and local structures and explore global citizenship	Critically analyze global governance systems, structures and processes and assess implications for global citizenship
2. Issues affecting interaction and connectedness of communities at local, national and global levels	List key local, national and global issues and explore how these may be connected	Investigate the reasons behind major common global concerns and their impact at national and local levels	Assess the root causes of major local, national and global issues and the interconnectedness of local and global factors	Critically examine local, national and global issues, responsibilities and consequences of decision-making, examine and propose appropriate responses
3. Underlying assumptions and power dynamics	Name different sources of information and develop basic skills for inquiry	Differentiate between fact/opinion, reality/fiction and different viewpoints/perspectives	Investigate underlying assumptions and describe inequalities and power dynamics	Critically assess the ways in which power dynamics affect voice, influence, access to resources, decision-making and governance

(to be continued)

Topics	Learning objectives			
	Pre-primary & lower primary (5-9 years)	Upper primary (9-12 years)	Lower secondary (12-15 years)	Upper secondary (15-18+years)
4. Different levels of identity	Recognize how we fit into and interact with the world around us and develop intrapersonal and interpersonal skills	Examine different levels of identity and their implications for managing relationships with others	Distinguish between personal and collective identity and various social groups, and cultivate a sense of belonging to a common humanity	Critically examine ways in which different levels of identity interact and live peacefully with different social groups
5. Different communities people belong to and how these are connected	Illustrate differences and connections between different social groups	Compare and contrast shared and different social, cultural and legal norms	Demonstrate appreciation and respect for difference and diversity, cultivate empathy and solidarity towards other individuals and social groups	Critically assess connectedness between different groups, communities and countries
6. Difference and respect for diversity	Distinguish between sameness and difference, and recognize that everyone has rights and responsibilities	Cultivate good relationships with diverse individuals and groups	Debate on the benefits and challenges of difference and diversity	Develop and apply values, attitudes and skills to manage and engage with diverse groups and perspectives
7. Actions that can be taken individually and collectively	Explore possible ways of taking action to improve the world we live in	Discuss the importance of individual and collective action and engage in community work	Examine how individuals and groups have taken action on issues of local, national and global importance and get engaged in responses to local, national and global issues	Develop and apply skills for effective civic engagement

(to be continued)

Topics	Learning objectives			
	Pre-primary & lower primary (5-9 years)	Upper primary (9-12 years)	Lower secondary (12-15 years)	Upper secondary (15-18+years)
8. Ethically responsible behaviour	Discuss how our choices and actions affect other people and the planet and adopt responsible behaviour	Understand the concepts of social justice and ethical responsibility and learn how to apply them in everyday life	Analyze the challenges and dilemmas associated with social justice and ethical responsibility and consider the implications for individual and collective action	Critically assess issues of social justice and ethical responsibility and take action to challenge discrimination and inequality
9. Getting engaged and taking action	Recognize the importance and benefits of civic engagement	Identify opportunities for engagement and initiate action	Develop and apply skills for active engagement and take action to promote common good	Propose action for and become agents of positive change

APPENDIX C

A semi-structured interview on teachers' perceptions toward GCE and metrolingualism in ELT textbooks and curriculum

Dear teacher,

This semi-structured interview is designed to gather information about your opinions on GCE and metrolingualism in ELT textbooks and curriculum. Your response to the interview questions will be kept confidential. The interview is for research purpose only. It is anonymous and there is no right or wrong answer. Please answer the following questions truthfully. Thank you for your participation!

Part 1 Personal information

Gender: ☐ Male ☐ Female

Age: ☐ 24 & below ☐ 25-30 ☐ 31-35 ☐ 36-40 ☐ 40 & above

Years of teaching:_____

Academic degree:_____

The grade you have taught: ☐ Grade 3 ☐ Grade 4 ☐ Grade 5 ☐ Grade 6

The series of the English textbook you teach: ☐ PEP ☐ Yilin

Part 2 Interview questions

1. What is your general impression of the textbooks and curriculum you are currently using?

2. What aspects of English teaching do you pay more attention to?

3. Have you heard about global citizenship education? What's your understanding of this concept?

4. How do you define your role and responsibility as an English teacher in preparing students as global citizens?

5. What types of teaching practices do you involve in your classroom in preparing students as global citizens? (If any)?

6. Do you think the ELT curriculum you are currently following educate students as global citizens? Why or why not?

7. Do you think the ELT textbooks you are currently teaching educate students as global citizens? Why or why not?

8. Is there anything that you do differently or add to the curriculum and textbooks at your classes to promote global citizenship education?

9. What do you see as challenges in ELT courses for preparing students to become global citizens?

10. What do you think of the linguistic codes used in posters and public signs in the illustrations of textbooks?

11. What do you think of the English code, Chinese code and other linguistic codes used in textbooks?

12. Do you agree or disagree that language teaching should come from life and be close to life? If agree, how do you practice this concept in actual English teaching?

13. Do you have anything else to say about today's interview?

APPENDIX D

Table 3　Example of coding procedures for GCE & metrolingualism in curriculum

Open coding		Axial coding	Selective coding
Sampling of statements	Initial codes	Categories	Themes
• Learning and using English plays an important role in absorbing the achievements of human civilization, learning advanced science and technology from foreign countries and enhancing mutual understanding between China and the world. • Offering English courses at the stage of compulsory education can lay a foundation for improving China's overall national literacy, cultivating talents with innovative ability and cross-cultural communication ability, and improving the international competitiveness of the country and the international communication ability of the people. • Learning English will not only help them better understand the world, learn advanced scientific and cultural knowledge, spread Chinese culture, enhance their communication and understanding with teenagers from other countries, but also provide them with more opportunities for education and career development.	• Absorbing the achievements of human civilization • Learning advanced science and technology • Broaden horizons • Enhancing mutual understanding between China and the world • Better understand the world • Enhance the understanding with teenagers from other countries • Understand the diversity of the world • Enhance international understanding • Cultivating talents with cross-cultural communication ability • Improving the international communication ability of the people • Enhance the communication with teenagers from other countries • Form cross-cultural awareness • Improving the international competitiveness of the country	• Expand international horizons • Enhance international understanding • Intercultural communicative competence and intercultural awareness • International competitiveness	• Global awareness

(to be continued)

Open coding		Axial coding	Selective coding
Sampling of statements	Initial codes	Categories	Themes
• Through English courses, students can broaden their horizons, enrich their life experience, form cross-cultural awareness, enhance patriotism, develop innovation ability, and form good character and correct outlook on life and values.	• Improving China's overall national literacy • Improving the international competitiveness of the country • Spread Chinese culture • Patriotism education	• National improvement • Chinese culture • Patriotism	• National awareness
• Learning a foreign language can promote people's mental development, help students understand the diversity of the world, form cross-cultural awareness through experiencing the similarities and differences between Chinese and foreign cultures, enhance international understanding, promote patriotism, form a sense of social responsibility and innovation, and improve humanistic quality. • Know the names of typical foods and drinks in English-speaking countries. • Know the capitals and flags of the major English-speaking countries. • Understand important symbols of major English-speaking countries, such as Big Ben in the United Kingdom. • Understand important holidays in English-speaking countries.	• Typical foods and drinks in English-speaking countries • The capitals and flags of the major English-speaking countries • Important symbols of major English-speaking countries • Important holidays in English-speaking countries • Spread Chinese culture • The similarities and differences between Chinese and foreign cultures • Popular entertainment and sports activities around the world • Popular festivals and their celebrations around the world	• Culture of English-speaking countries • Chinese culture • Global culture	• Cultural education
• Establishing students' self-confidence, developing the willpower to overcome difficulties... • Willing to cooperate with others, develop harmonious and healthy personalities...	• Correct outlook on life and values • Socialist core values • Patriotism education • Form a sense of social responsibility and innovation • Establishing students' self-confidence • Developing the willpower to overcome difficulties • Willing to cooperate with others • Traditional Chinese virtues	• Ideological education • Moral education	• Ideological and moral education

(to be continued)

Open coding		Axial coding	Selective coding
Sampling of statements	Initial codes	Categories	Themes
• Actively infiltrate patriotism education, socialist core values, traditional Chinese virtues, and education for democracy as well as rules of law.... • Interpenetrate and connect with other subjects to promote the comprehensive development of students' cognitive ability, thinking ability, aesthetic ability, imagination and creativity...	• Education and career development • Enrich life experience • Promote people's mental development • Develop harmonious and healthy personalities • Form good character • Develop innovation ability • Improve humanistic quality • Education for democracy as well as rules of law • Comprehensive development	• Personal development education • Physical and mental development education • Humanistic quality education	• Quality-oriented education
• Willing to imitate and daring to express as well as having a certain perception of English during the process of learning. • Be able to imitate the speech according to the recordings. • Be able to use correct pronunciation and intonation in oral activities. • Be able to make the pronunciation and intonation natural and appropriate in oral activities. • Be able to recognize mistakes and correct them when using English.	• Learning English through imitation • Imitate the recordings • Correct pronunciation and intonation • Natural and appropriate pronunciation and intonation • Recognize and correct mistakes	• Learning through imitation • Correct and natural pronunciation and intonation • Correct mistakes	• Native-speakerism norms

(to be continued)

233

Open coding		Axial coding	Selective coding
Sampling of statements	Initial codes	Categories	Themes
• Be able to understand common instructions and requirements as well as respond appropriately. • Be able to describe or tell simple stories with the help of teachers and the tips of pictures. • Be able to read stories or short passages correctly that have been learned. • Be able to write short sentences based on the hints of pictures, words or model sentences. • Understand English pronunciation phenomena such as liaison, rhythm, pause, intonation, etc. • Comprehend the ideographic functions of the above grammatical items in practice.	• Understand and respond to common instructions and requirements • Describe or tell simple stories • Read stories or short passages • Write short sentences • English pronunciation phenomena • Ideographic functions of grammatical items	• Listening require-ments • Speaking require-ments • Reading require-ments • Writing requirements • Requirements for linguistic knowledge	• Linguistic foci
• English courses should provide English learning resources close to students, close to life and close to times according to the needs of teaching and learning. • ...create as many opportunities as possible for students to use the language in real situations	• English learning resources close to students, close to life and close to times • Use the language in real situations	• Learning and using language close to daily lives	• Daily life-oriented resources

APPENDIX E

Table 4   Grading standards of cultural awareness (MOE, 2011, p.24)

Level	Standard description
Level 2	Know the simplest address forms, greetings and goodbyes in English.
	Respond appropriately to general compliments, requests, apologies, etc.
	Know the popular entertainment and sports activities around the world.
	Know the names of typical foods and drinks in English-speaking countries.
	Know the capitals and flags of the major English-speaking countries.
	Understand important symbols of major English-speaking countries, such as Big Ben in the United Kingdom.
	Understand important holidays in English-speaking countries.
	Be able to initially notice the similarities and differences between Chinese and foreign cultures in study and daily communications.
Level 5	Understand the body language commonly used in English communication, such as gestures, facial expressions, etc.
	Use address forms, greetings and goodbyes in English properly.
	Understand and distinguish common names and nicknames for different genders in English.
	Understand the dietary customs of English-speaking countries.
	Respond appropriately to compliments, requests, apologies, etc.
	Express a compliment, request, etc. in an appropriate way.
	Preliminarily understanding the geographical locations, climate features, histories, etc. in English-speaking countries.

(to be continued)

Level	Standard description
	Understand the customs of interpersonal communication in English-speaking countries.
	Understand the popular entertainment and sports activities around the world.
	Understand popular festivals and their celebrations around the world.
	Focus on the similarities and differences between Chinese and foreign cultures, and deepen the understanding of Chinese culture.
	Be able to introduce the major festivals and typical cultural customs in English.

APPENDIX F

Table 5 Grading standards for linguistic skills (Level 2) (MOE, 2011, p.14)

Level	Skills	Description for standards
Level 2	Listening	Be able to understand simple speech or recorded materials with the help of pictures, images and gestures. Be able to understand simple story with pictures. Be able to understand simple questions in activities during class. Be able to understand common instructions and requirements as well as respond appropriately.
	Speaking	Be able to pronounce clearly and the intonation basically conveys the meaning in oral expression. Be able to carry on brief conversations about familiar personal and family situations. Be able to use some of the most common daily expressions (e.g. greetings, goodbyes, thanks, apologies). Be able to give short narration on topics of daily life. Be able to describe or tell simple stories with the help of teachers and the tips of pictures.
	Reading	Be able to read the words that have been learned. Be able to read simple words according to the rules of spelling. Be able to read and understand brief requirements or instructions in textbooks. Be able to read simple messages such as greeting cards. Be able to read simple stories or short passages with pictures, and develop the habit of reading in meaning groups. Be able to read stories or short passages correctly that have been learned.

(to be continued)

Level	Skills	Description for standards
	Writing	Be able to use uppercase and lowercase letters and common punctuation marks correctly. Be able to write simple greetings and wishes. Be able to write short sentences based on the hints of pictures, words or model sentences.
	Playing, acting, audio visual	Be able to play games in simple English as required. Be able to act out short stories or plays with the help of teachers. Be able to sing about 30 simple English songs and ballads (including Level 1 requirements). Be able to understand English cartoons and English teaching programs at the same level, with no less than 10 hours of classroom audio-visual time per academic year (20-25 minutes per week on average).

APPENDIX G

Table 6   Grading standards for linguistic knowledge (Level 2) (MOE, 2011, pp.18-19)

Level	Knowledge	Description for standards
Level 2	Pronunciation	Pronounce the 26 English letters correctly. Understand simple spelling rules. Understand the word stress placement and tonic stress placement. Understand English pronunciation phenomena such as liaison, rhythm, pause, intonation.
	Vocabulary	Know that words are made up of letters. Know how to learn vocabulary according to their sounds, meanings and forms. Learn about 600-700 words and 50 idioms on the relevant topics of this level, and be able to preliminarily use about 400 words to express the corresponding topics stipulated in Level 2.
	Grammar	Understand the meaning and usage of the following grammatical items in context: Singular and plural forms of nouns and possessive nouns; Personal pronouns and adjectival possessive pronouns; Simple present tense, present progressive, past indefinite tense, simple future tense; Common prepositions indicating time, places, or locations; The basic form of simple sentences. Comprehend the ideographic functions of the above grammatical items in practice.
	Function	Be able to understand and use English expressions related to the following functions: greetings, introductions, goodbyes, requests, invitations, acknowledgments, apologies, feelings, preferences, suggestions, wishes, etc.

(to be continued)

Level	Knowledge	Description for standards
	Topic	Be able to understand and use English expressions related to the following topics: personal information, family and friends, body and health, school and daily life, recreational and sports activities, holidays, diet, clothing, seasons and weather, colors, animals, etc.

APPENDIX H

Table 7   Proportion of GCE in PEP vs. GCE in Yilin

Themes	Subthemes	Percentage in PEP series (occurrence number/493)	Percentage in Yilin series (occurrence number/277)
Social development and progress	N/A	0.61%	0.36%
Omnipotent artificial intelligence	N/A	6.9%	0.36%
Environmental responsibility and sustainable development	N/A	0.81%	4.33%
Harmonious coexistence of human-nature relations	N/A	5.48%	3.97%
Total in the domain of Education for sustainable development		13.79%	9.03%
Harmonious coexistence of human-human relations	Kinship	6.29%	10.11%
	Friendship	2.23%	1.81%
	Empathy	0.81%	0.72%
	Tolerance	0.41%	0
	Gratitude	0.81%	0.72%

(to be continued)

Themes	Subthemes	Percentage in PEP series (occurrence number/493)	Percentage in Yilin series (occurrence number/277)
Globality	N/A	0.61%	0
Cultural diversity	Anglophone cultures	13.39%	14.8%
	Chinese cultures	11.76%	11.91%
	Global cultures	2.23%	3.25%
	Other cultures	0.2%	0
Total in the domain of Inter/ multicultural education		38.74%	43.32%
Civic virtues & morality	Civilized manners	2.23%	3.61%
	Rule compliance	2.03%	3.97%
	Cooperation and solidarity	0.81%	0
	Diligence	0.61%	0.36%
	Honesty	0.2%	0.72%
	Being helpful	2.43%	3.61%
Total in the domain of Citizenship education		8.32%	12.27%
World geography	Anglophone geography	3.65%	4.69%
	Chinese geography	5.27%	7.22%
	Other geography	0.2%	0
Healthy diet & lifestyle	N/A	2.43%	3.97%
Leisure lifestyle	N/A	4.46%	7.94%
Native-speakerism	Native-speakerism prestige & supremacy	10.34%	1.44%

(to be continued)

Themes	Subthemes	Percentage in PEP series (occurrence number/493)	Percentage in Yilin series (occurrence number/277)
	Anti-native speakerism prestige	0	3.61%
Career planning	N/A	0.81%	2.17%
Commercialization	N/A	3.65%	2.89%
Everyday philosophy	N/A	0.81%	0
Chinese educational principles	N/A	7.51%	1.44%
Total in the domain of Emerging themes		39.15%	35.38%
Total		100%	100%

APPENDIX I

Table 8   Proportion of GCE among different grade levels

Themes	Subthemes	Percentage in Grade 3 (occurrence number/139)	Percentage in Grade 4 (occurrence number/153)	Percentage in Grade 5 (occurrence number/264)	Percentage in Grade 6 (occurrence number/214)
Social development and progress	N/A	0	0	0	1.87%
Omnipotent artificial intelligence	N/A	0	0.65%	8.33%	5.61%
Environmental responsibility and sustainable development	N/A	0.72%	0	0.38%	6.54%
Harmonious coexistence of human-nature relations	N/A	8.63%	4.58%	6.06%	1.4%
Total in the domain of Education for sustainable development		9.35%	5.23%	14.77%	15.42%
Harmonious coexistence of human-human relations	Kinship	11.51%	6.54%	7.58%	6.07%
	Friendship	2.16%	2.61%	1.14%	2.8%
	Empathy	0	1.96%	0	1.4%
	Tolerance	0	0	0	0.93%
	Gratitude	0	0	1.89%	0.47%

(to be continued)

Themes	Subthemes	Percentage in Grade 3 (occurrence number/139)	Percentage in Grade 4 (occurrence number/153)	Percentage in Grade 5 (occurrence number/264)	Percentage in Grade 6 (occurrence number/214)
Globality	N/A	0	1.96%	0	0
Cultural diversity	Anglophone cultures	21.58%	15.03%	13.26%	8.88%
	Chinese cultures	7.19%	10.46%	15.91%	10.75%
	Global cultures	3.6%	0	4.55%	1.4%
	Other cultures	0	0	0.38%	0
Total in the domain of Inter/ multicultural education		46.04%	38.56%	44.7%	32.71%
Civic virtues & morality	Civilized manners	3.6%	1.31%	2.27%	3.74%
	Rule compliance	2.88%	0	1.14%	6.54%
	Cooperation and solidarity	0.72%	0.65%	0	0.93%
	Diligence	0	0	0.76%	0.93%
	Honesty	0	0	0	1.4%
	Being helpful	0	4.58%	2.65%	3.74%
Total in the domain of Citizenship education		7.19%	6.54%	6.82%	17.29%
World geography	Anglophone geography	1.44%	3.92%	2.65%	7.48%
	Chinese geography	5.04%	6.54%	4.17%	8.41%
	Other geography	0	0.65%	0	0

(to be continued)

Themes	Subthemes	Percentage in Grade 3 (occurrence number/139)	Percentage in Grade 4 (occurrence number/153)	Percentage in Grade 5 (occurrence number/264)	Percentage in Grade 6 (occurrence number/214)
Healthy diet & lifestyle	N/A	2.88%	4.58%	3.03%	1.87%
Leisure lifestyle	N/A	9.35%	5.88%	4.17%	5.14%
Native-speakerism	Native-speakerism prestige & supremacy	13.67%	4.58%	9.47%	1.87%
	Anti-native speakerism prestige	2.16%	0.65%	0.76%	1.87%
Career planning	N/A	0	0	0	4.67%
Commercialization	N/A	2.16%	13.73%	0.38%	0.47%
Everyday philosophy	N/A	0.72%	0	0.76%	0.47%
Chinese educational principles	N/A	0	9.15%	8.33%	2.34%
Total in the domain of Emerging themes		37.41%	49.67%	33.71%	34.58%
Total		100%	100%	100%	100%

LIST OF ABBREVIATIONS

CDA	Critical Discourse Analysis
ECSCE	English Curriculum Standards for Compulsory Education
ELF	English as a Lingua Franca
ELT	English Language Teaching
GCE	Global Citizenship Education
LL	Linguistic Landscape
LLs	Linguistic Landscapes
MI	Metrolingual Interaction
MIs	Metrolingual Interactions
ML	Metrolingual Landscape
MLs	Metrolingual Landscapes
NNS	Non-native Speakers
NS	Native Speakers
OECD	Organization for Economic Cooperation and Development
PEP	People's Education Press
PEP3V1	PEP English textbook for Grade 3 Volume 1
PEP3V2	PEP English textbook for Grade 3 Volume 2
PEP4V1	PEP English textbook for Grade 4 Volume 1
PEP4V2	PEP English textbook for Grade 4 Volume 2
PEP5V1	PEP English textbook for Grade 5 Volume 1
PEP5V2	PEP English textbook for Grade 5 Volume 2
PEP6V1	PEP English textbook for Grade 6 Volume 1
PEP6V2	PEP English textbook for Grade 6 Volume 2
PISA	Programme for International Students Assessment
SLA	Second Language Aquisition
UNESCO	United Nations Educational, Scientific, and Cultural Organization
Yilin3V1	Yilin English textbook for Grade 3 Volume 1

Yilin3V2   Yilin English textbook for Grade 3 Volume 2
Yilin4V1   Yilin English textbook for Grade 4 Volume 1
Yilin4V2   Yilin English textbook for Grade 4 Volume 2
Yilin5V1   Yilin English textbook for Grade 5 Volume 1
Yilin5V2   Yilin English textbook for Grade 5 Volume 2
Yilin6V1   Yilin English textbook for Grade 6 Volume 1
Yilin6V2   Yilin English textbook for Grade 6 Volume 2